ELECTION FRAUD

ELECTION FRAUD

Detecting and Deterring
Electoral Manipulation

R. Michael Alvarez
Thad E. Hall
Susan D. Hyde

editors

BROOKINGS INSTITUTION PRESS
Washington, D.C.

ABOUT BROOKINGS

The Brookings Institution is a private nonprofit organization devoted to research, education, and publication on important issues of domestic and foreign policy. Its principal purpose is to bring the highest quality independent research and analysis to bear on current and emerging policy problems. Interpretations or conclusions in Brookings publications should be understood to be solely those of the authors.

Library of Congress Cataloging-in-Publication data
Election fraud : detecting and deterring electoral manipulation / R. Michael Alvarez, Thad E. Hall, Susan D. Hyde, editors.
    p.   cm.
    Summary: "Brings together experts on election law, election administration, and U.S. and comparative politics to examine the U.S. understanding of election fraud. With survey data, incident reports, and state-collected fraud allegations, measures the extent and nature of election fraud in U.S. Analyzes techniques for detecting and potentially deterring fraud"—Provided by publisher.
    Includes bibliographical references and index.
    ISBN 978-0-8157-0138-5 (cloth : alk. paper) — ISBN 978-0-8157-0139-2 (pbk. : alk. paper)
    1. Elections—Corrupt practices-United States.   2. Elections—Corrupt practices—United States—Prevention.   3. Ballot—Security measures—United States.   4. Elections—Corrupt practices—Case studies.   I. Alvarez, R. Michael, 1964–   II. Hall, Thad E. (Thad Edward), 1968–   III. Hyde, Susan D.   IV. Title.
  JK1994.E43 2008
  324.6'60973-dc22   2008005719

9 8 7 6 5 4 3 2 1

Typeset in Minion and Univers Condensed

Composition by R. Lynn Rivenbark
Macon, Georgia

Printed by R. R. Donnelley
Harrisonburg, Virginia

Contents

Part Two
Measuring Election Fraud: Learning from Observational Data

Part Three
Detecting Election Fraud: Techniques and Consequences

Foreword

In November of 2000, like millions of other Americans, we sat riveted while watching election officials in Florida recount presidential ballots. We closely followed the ensuing litigation and, ultimately, the decision handed down by the United States Supreme Court that decided the presidential contest. We then watched as advocates, academics, and election officials alike were summoned to briefings and hearings by Congress over a two-year period to discuss reforms to fix the real and perceived deficiencies.

On October 27, 2002, Congress passed the most sweeping election administration reform bill in the history of the country, now well known by its acronym, HAVA, or the Help America Vote Act of 2002. Given the well-established history of election administration by state and local governments, the law's passage showed that Congress was serious about ensuring uniformity in the conduct of federal elections. Both of us were honored to serve as commissioners to the new Election Assistance Commission (EAC), established by the law. Although we represented different political persuasions, we worked tirelessly in an attempt to put our nation's election administration system on a better footing.

Additionally, through HAVA, Congress appropriated more than $3 billion to be distributed to state and local governments to fund improvements to election administration, ending what some have called the "longest-running unfunded mandate in the history of our country." More recently, in late 2007

Congress appropriated millions in additional federal dollars to further implement many of the administrative improvements called for in HAVA.

The passage of the law, however, did not end the debate over how to improve election administration. If anything, that debate has become even more intense and has centered around two key components of election administration: the "technology" we use to capture and count our ballot choices and the "processes" that govern the administration of our elections from cycle to cycle. The emphasis on technology is not unexpected, given the specific (and renewed) financial incentives in HAVA for jurisdictions to replace antiquated voting systems and to implement statewide voter registration databases, among other improvements. The emphasis on process, likewise, reflects the new requirements in HAVA related to identifying first-time voters, providing for provisional voting, and ensuring that voters get enough information to cast ballots without errors.

As important as the focus is on election technology and processes, more and better research is needed on election administration. We both were excited when presented with an opportunity to participate in the Conference on Election Fraud cosponsored by the University of Utah and the Caltech/MIT Voting Technology Project. The conference was exciting for several reasons. First, it brought together many of the best and brightest academic scholars in the field of election administration, those who study elections in the United States but also scholars who study elections throughout the world. Most have been analyzing the conduct of elections for many years and have added greatly to the quality of the debate here. And by having individuals who study elections abroad, we were able not only to understand better the factors that make the U.S. electoral context unique, but also appreciate how much we can learn from election practices in other countries.

Second, the conference also brought together election officials—the practitioners of elections—with the academic community. Since the 2000 presidential election, academics, advocates, and election officials often have seemed to talk past each other. This conference brought together people who want to have a conversation and improve the process, not score political or advocacy points in some game. Over the course of the meeting, election officials better understood the interests, needs, and skills that academic scholars can bring to improve the task of election administration. At the same time, the academics learned about the political, technological, procedural, and monetary constraints that limit the ability of election officials to produce the data or technological changes that academics desire.

Finally, the chief topic, election fraud, is one that is highly controversial and has been, unfortunately, the subject of little rigorous research. We were presented with an opportunity to learn what we know and do not know about election fraud. More important, presentations laid out a research agenda for how to move the debate forward and new strategies for election officials to use for detecting and deterring election fraud. Although we both have taken opposite sides on some of the debates regarding election fraud, we recognize the importance of this issue because fraud—even allegations of fraud—can undermine public confidence in the electoral process and the long-standing work to improve elections in the United States.

There was a tremendous amount of give-and-take on questions of election fraud. For example, the question that is often asked—how much election fraud is there?—was put into stark relief by Peter Ordeshook, who noted that the anecdotal cases of serious election fraud in the United States would be considered comical in Russia and in many of its former republics, where election fraud has been committed on a scale that dwarfs anything in recent U.S. experience. Likewise, interesting debates covered how to detect fraud and what could be done once it was detected. As noted, election officials operate under the time constraints dictated by state law, leading to few chances for them to contemplate and analyze what might have gone wrong.

Scholars at the conference were able to answer some key questions and set a positive agenda for the future. First, it is clear that we can begin to identify and estimate election fraud systematically, given the correct data. Using data from lawsuits, election incident reports, and actual election results, scholars are able to determine when and how fraud occurs and what threats exist that can make it more or less likely. Academics can also use simple statistics to determine when election results do not match with what otherwise would be detected, providing election officials with a new tool in their election management tool kit. Given our role at the EAC in the development of a series of reports to improve election management, we were especially intrigued to hear scholars discuss how local and state election officials could quickly determine in which precincts election results might be problematic.

Second, we have a long way to go to realizing a complete understanding of election fraud. One of our biggest regrets is that while we were both serving as EAC commissioners, we were unable to obtain a larger budget to support academic research. Our nation needs to commit more resources to studying the election process, including election fraud. We need to understand the threats to the election system and how these threats can be minimized. This conference illustrated that such research is not difficult or costly to conduct, as long as there is a commitment to collect the data necessary for such studies. In 2006 two election scholars, Dan Tokaji and Thad Hall, put forward a simple proposal: Federal dollars could help pay for all federal elections if the states used some of the federal funds to collect better systematic election data. The federal government could play a key role in helping states develop a data-reporting system that is uniform across states and that harmonizes the idiosyncrasies of state election laws hindering such data collection. Congress recently took the first step in this direction, appropriating $10 million to the EAC's five pilot grant research programs to improve data collection efforts in the states.

We also think that the Election Assistance Commission has an important role in moving this discussion forward. It can provide the data from the pilot programs to the academic community and support further research, thus strengthening its role as a national clearinghouse for election information. And the EAC can serve as a neutral arbiter in the key debates surrounding election fraud, promoting collaboration among the key parties.

Although former EAC commissioners, we remain closely tied to the elections community. Policymakers, election officials, academics, and advocates can all learn much about election fraud here. No doubt debates about election fraud will continue well beyond the publication of this book. But *Election Fraud: Detecting and Deterring Electoral Manipulation* will help put the ongoing debates in perspective and assist readers in better appreciating the nuances of election administration and claims of election fraud.

PAUL DEGREGORIO
Chief Operating Officer for Everyone Counts, Inc.
Commissioner, Election Assistance Commission, 2003–07

RAY MARTINEZ
Director of Government Relations, Rice University
Commissioner, Election Assistance Commission, 2003–06

Acknowledgments

As volume editors, we have many people to thank for their help in making this project happen. The first phase involved the convening of a workshop in Salt Lake City, Utah, sponsored by the University of Utah and the Caltech/MIT Voting Technology Project. We wish to thank the entities whose financial support helped us put that event together: the Carnegie Corporation of New York, the John S. and James L. Knight Foundation, and the Institute of Public and International Affairs at the University of Utah. The University of Utah provided logistical support for the conference, and special thanks are due to Steve Ott and Steve Reynolds, who approved and funded this event for IPIA, and John Francis, who provided financial support as well. Aleta Tew, Shelley Kruger, and Jolaine Randall arranged the logistics of the event. Erin Peterson provided outstanding research support leading up to the event and helped throughout the conference. We thank Sarah Hill, who provided background research for the conference and for this volume. We also wish to thank the many other conference participants, whose questions, comments, and input helped to improve the research collected in this volume; in particular we want to thank Michael Caudell-Feagan, Doug Chapin, Geri Mannion, Charles Stewart, and Kim Wyman from Thurston County (Washington) for their participation in the conference.

For the second phase of the project, the collection of chapters herein and the editing of the volume, Alvarez wishes to acknowledge both Carnegie and Knight for continuing to support his work in this area. All three of the editors, finally, wish to express special thanks to Melissa Slemin, without whose assistance neither phase of this project would have been completed in such a rapid and efficient manner.

Introduction: Studying Election Fraud

R. Michael Alvarez, Thad E. Hall, and Susan D. Hyde

In 2006 alone, significant allegations of election fraud surrounded presidential elections in Italy, Mexico, and several former Soviet republics. In the United States, concerns have been raised regarding all aspects of elections, from voter registration fraud to voting machine security, especially since the 2000 presidential election, when accusations of electoral manipulation in Florida were heard around the world. The potential for election fraud overshadows elections in all election-holding countries, even long-established democracies.

Investigations by journalists, academics, lawyers, political parties, official nonpartisan observers, and interested citizens have drawn attention to cases of clear-cut voting fraud in many countries around the world, including the United States. These cases are troubling because fair and competitive elections are widely understood to be a necessary element of representative democracy. Electoral manipulation diminishes many of the assumed benefits of democratic governance, including public accountability, transparency, and representation. However, the concept of election fraud and electoral manipulation more generally remains remarkably understudied.

Policymakers and academics share an interest in election fraud, but several factors have made it difficult to formulate a coherent understanding of what election fraud is, much less how to detect and prevent it. There is still no widely accepted definition of election fraud because the applied understanding of fraud depends on the context: what is perceived as fraudulent manipulation of the electoral process differs over time and from country to country. Even within academia, the theoretical definitions of fraud have yet to be united across the fields of international and domestic law, comparative and American political science, and election administration in developed and developing countries.

As commitments to democratic governance have spread throughout the world, international organizations have tried to define democratic elections. They have established criteria for democratic elections, but there remain many points of contention between countries, regions, international organizations, NGOs, academics, and policymakers. Article 21 of the Universal Declaration of Human Rights adopted by the United Nations in 1948 states that the will of the people "shall be expressed in periodic and genuine elections which shall be by universal and equal suffrage and shall be held by secret vote or by equivalent free voting procedures." Beyond this relatively benign and widely cited commitment, there is limited agreement on the necessary elements of democratic elections.

Even well-established international election observers who are invited to countries in order to offer assessments on election quality maintain that their evaluations should be made within the historical and political context of the country in question. Further, since the early 1990s they have shied away from the efforts of journalists to classify elections as "free and fair." As Eric Bjornlund eloquently notes:

> Most people assume that the [election] observers' job is to determine whether an election is free and fair. Yet observation practice has not clearly established what this means. Measuring elections against a free and fair standard suggests a dichotomy—the elections either pass or fail a test of legitimacy—when elections are actually political processes more realistically judged along a continuum and placed in context. This focus on the free and fair determination has encouraged international election assessments to make categorical, "bottom-line" judgments that fail to take nuances and context into account. Such judgments imply, inaccurately, that elections in democratic countries are beyond reproach.[1]

In short, many allegations of election fraud may not be clear-cut, but will be context-dependent, falling along the continuum that Bjornlund outlines. Suspicious behavior may be the only "evidence" of election fraud, and it can be difficult to prove; the supposed fraud may instead be the result of administrative incompetence or simple misunderstandings. Finally, claims of fraud are typically made by the losing candidate or party, thus casting doubt on whether alleged cases of fraud are real or are the cries of a "sore loser."

Beyond identifying fraud, how to use the knowledge that it has occurred presents other challenges. For example, election observers must determine whether documented irregularities would have changed the outcome of an election. Neither academics nor policymakers have clearly defined how much fraud must take place in order to constitute a fraudulent election. As one noted scholar of comparative politics states:

> Democratic norms are not *perfectly* realized anywhere, even in advanced democracies. Access to the electoral arena always has a cost and is never perfectly equal; the scopes and jurisdictions of elective offices are everywhere limited; electoral institutions invariably discriminate against somebody inside or outside the party system; and democratic politics is never quite sovereign but always subject to societal as well as constitutional constraints. . . . There is much room for nuance and ambivalence . . . [and] bending and circumventing the rules may sometimes be considered "part of the game."[2]

Clearly, an election in which every vote is stolen should be considered fraudulent, but where should the line be drawn? Does a single manipulated vote constitute a fraudulent election? What about forms of election manipulation that do not pertain directly to the act of voting, such as intimidating potential political candidates or changing the electoral system to benefit one party over another? Is election fraud in a very close election more damaging than election fraud in an election with an overwhelming winner?

Given the substantive importance and widespread occurrence of election fraud around the world, and the central role that elections play in democratic governance, one might assume that sophisticated studies of election fraud would have proliferated. However, work to date includes little systematic research on how election fraud can be detected and deterred despite the frequent claims and anecdotes about election fraud found in the media and popular press. This comment is only partially a critique; detailed case studies or even anecdotes can provide important signals about where to look for election fraud, as well as information about the types of fraud that can be perpetrated.

Existing research includes well-documented cases of blatant election fraud and overt manipulation of the electoral process, including early twentieth-century Kentucky, New York from 1870 to 1916, and Costa Rica.[3] So called "electoral authoritarian" regimes often have used elections to legitimate their rule and, to the surprise of many observers, sometimes fail to win these elections. In these cases, regimes have to decide whether to cheat—to steal the election—or to submit to the will of the people and transfer power to the winner.[4]

When authoritarian regimes lose elections, power is not automatically transferred. These regimes commit a form of manipulation after election day if they fail to accept the results and retain power through other means. Philippine president Ferdinand Marcos engaged in well-documented fraud in the 1986 presidential elections that involved both retail fraud (bribery and intimidation) and postelection wholesale fraud (manipulating the vote tallies). Similarly, Zimbabwe's president Robert Mugabe has systematically engaged in violence and intimidation to ensure that the opposition is weakened, and he continues to win elections. Of course, not all authoritarian governments resort to fraud in order to hold on to power; the party of the Sandinistas in Nicaragua handed over power to the opposition when they lost elections in 1990. Likewise, many nations with long histories of democratic government have held elections where irregularities and administrative problems raised questions about the integrity of elections where existing governments have tried to retain power, such as in the 2006 parliamentary elections in Italy.

Social scientists have an important opportunity (and, some would argue, a responsibility) to contribute to the detection and deterrence of election fraud. In the context of elections in the United States, the most outspoken commentators on the subject of election fraud are divided into two camps. On the one hand there are individuals who argue that election fraud is rampant and that U.S. elections are completely corrupt. On the other hand there are individuals who dismiss all claims of election fraud as partisan and instead argue that election fraud is nonexistent in U.S. elections.

In our view, these competing claims can be examined scientifically, relying primarily on tools from the social sciences. Without a doubt, election fraud has occurred in the United States, as shown in studies by Tracy Campbell, Gary Cox, and J. Morgan Kousser.[5] However, it is also true that many claims of election fraud may be initiated for purely political reasons and that some irregularities really are just administrative errors or oversights. By articulating legal definitions of fraud and by providing a menu of new techniques for fraud detection, we hope to find a middle ground in which election fraud is taken seriously but not all claims are assumed to be true, either in or outside the United States. By studying methods of fraud prevention and by examining the consequences of election fraud and efforts to prevent it, we also hope that this volume provides valuable information to election officials who are interested in increasing public confidence in elections. Even in jurisdictions where elections are run perfectly, unfounded accusations of fraud can undermine public confidence in the electoral process and complicate an already difficult job. It is in this spirit that we offer recommendations to election officials that can increase transparency and thus public confidence in the electoral process.

This volume brings together a collection of scholars who attempt to address several critical questions. First, what is election fraud and how does context matter in the conceptualization of what constitutes election fraud and what does not? Second, what is the empirical record regarding fraud, and how can voters and interested observers identify election fraud in the United States? Third, what lessons can we learn from elections outside the United States about the incidence and detection of election fraud? Finally, what are the most effective new statistical methodologies for detecting election anomalies, which then can be used as the basis for subsequent analysis to ferret out election fraud? We conclude the volume with a discussion of directions for future research and policy changes that are necessary so that we can better study and prevent election fraud.

The one limitation that all scholars face is a lack of transparency in the electoral process, and we discuss this important issue at length in our conclusion. Critical to this transparency is access to election data that, we argue, should be reported efficiently and in a consistent format over time and across jurisdictions. In addition, we advocate greater access by scholars and researchers to the voting process and to vote-counting procedures as a means to enhance the empirical study of election fraud.

What Is Election Fraud and How Can It Be Quantified?

In studying election fraud, it becomes immediately clear that understandings of the concept are rooted in each country's cultural and political milieu. Consider, for example, the allegations of fraud in Mexico's 2006 presidential election. Some charges centered on the use of door-to-door canvassing by one of the political parties and whether such campaigning constituted undue partisan pressure on voters. Similarly, the decision by President Vicente Fox to endorse one of the candidates running to replace him was perceived within Mexico as illegitimate pressuring of voters and an unfair use of state funds to promote one candidate. In the United States, both of these activities have long been commonplace; parties and candidates are expected to go door-to-door attempting to persuade and mobilize voters, and endorsements by officeholders are a non-controversial part of the electoral process. By contrast, the U.S. campaign finance system—where groups and individuals with an interest in particular policies can make direct contributions to the campaigns of decisionmakers— is legal in the United States, but in other counties similar contributions by groups and individuals would constitute campaign and election fraud. As these examples show, differences in countries' electoral laws and differences in political culture contribute to whether a given activity is perceived as election fraud.

Even in the United States, views of election fraud have varied over time and across states. We often forget that it was only in the 1960s that the United States ended the practice of systematically disenfranchising entire classes of voters. This was the ultimate form of election fraud; the use of state power to keep eligible voters from casting a ballot. In the 1800s, low-level violence and intimidation at the polls were commonplace in many regions of the country and were seen as part of electoral competition. Vote buying, a concern today, was conducted out in the open in the mid-1800s, with voters often able to receive "bids" for their votes from competing political parties. In the late 1890s, U.S. voters in some parts of the country were paid to stay home on election day.[6] Various reforms have addressed such election fraud, including the adoption of the secret ballot and the use of voting machines for casting and counting ballots.

Culture also affects how different countries view the same election reforms. Estonia conducts elections using the Internet, something that critics of electronic voting in the United States have argued is a recipe for election fraud. Likewise, India adopted electronic voting because it helped to mitigate the rampant practice of armed gunmen's stuffing ballot boxes in certain regions of the country. In the United States, electronic voting equipment, similar to that used successfully in India, is viewed as a potential source of fraud by a subset of voters and activists. In each of these cases, history, politics, and culture together shape how a given reform is viewed in the context of election fraud.

Perhaps due to a lack of consistent data and definitions about election fraud, there has been relatively little empirical analysis of election fraud in the research literature. Most election fraud studies in the United States are historical, focusing on historical epochs or case studies. One epoch of great interest is the "Gilded Age," during the late 1800s; many of these studies try to estimate the extent of election fraud. Geographic, case-based historical studies of American election fraud include studies of the early twentieth century in Pittsburgh and studies of nineteenth-century New York, Texas, South Carolina, and Mississippi.[7] George Miller is one scholar who focused on fraud in specific election modes by examining fraud allegations in absentee voting;

others have studied historic allegations of fraudulent voter registration.[8] Contemporary considerations of election fraud can be found in a book by Larry Sabato and Glenn Simpson, as well as in studies by John Fund, Tracy Campbell, and Andrew Gumbel.[9]

Outside the United States there have been studies of election fraud, especially in what Fabrice Lehoucq refers to as "pre-reform political systems."[10] These are nations that do not meet minimal requirements for a functioning democracy, and whose electoral administration systems appear to allow for much more rampant election fraud. Important examples include Costa Rica, Imperial Germany, Argentina, and Brazil.[11] The general conclusions from this literature are that there are many different ways in which political agents attempt to illegally manipulate election outcomes; however the evidence is weak that many of these manipulations are in fact decisive in determining electoral winners or losers.

Lehoucq and Ivan Molina have also conducted an in-depth longitudinal study of electoral fraud in Costa Rica for an almost fifty-year period in the development of the country.[12] They found that changes in social structure dramatically changed the nature of election fraud. Population movements, changes in economic conditions and labor markets, and educational attainment all can lead to changes in the types and level of fraud. Fraud is also a function of the legal framework in which elections occur. Party competition, how legislative seats are allocated, and the forms of representation that exist can all affect whether the political environment is likely to be a problem.

Last, there is an extensive and growing literature on political corruption. This literature focuses on historical political machines and corruption in American cities, including Tammany Hall in New York. Political corruption is also explored in comparative perspective. As this literature tends to cover more general issues of political corruption, some works examine types of corruption that take place in the electoral arena.[13]

Political factors, especially political competition, have been shown to explain some of the observed variation in election fraud, with a positive correlation between competitiveness and various measures of election fraud, with some important exceptions.[14] Institutional factors, in particular the specific mechanisms used for legislative elections (for example, majoritarian versus proportional systems), appear to explain much of the variance in election fraud in Costa Rica, with more fraud occurring under majoritarian rules. Economic interests, partisanship and incumbency, and urbanization also appear to correlate with the extent of election fraud.[15]

Plan of the Book: Defining, Measuring, and Detecting Fraud

It will become clear to the reader that there are a number of competing definitions of election fraud. Even scholars who are at the forefront of research on election fraud do not agree on a general conceptual definition. We return to this issue in the final chapter of this volume, where we delineate the steps that we view as essential in working toward a stronger body of research on election fraud and for improving public policies for the detection and prevention of election fraud.

Although the volume includes research informed by elections in dozens of countries, it was motivated primarily by a desire to systematically evaluate the heightened attention to claims of election fraud in the United States since the controversial 2000 presidential election. These claims and much of the literature on election fraud in both domestic and international contexts is atheoretical and anecdotal, designed to make a specific case about election fraud or give examples about the continuity of fraud cases over time. Such works are helpful to the overall understanding of election fraud, but have been most useful in documenting the historical occurrences of fraud.

We are interested in developing a more comprehensive framework for examining election fraud. In many ways, the election fraud problem is similar to many "black box" problems. Elections have inputs (voters, parties, candidates, the media) and outputs (the vote share for each competitor). In the middle there is a process that is not inherently transparent. The secret ballot minimizes voter coercion by ensuring that a given vote cannot be attributed to a given voter. However, it also means that the election process is not auditable in the same way that a banking system is auditable. The procedures that govern the election can also make the process more or less transparent and more or less open to public scrutiny.

Given that we can never truly measure whether each voter's intention was successfully transmitted through the electoral process, this book examines the array of potentially illegal or unfair inputs and outputs of the electoral process. This requires defining the electoral process and the bounds for legal and illegal election activities. Next, given that the electoral process can be viewed as a black box problem, we are also interested in examining techniques that can be employed to determine whether the activities that occurred "inside" the black box are outside the bounds of what we would expect in a democratic election. Finally, we consider how to make an election free and fair through procedural and legal measures.

Defining Election Fraud

Research on election fraud, both in the United States and internationally, is difficult. Even in a purely legal sense, definitions of election fraud differ widely in different jurisdictions. Comparatively, activities viewed as normal behavior during elections in the United States would be considered fraud in other countries. Even in the United States, acceptable actions in one state may be explicitly banned in others. The relative nature of election fraud and the widely variant historical, cultural, and institutional contexts in which election fraud has occurred make the development of a clear and consistent definition a complicated, if not impossible, undertaking. In this part of the book, we examine understandings of election fraud in the United States, focusing primarily on legal definitions of fraud. Even within the rather narrow U.S. legal context, federal and state laws differ, and case law continues to contribute new information. New voting technologies have generated new legal challenges, and some questionable practices remain untested within the judicial system. The chapter by Craig Donsanto provides a helpful legal framework for understanding U.S. federal election laws and the activities that are considered election fraud. Donsanto cuts through the legalese to explain what is actually outlawed in U.S. elections. Tellingly, we again see here that definitions of election fraud, as established by the courts, have evolved over time, and Congress has worked to tune the laws related to election fraud for more than 100 years.

One of the more vital consequences of election fraud may be the negative effect it has on public confidence in the electoral process. This consequence may occur even when no election fraud actually takes place. Simple allegations of fraud can be enough to depress citizen participation and harm the reputation of the institutions charged with administering elections. Such allegations also give politicians the ability to offer reforms, which may serve either to improve elections or to entrench some bias in the electoral system. With this in mind, Thad Hall and Tova Wang examine what might be learned from the international democracy promotion community about normative principles for the prevention of election fraud. Although not law, these documents may provide guidance to those interested in applying lessons from abroad in the U.S. context.

A looming unknown question is whether efforts to reduce election fraud through prevention, deterrence, or detection are analogous to plugging a small hole in a leaky dam or throwing a boulder in the middle of a river. In other words, do efforts to prevent or deter election fraud actually eliminate it or do they merely displace it? In some contexts, particularly in the more undemocratic settings, persons planning to engage in election fraud will simply circumvent any barriers put in their way. In other cases, it is possible that only minor reforms could eliminate fraudulent practices altogether.

The final contribution in this section only begins to answer this question, and does so by raising important questions about election fraud in a broader theoretical context. Through case studies of Iraqi and Palestinian elections, Gamze Çavdar shows how procedurally acceptable elections may be affected by the broader context, specifically when elections take place under foreign occupation. Given the lively current debate about the importance of transitioning to democratic elections in the Middle East, Çavdar's chapter provides important theoretical analysis of the issues that must be considered as countries move to democratic elections.

Measuring Election Fraud

Debates about election reform and proposed changes to election procedures are generally infused with questions about election fraud. For example, following the 2000 U.S. presidential election, when debate began over the legislation that became the "Help America Vote Act," significant attention was paid to the question of whether the voter registration process in some states invited certain forms of election fraud. In recent years, as many states have moved toward stricter voter identification procedures, the rationale for stricter identification requirements has been that they will prevent voter fraud. Some experts have criticized these debates, arguing that there is little empirical evidence documenting widespread election fraud, at least of the sort that stricter voter identification requirements would prevent.[16]

This empirical debate is quite important because, if fraud is a problem, we should be able to see evidence of it in legal proceedings and in data from elections. The debate over fraud requires having some baseline data on the types of fraud that occur, the frequency of these various types of fraud, the types of individuals who perpetrate fraud, and the rationale for committing fraud. Given the mostly anecdotal nature of the debate over fraud, any effort to systematically collect and analyze data on election fraud—at the federal, state, or local level—moves the study of election fraud forward. To use an analogy, are fraud accusations like airplane crashes—infrequent but focusing events that we remember; or are accusations of fraud more like car accidents, events that occur frequently but where only the most dramatic make the news?

The contributions in the second part of the book consider a seemingly simple yet vexing question: how much election fraud is there? This part focuses on measuring election fraud in the United States; we would encourage readers to examine chapter 11, by Mikhail Myagkov, Peter Ordeshook, and Dimitry Shaikin, to appreciate the issues associated with fraud in the post-Soviet context. We start this part with attitudinal data regarding election fraud; Michael Alvarez and Thad Hall take readers on a tour of these perceptions, discussing how both the elite and the general population view fraud. Unlike many discussions of election fraud, they ground this discussion in a theoretical framework of risk assessment and how risk is communicated and amplified through society. The survey data presented by the authors allow us to see how Americans perceive fraud and what types of fraud are most worrisome to the general public.

The next four chapters are specific empirical analyses of fraud. Delia Bailey looks at the record of federal election fraud litigation to examine how many cases have been brought into the national court system, what types of fraud have been alleged, and how extensive the election fraud might have been. Given the political debate in Washington in 2007 regarding the role of U.S. attorneys in prioritizing voting fraud prosecutions, the findings in this chapter shed important light on the prosecution of federal election fraud. Michael Alvarez and Frederick Boehmke examine records of fraud allegation from California and Georgia in order to document the rates of different forms of election fraud. As in the chapter by Delia Bailey, the systematic examination of election fraud at the state level provides a baseline for understanding the frequency with which fraud is actually prosecuted as well as evidence of the types of fraud that occur.

Roderick Kiewiet, Thad Hall, Michael Alvarez, and Jonathan Katz consider a simple but potentially powerful methodology for finding problems in a given jurisdiction's elections: asking the local elections administrators to fill out "incident reports." Using these incident reports from a recent election in Ohio, Kiewiet and his colleagues are able to document a number of potential points of failure and some important procedural vulnerabilities. These data provide insights both into the types of administrative problems that occur in elections as well as the types of fraud that can occur if simple procedures for election security are not followed. Finally, Todd Donovan and Daniel Smith present and analyze new data on signature fraud in ballot measure petitions. Given the growing number of ballot initiatives in many U.S. states and the role that they can play in setting the policy agenda, understanding how fraud is perpetrated in the signature collection process, its frequency, and the effectiveness of efforts to ameliorate this problem are critical in evaluating direct democracy.

Detecting Election Fraud

Detecting election fraud can be a difficult task. Except in cases of blatant fraud—such as the case examined by Mikhail Myagkov, Peter Ordeshook, and Dimitry Shaikin in their chapter on Russia—it can be difficult to distinguish between blatant attempts to manipulate the election and isolated anomalies, incidents, or irregularities that may be completely unintentional. Many methods of detecting election fraud require a transparent electoral process and high-quality data reported in a timely manner. Detection also requires knowing where to look for election manipulation. For example, fraud is a more cost-effective activity in an election where only a small number of stolen votes are needed to change the outcome of a race. Local races and very close elections are often the places to look for fraud within relatively democratic contexts.[17]

The 2000 U.S. presidential election and the subsequent attention paid to observed electoral irregularities in that election (especially in Florida) generated renewed interest in the United States in studying electoral irregularities and fraud. The problem with such research is that it is often predicated on suppositions or assumptions that may have little to do with fraud. The 2004 election was rife with allegations not necessarily founded on evidence; the *New York Times* even printed a story about conspiracy theories on the Internet, including allegations that optical scan balloting was the source of fraud in Florida, and that long lines in Ohio were a sure sign of fraud there.[18] These studies often failed to consider basic, well-established, information about party identification, bipartisan election administration, and statistics. For example, the *New York Times* article quotes Clay Shirky of the interactive telecommunications program at New York University, who suggests "that the online fact-finding machine has come unmoored, and that some bloggers simply 'can't imagine any universe in which a fair count of the votes would result in George Bush being re-elected president.'"

Addressing the question of election fairness requires models of elections that allow researchers to determine if election outcomes look like what we would expect in a fair election. There is growing interest in using sophisticated statistical or econometric techniques to model election regularities—and to then identify election irregularities, or "outliers."[19] Detected outliers, say in precinct-by-precinct or county-by-county analyses, can then be examined in further detail to determine if their outlier status is due to fraud or to other benign or idiosyncratic factors.

This is a promising avenue for future studies of election fraud and one that is explored in five of the chapters presented here. Each chapter uses a different method to answer the same question: were the data that were produced by the election—the vote totals, turnout, and the like—what we would expect in a democratic election? Represented in this final part of the book are several different statistical methodologies that can be used to look for anomalies and problems in elections and election administration—results that might provide the a priori evidence for further investigation of potential election fraud.

This section begins with an analysis by Michael Alvarez and Jonathan Katz, who examine the 2002 gubernatorial and senatorial elections in Georgia in which problems were alleged. Alvarez and Katz show that the combination of political science knowledge of elections and simple but powerful statistical tools can be used to look for anomalies in county-level data. Using historical data and regression analysis, they show how it is possible to determine whether a given election outcome is within the bounds of what would be predicted by previous events.

Walter Mebane modifies the use of Benford's Law—a statistical technique that was originally developed to detect financial fraud—to examine election fraud. This little-known but potentially powerful test can be used to study the distribution of election returns across geographic units and test whether they differ from expected patterns. He has applied this technique to both domestic and international election data and shows how Benford's Law not only identifies traditional localities with a history of fraud but also identifies localities that have been the center of election controversies.

Mikhail Myagkov, Peter Ordeshook, and Dimitry Shaikin use data from recent elections in Russia and a "flow of votes" analysis to look for evidence of anomalies and potential manipulation. Susan Hyde considers how international election observation can detect and deter election fraud and advocates random assignment of observers as an improvement to existing methodology. Raising a number of thought-provoking questions in the final chapter in this section, Alberto Simpser considers the potential unintended consequences of high-quality election observation.

Recommendations for Reform

In the final chapter we propose a series of simple reforms that could be put into place to detect and prevent election fraud. Even where the probability of election fraud is low, doubts surrounding the legitimacy and fairness of an electoral process should still compel strong public policy action. Low voter confidence in an electoral process, even if unfounded, can have a depressing effect on turnout and other civic action. Therefore, we argue that policy-makers in the United States should enact reforms that are likely to increase voter trust and confidence in the electoral process. Given persistent suspicions about the integrity of U.S. elections, steps should be taken to ensure that the public—not just the insular world of election officials and political parties—is confident that elections are free and fair, and that their outcomes are accurate.

Our first recommendation is that elections, especially U.S. elections—should be made more transparent to observation by impartial and nonpartisan observers. In most American states, the role of election observation has been delegated to political parties. Although this is helpful, parties are not neutral observers; they want to ensure that *their own voters* get to vote but are likely to be indifferent, or even hostile, to voters from other parties. States should adopt laws that allow for neutral organizations to observe voting in order to signal that the elections are being conducted in a free and fair manner. An additional benefit of such observation is that scholars and interested students of elections will gain access to information about the mechanics of voting operations at polling places and thus study the efficacy of election administration practices that relate to election fraud prevention. Presently, lack of access by nonpartisan observers to a diverse sample of polling stations is one of the barriers to scholarly evaluation of election administration.

Second, election officials should report more data in real time. The basic data on elections—how many voters were eligible to vote in each precinct, how many voters voted, and the vote totals for each race—are needed for a transparent electoral process and for some methods of fraud detection. We understand that this recommendation may require significant upgrading of the technical infrastructure in many U.S. counties. Many of the most powerful techniques for fraud detection, identified in this volume, require access to precinct-level election results. Many other countries, including developing democracies, already compile and release precinct-level election results. Proper analysis of those results may be one of the best ways to deter fraud, and greater transparency is likely to increase voter confidence in the electoral process. It would be ideal if these data could be reported electronically, in a common format. Even without this reform, better reporting of existing data would improve our ability to analyze them.

Finally, we also strongly urge our colleagues—and the public and private organizations that fund their research—to expand the research literature on election fraud. As scholars, we need to develop new ways to study election fraud, we need new publication outlets for academic research on a question that is inherently multidisciplinary and methodologically complex, and we need to develop theoretical approaches for defining and understanding what we mean by election fraud, when it might occur, and how it might be perpetrated. These are tall orders, but we are hopeful that the collection of ideas in this volume will spark interest in what we see as a potentially exciting new field for new social science research.

Notes

1. Eric C. Bjornlund, *Beyond Free and Fair: Monitoring Elections and Building Democracy* (Johns Hopkins University Press, 2004), pp. 97–98.

2. Andreas Schedler, "The Menu of Manipulation," *Journal of Democracy* 13, no. 2 (2002): 36–50; emphasis in original.

3. Tracy Campbell, "Machine Politics, Police Corruption, and the Persistence of Vote Fraud: The Case of the Louisville, Kentucky, Election of 1905," *Journal of Policy History* 15, no. 3 (2003): 269–300; Gary W. Cox and J. Morgan Kousser, "Turnout and Rural Corruption: New York as a Test Case," *American Journal of Political Science* 25, no. 4 (1981): 646–63; Fabrice E. Lehoucq and I. Molina, *Stuffing the Ballot Box: Fraud, Electoral Reform, and Democratization in Costa Rica* (Cambridge University Press, 2002).

4. For a comprehensive examination of this issue, see Mark R. Thompson and Philipp Kuntz, "After Defeat: When Do Rulers Steal Elections?" in *Electoral Authoritarianism: The Dynamics of Unfree Competition*, edited by Andreas Schedler (Boulder, Colo.: Lynne Rienner, 2006).

5. Tracy Campbell, *Deliver the Vote* (New York: Carroll and Graf, 2005); Cox and Kousser, "Turnout and Rural Corruption."

6. Cox and Kousser, "Turnout and Rural Corruption."

7. Peter H. Argersinger, "New Perspectives on Election Fraud in the Gilded Age," *Political Science Quarterly* 100 (1985–86): 699–87; Dale Baum, "Pinpointing Apparent Fraud in the 1861 Texas Succession Referendum," *Journal of Interdisciplinary History* 22 (1991): 201–21; Cox and Kousser, "Turnout and Rural Corruption"; R. F. King, "Counting the Votes: South Carolina's Stolen Election of 1876," *Journal of Interdisciplinary History* 32 (2001): 169–91; Loomis Mayfield, "Voting Fraud in Early Twentieth-Century Pittsburgh," *Journal of Interdisciplinary History* 24 (1993): 59–94.

8. George F. Miller, *Absentee Voters and Suffrage Laws* (Washington: Daylion, 1948).

9. Campbell, *Deliver the Vote*; John Fund, *Stealing Elections* (New York: Encounter Books, 2004); Andrew Gumbel, *Steal This Vote* (New York: Nation Books, 2004);

Joseph P. Harris, *Registration of Voters in the United States* (Washington: Brookings, 1929); Alexander Keyssar, *The Right to Vote: The Contested History of Democracy in the United States* (New York: Basic Books, 2000); Larry J. Sabato and Glenn R. Simpson, *Dirty Little Secrets: The Persistence of Corruption in American Politics* (New York: Random House, 1996).

10. Fabrice Lehoucq, "Electoral Fraud: Causes, Types, and Consequences," *Annual Review of Political Science* 6 (2003): 233–56.

11. M. L. Anderson, *Practicing Democracy: Elections and Political Culture in Imperial Germany* (Princeton University Press, 2000); R. Graham, *Politics and Patronage in Nineteenth-Century Brazil* (Stanford University Press, 1990); Lehoucq and Molina, *Stuffing the Ballot Box*; and Hilda Sábato, *The Many and the Few: Political Participation in Republican Buenos Aires* (Stanford University Press, 2001). For a more extensive literature review, covering sources in French and Spanish in addition to English, see Lehoucq, "Electoral Fraud."

12. Lehoucq and Molina, *Stuffing the Ballot Box*.

13. Richard L. Hasen, "Vote Buying," *California Law Review* 88 (2000): 1323–71; Roger Myerson, "Effectiveness of Electoral Systems for Reducing Government Corruption: A Game–Theoretic Analysis," *Games and Economic Behavior* 5 (1993): 118–32; Torsten Persson and Guido Tabellini, *Political Economics: Explaining Economic Policy* (MIT Press, 2000); William L. Riordan, *Plunkitt of Tammany Hall* (New York: St. Martin's, 1994); Susan Rose-Ackerman, *Corruption and Government: Causes, Consequences and Reform* (Cambridge University Press, 1999).

14. Alberto Simpser, "Making Votes Not Count" (Ph.D. dissertation, Stanford University, 2005). Simpser shows that election fraud occurs in many noncompetitive elections, arguing that it can be a means by which autocrats demonstrate their dominance of the system.

15. See Anderson, *Practicing Democracy*; J. I. Dominguez and J. A. McCann, *Democratizing Mexico: Public Opinion and Electoral Choices* (Johns Hopkins University Press, 1996).

16. Spencer Overton, *Stealing Democracy* (New York: W. W. Norton, 2006).

17. Although fraud is more likely to change the outcome of an election that is close, Alberto Simpser has demonstrated that in some countries candidates may have an incentive to engage in widespread electoral fraud even in elections that are not likely to be close. See Simpser, "Making Votes Not Count."

18. Tom Zeller, "Vote Fraud Theories, Spread by Blogs, Are Quickly Buried," *New York Times*, November 12, 2004, p. A-1.

19. See Walter R. Mebane and Jasjeet S. Sekhon, "Robust Estimation and Outlier Detection for Overdispersed Multinomial Models of Count Data," Harvard University, manuscript; Jonathan N. A. Wand, Jasjeet S. Sekhon, and Walter R. Mebane, "A Comparative Analysis of Multinomial Voting Irregularities: Canada 2000," paper presented at the 2001 Joint Statistical Meetings, American Statistical Association, Social

Statistics Section, Atlanta, Georgia. While this new interest is developing among methodologically sophisticated social scientists, the basic idea of using outlier detection to identify potential electoral fraud has appeared earlier in some historical studies of fraud, including Baum, "Pinpointing Apparent Fraud"; Robert C. Oberst and Amy Weilage, "Quantitative Tests of Electoral Fraud: The 1982 Sri Lankan Referendum," *Corruption and Reform* 5 (1990): 49–62; and L. N. Powell, "Correcting for Fraud: A Quantitative Reassessment of the Mississippi Ratification Election of 1868," *Journal of Southern History* 5 (1989): 633–58.

part one

Defining Election Fraud: The United States in Comparative Perspective

one

Corruption of the Election Process under U.S. Federal Law

Craig C. Donsanto

Election fraud can be viewed as a purely legal phenomenon. In this context, election fraud is whatever is defined in the law as such, though its definition can change as the social, political, and technological aspects of elections change. For example, you cannot have election fraud in the voter registration process until after states have adopted and developed voter registration requirements and lists. Even once voter registration systems are developed, the laws that govern fraud may change over time as conditions and technologies change.

In this chapter, I focus on election fraud as defined under federal law. These laws are intended to ensure that elections are free from corruption. This focus excludes two important areas from consideration: (1) state laws dealing with election fraud; and (2) efforts under federal law to prevent discrimination against minorities at the ballot box. State election laws may define fraud differently and cover different actions than federal law. And federal antidiscrimination issues involve entirely different constitutional and

Craig Donsanto is director of the Election Crimes Branch at the United States Department of Justice. The views expressed in this chapter are solely those of the author and do not necessarily reflect the position or view of the United States Department of Justice concerning the issues addressed. Nothing herein is intended to confer rights or defenses to those whose activities may be addressed by this chapter. Readers are encouraged to consult Donsanto and Simmons, *Federal Prosecution of Election Offenses,* 7th edition, from which this chapter was excerpted, for the official view of the Department of Justice (available to the public at www.usdoj.gov/criminal).

federal interests that center largely on implementation of the Voting Rights Act and its amendments.

What Is (and Is Not) Election Fraud?

Election fraud, as a criminal law concept, involves a substantive irregularity relating to the act of voting—such as bribery, intimidation, or forgery—that has the potential to taint the election. Over the past century and a half, Congress and the federal courts have articulated the following constitutional principles concerning the right to vote in the United States. Any activity intended to interfere corruptly with any of the following principles may be actionable as a federal crime:

—All qualified citizens are eligible to vote.

—All qualified voters have the right to have their votes counted fairly and honestly.

—Invalid ballots dilute the worth of valid ballots and therefore will not be counted.

—Every qualified voter has the right to make a personal and independent election decision.

—Qualified voters may opt not to participate in an election.

—Voting shall not be influenced by bribery or intimidation.

Simply put, election fraud is conduct intended to corrupt the process by which ballots are obtained, marked, or tabulated; the process by which election results are canvassed and certified; or the process by which voters are registered. Schemes that involve corruption of other political processes (for example, political campaigning or the circulation of nominating petitions) do not normally serve as the basis for a federal election crime.

The following activities provide a basis for federal prosecution for election fraud. The laws are loosely categorized as follows:

Vote buying consists of paying voters to register to vote, or to participate in elections, in which a federal candidate is on the ballot.[1]

Voter intimidation, in the context of a criminal case, can consist of preventing a voter from participating in an election where a federal candidate is on the ballot or encouraging a voter to participate in such an election through the application or threat of physical or economic duress.

Illegal voting and ballot box stuffing are both crimes. Illegal voting consists of voting in federal elections on behalf of individuals who do not personally participate in, and assent to, the voting act attributed to them. It also covers impersonating voters or casting ballots in the names of voters who do not vote in federal elections.[2] Malfeasance by election officials acting "under color of law" by performing such acts as diluting valid ballots with invalid ones (ballot box stuffing), rendering false tabulations of votes, or preventing valid voter registrations or votes from being given effect in any election, federal or nonfederal, as well as in elections in which federal candidates are on the ballot, is illegal as well. Finally, knowingly making a false claim of U.S. citizenship in order to register to vote or to vote in any election, or falsely and willfully claiming U.S. citizenship for, inter alia, registering or voting in any election is a form of illegal voting.

Voter registration fraud can take several forms, including: (a) submitting fictitious names on voter registration rolls and thereby qualifying the ostensible voters to vote in federal elections;[3] (b) knowingly procuring eligibility to vote for federal office by persons who are not entitled to vote under applicable state law, notably persons who have committed serious crimes (a law in approximately forty states) and persons who are not U.S. citizens (currently a law in all states); (c) providing false information concerning a person's name, address, or period of residence in a voting district in order to establish that person's eligibility to register or to vote in a federal election; or (d) causing the production of voter registrations that qualify alleged voters to vote for federal candidates, or the production of ballots in federal elections, that the actor knows are materially defective under applicable state law.

Various types of conduct that might adversely affect the election of a federal candidate may not constitute federal election crimes, despite what may be their reprehensible character. For example, a federal election crime does not currently involve irregularities relating to: (1) issuing inaccurate campaign literature; (2) campaigning too close to the polls; (3) the process by which a candidate obtains the withdrawal of an opponent; and (4) negligently failing to comply with state-mandated voting procedures (in the case of election officers). Also, "facilitation payments," things of value that are given to voters to make it easier for the voter to cast a ballot but that are not intended to stimulate or reward the voting act itself (for example, a ride to the polls, a stamp to mail in an absentee ballot) do not ordinarily constitute a federal crime.

Participating in Fraud

As a practical matter, election frauds fall into two categories: those in which individual voters do not participate in the fraud, and those in which they do. The investigative approach and prosecutive potential are different for each type of case. The first category involves voters who do not participate, in any way, in the voting act attributed to them. These offenses include ballot box stuffing, ghost voting, and "nursing home" voter fraud. Proof of these crimes depends largely on evidence generated by the voting process, or on hand-writing examples taken from persons who had access to voting equipment and thus the opportunity to misuse it. Some of the more common ways these crimes are committed include placing fictitious names on the voter rolls, which allows for fraudulent ballots to be used to stuff the ballot box; casting bogus votes in the names of persons who did not vote; obtaining and mark-ing absentee ballots without the active input of the voters involved;[4] and fal-sifying vote tallies.

The second category of election fraud includes cases in which the voters do participate, at least to some extent, in the voting acts attributed to them. Com-mon examples include vote-buying schemes; voter intimidation schemes; migratory voting (or floating voter) schemes; and voter "assistance" fraud, in which the wishes of the voters are ignored or not sought. Successful prosecu-tion of these cases usually requires the cooperation and testimony of the vot-ers whose ballots were corrupted. This requirement presents several difficul-ties. One problem is that the voters themselves may be technically guilty of participating in the scheme. However, because these voters can often be con-sidered victims, federal prosecutors usually consider declining to prosecute them in exchange for truthful cooperation against organizers of such schemes.

A second difficulty encountered in cases where voters participate is that the voter's presence alone may suggest that he or she "consented" to the defendant's conduct (marking the ballot, taking the ballot, choosing the can-didates, and so on). For example, in *United States* v. *Salisbury* (1993) the court left unanswered the question whether a voter who signs a ballot envelope at the defendant's instruction but is not allowed to choose the candidates has consented to having the defendant mark his or her ballot; but in *United States* v. *Cole* (1994) the court found that voters who merely signed ballots subse-quently marked by the defendant were not expressing their own electoral preferences.[5]

Although the presence of the ostensible voter when another marks his or her ballot does not negate whatever crime might be occurring, it may increase the difficulty of proving the crime. This difficulty is compounded when those who commit this type of crime target vulnerable members of society, such as persons who are uneducated, socially disadvantaged, or with little means of livelihood. Therefore, if the voter is present when another person marks his or her ballot, the evidence should show that the defendant either procured the voter's ballot through means that were themselves corrupt (such as bribery or threats), or that the defendant marked the voter's ballot without the voter's consent or input.

The Evolution of Federal Election Fraud Law

Federal interest in the integrity of the franchise dates back to Reconstruction, when Congress passed the Enforcement Acts, with the goal of protecting the political rights of newly enfranchised African Americans. These acts served as the basis for federal activism in prosecuting corruption of the franchise until most of them were repealed in the 1890s. They had broad jurisdictional predicates that allowed them to be applied to a wide variety of corrupt election practices as long as a federal candidate was on the ballot. The Supreme Court upheld this principle in *Ex parte Coy* (1888) by ruling that Congress had authority under the Constitution's "necessary and proper" clause to regulate any activity during a mixed federal/state election that exposed the federal election to potential harm, whether that harm materialized or not. *Coy* is still applicable law.[6]

After Reconstruction, federal activism in election matters retrenched. The repeal of most of the Enforcement Acts eliminated the statutory tools that had encouraged federal activism in election fraud matters. Two surviving provisions of these acts, now embodied in Sections 241 and 242 of the U.S. Code, made it unlawful to intentionally deprive anyone of rights guaranteed directly by the Constitution or federal law. However, contemporary interpretations made it difficult to use these provisions to prosecute election fraud. Courts during this period held that the Constitution directly conferred a right to vote only for federal officers and that conduct aimed at corrupting nonfederal contests was not prosecutable in federal courts. Federal attention to election fraud was further limited by case law holding that primary elections were not part of the official election process (*Newberry* v. *United States* (1921)) and by cases like *United States* v. *Bathgate* (1918), which read the entire subject of vote buying out of federal criminal law, even when it was directed at federal contests.[7]

In 1941, Supreme Court rulings in several cases began to expand and reshape federal involvement in elections. In *United States* v. *Classic,* the Court reversed direction and overturned the *Newberry* decision, recognizing that primary elections are an integral part of the process by which candidates are elected to office.[8] In so doing, the Court ushered in a new period of federal activism. By the late 1960s, prosecutors had begun to expand their use of Section 241 to address election fraud. Since then, this statute has been successfully applied to prosecute election fraud that occurs "under color of law" (through corrupt official misconduct usually by election officials) in nonfederal elections as well as in elections where there are federal candidates on the ballot.

For decades, prosecutors also successfully used Section 1341, popularly known as the mail fraud statute, to target local election fraud, under the theory that such schemes defrauded citizens of their right to fair and honest elections. However, the mail fraud theory has been barred since 1987 when the Supreme Court held in *McNally* v. *United States* that Section 1341 did not apply to schemes to defraud someone of intangible rights, such as the right to honest provision of public services. Congress responded to *McNally* by enacting a provision that specifically defined Section 1341 to include schemes to defraud someone of "honest services."[9] However, subsequent attempts by the Justice Department to apply the mail fraud statute to election crimes have proven largely unsuccessful.[10]

In addition to these broad statutes, since the late 1950s Congress has enacted new criminal laws to combat false registrations, vote buying, multiple voting, and fraudulent voting in elections. These statutes rest on Congress's power to regulate federal elections and on its power under the "necessary and proper" clause to enact laws to protect the federal election process from the potential of corruption.[11] They can be applied as long as either the name of a federal candidate is on the ballot or the fraud involves corruption of the voter registration process in a state where individuals register to vote simultaneously for federal and other offices.

Applying Election Fraud Statutes

There are two classes of federal criminal statutes related to election fraud, as shown in table 1-1. The first class applies to both federal and nonfederal elections. The second class of statutes is applicable to federal elections—including "mixed" elections that have both federal and nonfederal candidates—but not to purely nonfederal elections. In this section, I review these statutes to illustrate the types of election crimes that they are designed to address.

Conspiracy against Rights: 18 U.S.C. §241

Section 241 makes it unlawful for two or more persons to "conspire to injure, oppress, threaten, or intimidate any person in any state, territory or district in the free exercise or enjoyment of any right or privilege secured by the Con-

Table 1-1. Federal Election Crime Statutes

Statute	Offense
Statutes applicable to federal and nonfederal elections	
42 U.S.C. §1973i(c), §1973gg-10, and 18 U.S.C. §1015(f)	Any fraud that is aimed at the process by which voters are registered, notably those to furnish materially false information to election registrars
18 U.S.C. §§241 and 242	Any scheme that involves the necessary participation of public officials, usually election officers or notaries, "acting under color of law," which is actionable as a derogation of the "one person, one vote" principle of the 14th Amendment—that is, "public schemes"[a]
18 U.S.C. §245(b)(1)(A)	Physical threats or reprisals against candidates, voters, poll watchers, or election officials
18 U.S.C. §592	"Armed men" stationed at the polls
18 U.S.C. §609	Coercion of voting among the military
18 U.S.C. §610	Coerced political activity by federal employees
18 U.S.C. §911	Fraudulent assertion of U.S. citizenship
18 U.S.C. §1341	Schemes involving the U.S. mails to corrupt elections that are predicated on the post-McNally "salary" or "pecuniary loss" theories[b]
18 U.S.C. §1952	Schemes to use the mails in furtherance of vote-buying activities in states that treat vote buying as bribery
Statutes applicable to federal elections only	
18 U.S.C. §594	Intimidation of voters
18 U.S.C. §597	Payments to persons to vote, or to refrain from voting, for a federal candidate
18 U.S.C. §608(b)	Vote buying and false registration under the Uniformed and Overseas Citizens Absentee Voting Act
18 U.S.C. §611	Voting by aliens
42 U.S.C. §1973i(c)	Payments for registering to vote or voting, fraudulent registrations, and conspiracies to encourage illegal voting
42 U.S.C. §1973i(e)	Voting more than once
42 U.S.C. §1973gg-10(1)	Voter intimidation
42 U.S.C. §1973gg-10(2)	Fraudulent voting or registering

a. Federal prosecutors should also evaluate whether a public scheme involves a deprivation of honest services. 18 U.S.C. §§1341, 1343, 1346.

b. This theory of mail fraud was recently rejected as applied to election fraud cases in *United States* v. *Turner*, 459 F.3d 775 (6th Cir. 2006); *United States* v. *Ratcliff*, 488 F.3d 639, C.A.5 (2007).

stitution or laws of the United States." Violations are punishable by imprisonment for up to ten years or, if death results, for any term of years or for life. The Supreme Court long ago recognized that the right to vote for federal offices is among the rights secured by Article I, Sections 2 and 4, of the Constitution, and hence is protected by Section 241. Although the statute was enacted just after the Civil War to address efforts to deprive the newly emancipated slaves of the basic rights of citizenship, such as the right to vote, it has been interpreted to include any effort to derogate any right that flows from the Constitution or from federal law. Section 241 has been an important statutory tool in election crime prosecutions. Originally held to apply only to schemes to corrupt elections for federal office, it has recently been success-fully applied to nonfederal elections as well, provided that state action (action by an individual or entity representing the state) was a necessary feature of the fraud. This state action requirement can be met not only by the partici-pation of poll officials, but also by activities of persons who clothe themselves with the appearance of state authority (for example, with uniforms, creden-tials, and badges).

Section 241 embraces conspiracies: (1) to stuff a ballot box with forged ballots; (2) to impersonate qualified voters; (3) to alter legal ballots; (4) to fail to count votes and to alter votes counted; (5) to prevent the official count of ballots in primary elections; (6) to destroy ballots; (7) to destroy voter regis-tration applications; (8) to illegally register voters and cast absentee ballots in their names; and (9) to injure, threaten, or intimidate a voter in the exercise of his right to vote. Section 241 does not require that the conspiracy be suc-cessful or that there be proof of an overt act. Section 241 reaches conduct affecting the integrity of the federal election process as a whole and does not require fraudulent action with respect to any particular voter. On the other hand, Section 241 does not reach schemes to corrupt the balloting process through voter bribery, even schemes that involve poll officers to ensure that the bribed voters mark their ballots as they were paid to do. Section 241 pro-hibits only conspiracies to interfere with rights flowing directly from the Constitution or federal statutes. This element has led to considerable judicial speculation over the extent to which the Constitution protects the right to vote for candidates running for nonfederal offices. Although *dicta* in *Reynolds* v. *Sims* cast the parameters of the federally protected right to vote in ex-tremely broad terms, in a ballot fraud case ten years later the Supreme Court specifically refused to decide whether the federally secured franchise ex-tended to nonfederal contests.[12]

The use of Section 241 in election fraud cases has generally been confined to two types of situations: "public schemes" and "private schemes." A public scheme is one that involves the necessary participation of a public official acting under the color of law. In election fraud cases, this public official is usually an election officer using his office to dilute valid ballots with invalid ballots or to otherwise corrupt an honest vote tally in derogation of the equal protection and due process clauses of the 14th Amendment. A private scheme is a pattern of conduct that does not involve the necessary participation of a public official acting under color of law, but one that can be shown factually to have adversely affected the ability of qualified voters to vote in elections in which federal candidates were on the ballot. Examples of private schemes include: (1) voting fraudulent ballots in mixed elections, and (2) thwarting get-out-the-vote or ride-to-the-polls activities of political factions or parties through such methods as jamming telephone lines or vandalizing motor vehicles.

Deprivation of Rights under Color of Law: 18 U.S.C. §242

Section 242, also enacted as a post–Civil War statute, makes it unlawful for anyone acting under color of law, statute, ordinance, regulation, or custom to willfully deprive a person of any right, privilege, or immunity secured or protected by the Constitution or laws of the United States. Violations are misdemeanors unless bodily injury occurs, in which case the penalty is ten years, or unless death results, in which case imprisonment may be for any term of years or for life. Prosecutions under Section 242 need not show the existence of a conspiracy. However, the defendants must have acted illegally "under color of law" (that is, the case must involve a public scheme, as discussed above). This element does not require that the defendant be a de jure officer or a government official; it is sufficient if he or she jointly acted with state agents in committing the offense, or if his or her actions were made possible by the fact that they were clothed with the authority of state law.

False Information in, and Payments for, Registering and Voting: 42 U.S.C. §1973i(c)

Section 1973i(c) makes it unlawful, in an election in which a federal candidate is on the ballot, to knowingly and willfully (1) give false information as to name, address, or period of residence to an election official for the purpose of establishing one's eligibility to register or to vote; (2) pay, offer to pay, or accept payment for registering to vote or for voting; or (3) conspire with another person to vote illegally. Violations are punishable by imprisonment for up to five years.

The "false information" provision of Section 1973i(c) prohibits any person from furnishing certain false data to an election official to establish eligibility to register or vote. The statute applies to three types of information: name, address, and period of residence in the voting district. False information concerning other factors (such as citizenship, felon status, and mental competence) is not covered by this provision. The clause of Section 1973i(c) that prohibits "vote buying" does so in broad terms, covering any payment made or offered to a would-be voter "to vote or for voting" in an election where the name of a federal candidate appears on the ballot, as well as payments made to induce unregistered persons to register. Section 1973i(c) applies as long as a pattern of vote buying exposes a federal election to potential corruption, even though it cannot be shown that the threat materialized.

Voting More than Once: 42 U.S.C. §1973i(e)

Section 1973i(e), enacted as part of the 1975 amendments to the Voting Rights Act of 1965, makes it a crime to vote "more than once" in any election in which a federal candidate is on the ballot. Violations are punishable by imprisonment for up to five years. In addition to its obvious use against individuals who vote more than once by casting two or more ballots in the same election, Section 1973i(e) is useful as a statutory weapon against fraud that does not involve the participation of voters in the balloting acts attributed to them. Examples of such fraud are schemes to cast ballots in the names of voters who were deceased or absent, schemes to exploit the infirmities of the mentally handicapped by casting ballots in their names, and schemes to cast absentee ballots in the names of voters who did not participate in and consent to the marking of their ballots by the offender.

Most cases prosecuted under the multiple voting statute have involved defendants who physically marked ballots outside the presence of the voters in whose names they were cast—in other words, without the voters' participation or knowledge. The statute may also be applied successfully to schemes when the voters are present but do not participate in any way, or do not otherwise consent to the defendant's assistance, in the voting process. However, when the scheme involves "assisting" voters who are present and who also marginally participate in the process, such as by signing a ballot document, prosecuting the case under Section 1973i(e) may present difficulties. Recent court decisions in cases based on 1973i(e) suggest that Section 1973i(e) most clearly applies to cases of "ballot theft." Examples of such situations are when the defendant marked the ballots of others without their input; when voters did not knowingly consent to the defendant's participation in their voting transactions; when the voters' electoral preferences were disregarded; or when the defendant marked the ballots of voters who lacked the mental capacity to vote or to consent to the defendant's activities.

Voter Intimidation: 42 U.S.C. §§1973gg-1973gg-10, 18 U.S.C. §594, 18 U.S.C. §241

Voter intimidation schemes are the functional opposite of voter bribery schemes. In the case of voter bribery, voting is stimulated by offering or giving something of value to individuals to induce them to vote or reward them for having voted. The goal of voter intimidation, in contrast, is to deter or influence voting through threats to deprive voters of something they already have, such as jobs, government benefits, or, in extreme cases, their personal safety. Another distinction between voter bribery and intimidation is that bribery generates concrete evidence: the bribe itself (generally money). Intimidation is amorphous and largely subjective, and often generates no concrete evidence.

Voter intimidation is an assault against both the individual and society, warranting prompt and effective redress by the criminal justice system. Yet a number of factors make it difficult to prosecute. Intimidation is likely to be subtle and to be conducted without witnesses. Furthermore, voters who have been intimidated are not merely victims; they provide the testimony that proves the crime. These voters must testify, publicly and in an adversarial proceeding, against the very person who intimidated them. Proving the crime of voter intimidation normally requires evidence of threats, duress, economic coercion, or some other aggravating factor that improperly induces conduct on the part of the victim.

There are three laws of interest in regard to intimidation. First, when Congress enacted the National Voter Registration Act (NVRA), 42 U.S.C. §§1973gg-1973gg-10, in 1993—which requires that the states provide prospective voters with uniform and convenient means by which to register for the federal franchise—there were concerns that relaxing registration requirements might lead to an increase in election fraud. In response to this concern, the NVRA included a new series of election crimes, one of which prohibited knowingly and willfully intimidating or coercing prospective voters for registering to vote, or for voting, in any election for federal office. Violators are subject to imprisonment for up to five years.

Second, Section 594 prohibits intimidating, threatening, or coercing anyone, or attempting to do so, for the purpose of interfering with an individual's right to vote or not vote in any election held solely or in part to elect a federal candidate. The statute does not apply to primaries. Violations are one-year misdemeanors. The operative words in Section 594 are "intimidates," "threatens," and "coerces." Section 594 was enacted as part of the original 1939 Hatch Act, which aimed at prohibiting the blatant economic coercion used during the 1930s to force federal employees and recipients of federal relief benefits to perform political work and to vote for and contribute to the candidates supported by their supervisors.

Third, Section 241 makes it a ten-year felony to "conspire to injure, oppress, threaten, or intimidate any person in any state, territory or district in the free exercise or enjoyment of any right or privilege secured by the Constitution or laws of the United States"—including the right to vote. The statute, which is discussed in detail above, has potential application in two forms of voter intimidation: a conspiracy to prevent persons whom the subjects knew were qualified voters from entering the polls to vote in an election when a federal candidate is on the ballot, and a conspiracy to misuse state authority to prevent qualified voters from voting for any candidate in any election.

Fraudulent Registering and Voting: 42 U.S.C. §1973gg-10(2)

This provision was enacted as part of the National Voter Registration Act of 1993. As discussed above, Congress enacted the NVRA to ease voter registration requirements throughout the country. In addition to providing new protections against voter intimidation in federal elections, the NVRA prohibits individuals from furnishing materially false information (such as citizenship or felon status information) to election officials when registering to vote or when voting in federal elections. Violations of this statute are punishable by imprisonment for up to five years. The NVRA's criminal statute resulted from law enforcement concerns expressed during congressional debates on the proposed law. Opponents and supporters of the NVRA alike recognized that relaxing requirements for registering to vote had the unavoidable potential to increase the occurrence of election crime by making it easier for the unscrupulous to pack registration rolls with fraudulent applications and ballots.[13]

Registering to Vote and Voting by Noncitizens: 18 U.S.C. §§611, 911, 1015(f), 42 U.S.C. §1973gg-10

Neither the Constitution nor federal statutory law requires that persons be U.S. citizens in order to vote. Eligibility to vote for both federal and nonfederal offices is a matter that the Constitution leaves primarily to the states. At the time this chapter was written, all states required that prospective voters be U.S. citizens, although some localities do allow noncitizens to vote in local elections and, in some instances, on bond referendums.

Federal laws do, however, have quite a bit to say about citizenship and voting. Specifically, in 1993 the federal role in the election process expanded significantly with the enactment of the National Voter Registration Act (NVRA). This legislation required, among other things, that forms used to register persons to vote in federal elections clearly state "each eligibility requirement (including citizenship)" and that persons registering to vote in federal elections affirm that they meet "each eligibility requirement (including citizenship)." Nine years later, Congress passed the Help America Vote Act of 2002

(HAVA). HAVA reemphasized these requirements for voters who register to vote by mail by requiring the states to place a citizenship question on forms used by individuals under the "registration by mail" feature of NVRA.

Troops at Polls: 18 U.S.C. §592

This statute makes it unlawful to station troops or "armed men" at the polls in a general or special election (but not a primary), except when necessary "to repel armed enemies of the United States." Violations are punishable by imprisonment for up to five years and disqualification from any federal office. Section 592 prohibits the use of official authority to order armed personnel to the polls; it does not reach the troops who actually go in response to those orders. The effect of this statute is to raise doubt as to whether the FBI may conduct investigations within the polls on election day and whether U.S. marshals may be stationed at open polls, as both are required to carry their weapons while on duty. This statute applies only to agents of the U.S. government. It does not prohibit state or local law enforcement agencies from sending police officers to quell disturbances at polling places; nor does it preempt state laws that require police officers to be stationed in polling places.

Retention of Federal Election Records: 42 U.S.C. §1974

The detection, investigation, and proof of election crimes—and in many instances Voting Rights Act violations—often depends on documentation generated during the voter registration, voting, tabulation, and election certification processes. In recognition of this fact, and the length of time it can take for credible election fraud predication to develop, Congress enacted Section 1974 to require that documentation generated in connection with the voting and registration process be retained for twenty-two months if it pertains to an election that included a federal candidate. Absent this statute, the disposition of election documentation would be subject solely to state law, which in virtually all states permits its destruction within a few months after the election is certified.

Section 1974 requires that election administrators preserve for twenty-two months "all records and papers that come into their possession relating to any application, registration, payment of poll tax, or other act requisite to voting." This retention requirement applies to all elections in which a candidate for federal office was on the ballot—that is, a candidate for the United States Senate, the United States House of Representatives, president or vice president of the United States, or presidential elector. Section 1974 does not apply to records generated in connection with purely local or state elections. Retention and disposition of records in purely nonfederal elections (those where no federal candidates were on the ballot) are governed by state document retention laws.

However, Section 1974 does apply to all records generated in connection with the process of registering voters and maintaining current electoral rolls. This is because voter registration in virtually all U.S. jurisdictions is "unitary" in the sense that a potential voter registers only once to become eligible to vote for both local and federal candidates.[14] Thus, registration records must be preserved as long as the voter registration to which they pertain is considered an "active" one under local law and practice, and those records cannot be disposed of until the expiration of twenty-two months following the date on which the registration ceased to be "active."

Section 1974 requires that covered election documentation be retained either physically by election officials themselves or under the direct administrative supervision of election officers. This is because the document retention requirements of this federal law place the retention and safekeeping duties squarely on the shoulders of election officers, and Section 1974 does not contemplate shifting this responsibility to other government agencies or officers.

Conclusion

At the time this chapter was written in 2007, the investigation and prosecution of election crimes ranked near the very top of the Justice Department's law enforcement priorities. It was outranked only by crimes involving terrorism and espionage. This focus has much to do with the critical role that elections play in the basic functioning of American democracy.

Elections serve a greater role than simply determining the winners and the losers of elective contests for public offices. More important, elections serve to legitimize the transfer of governmental power. Simultaneously, they work to hold the government accountable to the body politic that elected it. Indeed, when they are conducted fairly and inclusively, elections provide the most effective means known to modern society by which the people can effect political change peacefully.

Where the integrity of the ballot box and the voting process breaks down through corruption and fraud, the legitimacy of the state can easily be called into question. Corruption and arbitrary government inevitably follow. Voter fraud is, therefore, a crime of the first order of magnitude against the social order of any democratic state.

The importance of the societal interests involved requires constant vigilance and impartial (politically neutral) adjudication of criminal charging decisions. Those interests also require that election systems be designed to make the commission of this sort of offense as difficult as possible and to provide law enforcement authorities with the tools they require to find those responsible for voter frauds and to bring them to justice. No democracy is immune from voter fraud, for as long as the stakes involved in the election process are the allocation of governmental power, there will be criminals bent on exploiting the voting process to selfish and venal ends. There is no substitute for constant vigilance where the integrity of the election process is concerned.

In the United States, the criminal prosecution of election-related crimes is not designed to determine who won an election or to resolve election disputes. However, it can deter those contemplating corrupting the voting process. That, in turn, can and should lead to greater public confidence in the voting process itself, as well as in the ability of the elective process to perform its central functions: legitimizing the transfer and exercise of political power and holding the government accountable to the people.

Notes

1. 42 U.S.C. §1973i(c); 18 U.S.C. §597; 18 U.S.C. §1952; 42 U.S.C. §1973gg-10.

2. The code sections referred to in this section are, respectively: 42 U.S.C. §§1973i(c), 1973i(e), 1973gg-10; 18 U.S.C. §§241, 242 and 42 U.S.C. §§1973i(c), 1973i(e), 1973gg-10; and 18 U.S.C. §1015(f) and 18 U.S.C. §911.

3. The code sections referred to in this section are, respectively: 42 U.S.C. §§1973i(c), 1973gg-10; 42 U.S.C. §§1973i(c), 1973gg-10; 42 U.S.C. §§1973i(c), 1973gg-10; 18 U.S.C. §§1015(f), 611; 42 U.S.C. §§1973i(c), 1973gg-10; and 42 U.S.C. §1973gg-10.

4. Absentee ballots are particularly susceptible to fraudulent use because, by definition, they are marked and cast outside the presence of election officials.

5. *United States* v. *Salisbury*, 983 F.2d 1369 (6th Cir., 1993); *United States* v. *Cole*, 41 F.3d 303 (7th Cir., 1994).

6. In *Ex parte Coy*, 127 U.S. 731, 1888.

7. *Newberry* v. *United States*, 256 U.S. 232 (1918); *United States* v. *Bathgate*, 246 U.S. 220 (1918).

8. *United States* v. *Classic*, 313 U.S. 299 (1941).

9. The mail fraud statute, 18 U.S.C. §1341, *McNally* v. *United States*, 483 U.S. 350 (1987).

10. *United States* v. *Turner*, 459 F.3d 775 (6th Cir. 2006); *United States* v. *Ratcliff*, 488 F.3d 639 (5th Cir. 2007).

11. Such crimes include 42 U.S.C. §§1973i(c), 1973i(e), and 1973gg-10. The Commerce and Necessary and Proper Clauses are at U.S. Const. art. I, §4, and U.S. Const. art. I, §8, cl. 18.

12. *Reynolds* v. *Sims*, 377 U.S. 533 (1964).

13. The key sections of NVRA referred to in this section are 42 U.S.C. §1973gg-10(1); 42 U.S.C. §1973gg-10(2); 42 U.S.C. §§1973gg-3(c)(2)(c), 1973gg-5(a)(6)(A)(i), 1973gg-7(b)(2), and 42 U.S.C. §1973gg-4); also see 42 U.S.C. §15483(b)(4)(A)(i).

14. See *United States* v. *Cianciulli*, 482 F.Supp. 585 (E.D.Pa. 1979).

two

International Principles for Election Integrity

Thad E. Hall and Tova Andrea Wang

Election fraud, as currently defined, was a routine occurrence in the early history of the United States. George Washington won an election in colonial Virginia in part by spending lavishly on alcohol for voters on election day, and his fellow Founding Father, James Madison, lost an election in Virginia in part because he refused to spend money on such things. These were not isolated instances. Balloting in the early and mid-1800s was rife with potential for manipulation. Elections were not conducted on secret ballots, which raised concerns about voter intimidation and vote buying. The use of paper ballots and the lack of effective rules governing how ballots were handled led to questions about ballot box stuffing. The lack of voter registries raised questions about voters' eligibility to vote in the jurisdiction where they cast ballots.

In comparison, elections in the United States today are much more effectively run. With few exceptions, all citizens who are eighteen years old or older are eligible to vote. Votes are cast by secret ballot, and statewide voter registration databases have become the norm. But recent controversies have demonstrated that problems remain, and reform proposals continue to proliferate. Some, such as plans to strengthen voter identification requirements at polling places, are intended to target fraud. Others, such as measures to expand early and absentee voting, are aimed more broadly at increasing election participation or fairness. Both types of proposals often generate debate. For example, the voter identification laws in Georgia and Indiana that require every voter to present government-issued photo identification have been touted by Republicans as an effort to stop voting fraud at polling places and decried by Democrats as an attempt to suppress voting.[1]

In light of such controversy, how can we determine whether particular reform proposals will increase or reduce the quality of elections? To answer this question, we examine three sets of norms for election integrity that have been established by international institutions: the Organization for Security and Cooperation in Europe's (OSCE) Office for Democratic Institutions and Human Rights (ODIHR); the United Nations, through its Declaration of Principles for International Election Observation (DPIEO); and the Administration and Cost of Elections (ACE) project. The ACE project's work focuses specifically on vote counting; the DPIEO and ODIHR deal with election monitoring and observation more broadly. We discuss how the principles articulated by these three organizations can be used to create a framework for evaluating proposed election law reforms. We also consider how these criteria can be used to evaluate U.S. election law more broadly.

Democratic Norms for Elections

Through commitments made in treaties and protocols, the OSCE's Office for Democratic Institutions and Human Rights has identified characteristics of elections that meet democratic norms. The top panel of table 2-1 lists the OSCE commitments on elections that were articulated in the Copenhagen Document of 1990. Member states are required to meet these commitments in the conduct of their elections. The table also lists "the principal and emerging areas [of concern for the OSCE] where the conduct of democratic election requires further attention and improvement."[2] OSCE/ODIHR election observers developed this list on the basis of their work over the past decade. The list of commitments from the Copenhagen Document includes areas the United States has dealt with historically, either illicitly or within a legal framework, in its efforts to conduct free democratic elections. For example, the historical exclusion of minority voters and minority candidates under the rubric of state or political party voting eligibility requirements would have violated these principles, as would the violence that was associated with such discrimination. In the nineteenth century, the lack of secret ballots in elections would have violated the principles associated with this agreement, as would the exclusion of women from voting before the passage of the Nineteenth Amendment.

The Copenhagen Document can also be viewed as articulating international standards for democratic elections. For example, laws or activities that

Table 2-1. OSCE Election Protocols

Copenhagen document requirements
Elections to be held at reasonable intervals
All seats in one legislative chamber to be popularly elected
Guaranteed universal and equal suffrage
Respect for the right of citizens to seek office
Respect for the right to establish political parties and ensure the parties
    can compete on the basis of equal treatment before the law
Ensure that political campaigning can be conducted in a free and fair
    atmosphere without administrative action, violence, intimidation, or fear
    of retribution against candidates, parties, or voters
Ensure unimpeded access to the media on a nondiscriminatory basis
Ensure that votes are cast by secret ballot, and are counted and reported
    honestly, with the results made public
Ensure that candidates who win the necessary votes to be elected are duly
    installed and are permitted to remain in office until their terms expire

OSCE areas of concern
Respect for the civil and political rights of candidates and voters
Compilation of accurate voter lists
Equitable access to the media
Access for international and domestic election observers
Participation of women
Inclusion of national minorities
Access for disabled voters
Honest counting and tabulation of votes
Effective complaint and appeals process with independent judiciary
Overall transparency and accountability that instills public confidence
Development and implementation of new voting technologies

Source: *Election Observation. A Decade of Monitoring Elections: The People and the Practice* (Warsaw: OSCE/ODIHR, 2005).

prevent one set of voters who do not meet a given requirement from voting can be viewed as violating the international norm of equal suffrage. In this frame, discrimination is a form of fraud within the electoral process because it intentionally excludes a class of potential adult voters. The class of voters that is being excluded cannot make its voice heard in the electoral process. Likewise, dirty tricks in campaigning—including activities that lead to voter suppression such as disseminating misinformation about the voting process or where to vote on election day—also violate one of the principles in the Document.

The OSCE/ODIHR's "areas of concern" apply to elections in both established and emerging democracies. One key concern in the United States is the transparency of election day procedures. The OSCE/ODIHR principles for election observation require a highly transparent electoral process, one that allows observers with proper accreditation to collect data and information about the election process and to observe elections without restriction or prior notification. But many states deny independent observers access to polling places; the only observers allowed are those who are affiliated with a political party. Lack of access to polling places by independent outside observers can create an atmosphere of distrust and foster allegations of fraud if there are accusations of problems at the polls that cannot be independently examined and verified.

Several other issues identified by OSCE/ODIHR are also concerns in the United States. When transparency is limited, it is difficult to determine whether votes are counted and reported honestly, and disaggregated election results are difficult for the public to access. More and better data from election officials should be reported promptly and in usable formats so that they can be analyzed for evidence of anomalous results and possible election fraud. Such data reporting would promote the accountability that is needed for the public to be confident that the results of elections are accurate. Likewise, as the United States adopts new voting technologies and modes of voting, greater consideration needs to be given to securing voting equipment, to developing verifiable chains of custody for ballots, and to auditing election results. It is critical that any new rules and laws do not discriminate against certain technologies. For example, paper ballot voting systems should be subject to the same security requirements as electronic machines and should be audited according to the same set of principles as those used to audit electronic voting systems.

In observing elections, OSCE/ODIHR representatives typically analyze whether the jurisdiction's laws comply with OSCE and universal principles and whether those laws are implemented properly, consistently, and impartially. This legal analysis is important because it reminds us that, although a specific electoral requirement may be established in law, it may still violate a principle associated with the appropriate democratic conduct of elections. For example, the poll taxes and all-white primaries that existed in the South, and the literacy test requirements that were in place in New York before the passage of the Voting Rights Act of 1965, were legally established voting requirements that were also discriminatory according to international principles.

The legal evaluation is also important because laws that are designed to prevent fraud might inadvertently create loopholes that make it easier to commit. Consider the following two examples. First, many states that have adopted electronic voting technologies have also adopted election audit requirements only for electronic voting machines. Although such audits are important, they should not exclude paper-based voting. Second, in Georgia, the state's voter identification law intentionally creates different identification requirements for in-precinct and absentee voters; in-precinct voters must present documentation to verify their eligibility to vote, but absentee are not required to prevent any such proof. In both instances the law designed to prevent fraud instead creates exclusions that favor one set of voters or technology over others.

In order to conduct such a legal analysis, election law information for each state should be readily available online. It is difficult to know whether election fraud or problems have occurred if a jurisdiction's laws and regulations are not accessible to the public. Although many states have put their election codes online, in some it is very difficult to locate election law information, especially regulatory and administrative information intended to guide local election officials.[3] Easy access to this legal information provides transparency by allowing everyone to understand the rules of the game.

The election observation principles articulated by more than twenty election observation organizations in the DPIEO are similar to those in the Copenhagen Document. In the United States, the Carter Center and the National Democratic Institute, jointly with the United Nations, sponsored the creation of the document and were the first endorsing organizations.[4] The DPIEO report contains a set of principles that provide the rationale for election observation and the goals of such observation. It also articulates the necessary elements of democratic elections. These include many of the items included in the Copenhagen Document—universal and equal suffrage, respect for rights to seek office, respect for the rights of political parties, appropriate access to the media, and elections held at reasonable intervals. Most beneficially, the DPIEO provides a clear definition of international election observation and a description of what can be achieved through election observation:

> International election observation evaluates pre-election, election-day and post-election periods through comprehensive, long-term observation, employing a variety of techniques. . . . All observer missions must make concerted efforts to place the Election Day into its context and not to over-emphasize the importance of Election Day observations.
>
> International election observation examines conditions relating to the right to vote and to be elected, including, among other things, discrimination or other obstacles that hinder participation in electoral processes based on political or other opinion, gender, race, colour, ethnicity, language, religion, national or social origin, property, birth or other status, such as physical disabilities.

In short, election observers do look for fraud on election day, but they are equally concerned about structural obstacles—including laws and practices—that hinder the participation of any group or class of voters in the electorate. Voter registration and the handling of ballots upon completion of the election are just as important for confidence in the fairness of the election as voting itself. In fact, fraud would be much easier to perpetrate at other times. For example, it is easier to deny voters the right to vote by not allowing them to register than it is to disenfranchise them on election day at the polling place.

Both the ODIHR and DPIEO documents are intended to articulate the features of a legitimate, fair election and how elections should be observed. They provide a set of baseline principles for evaluating when an election is or is not fair. With these principles in hand it is possible to determine when a law might hinder the fair conduct of an election in a state or nation.

The ACE project emphasizes the casting and counting of ballots as principles of democratic elections, as well as broader considerations. ACE is a collaboration of three internationally recognized organizations involved in elections: (1) IFES, an international nonprofit organization that supports the building of democratic societies; (2) the International Institute for Democracy and Electoral Assistance (IDEA); and (3) the United Nations Department of Economic and Social Affairs (UNDESA). The project recognizes that one very important component of elections is public perception—which may or may not correlate with objective reality: "to establish and maintain public confidence in the electoral process, vote counting systems and procedures should incorporate the fundamental principles of vote counting in a democratic election."[5]

The ACE project identifies eight guiding principles for vote counting: transparency, security, professionalism, accuracy, secrecy, timeliness, accountability, and equity. It includes similar guidelines for other election-related topics, including voter registration, voting operations, the media and elections, and voter education. Before we discuss each of these subjects in relation to vote counting, we explain how each concept is used in voting, as articulated by ACE:

(1) *Transparency.* For the counting process to be open and transparent, representatives of political parties and candidates should be allowed to witness and/or participate in the process, and permitted to copy the statement of the results of the counting process. National and international electoral observers should also be allowed to witness the process and permitted to copy the statement of the results of the counting process. In some countries, ordinary citizens are encouraged to watch the counting

process. Manual counting is by its nature more transparent than computerized counting. If vote counting is computerized, new mechanisms for ensuring transparency, such as external audits, need to be introduced.

(2) *Security.* The security of the ballots and the ballot boxes, from the time voting begins to the completion of the count, is fundamental to the integrity of the counting process. Polling and counting officials, representatives of political parties and candidates, and national and international electoral observers should carefully watch the ballots and the boxes at all times, and accompany them if they are moved from one location to another. Individually numbered, tamper-proof seals or bags should be used to ensure the secure transport of ballots.

(3) *Professionalism.* Polling and counting officials must act in a professional manner. They should be thoroughly trained in the counting process, as distinct from the voting process; thorough in their procedures; and committed to treating electoral materials with care and respect. Once a person accepts work as a counting official, he or she must be non-partisan throughout the entire process. Some jurisdictions require that all counting officials (as well as poll officials) sign an oath to this effect, creating awareness that they can be legally prosecuted if their work is proved to be partisan.

(4) *Accuracy.* Accuracy is directly related to the integrity of the count, and of the elections themselves. Later discovery of errors and correction of mistakes can lead to accusations of manipulation or fraud. The accuracy of the count will depend on clear procedures and manuals, adequate staff training, and a commitment on the part of elections officials to adhering to the process. Clear audit trails of ballots and ballot boxes, as well as checking and rechecking mechanisms, will contribute to the accuracy of the results. While mechanical voting or computerization may enhance accuracy this must be balanced against the resulting apparent loss of transparency.

(5) *Secrecy.* Secrecy of the vote is important because it ensures that voters cannot be punished for the way they vote, or intimidated into voting a particular way. To preserve the secrecy of the vote, voters' identification must be protected during the count. If their identity and choice on the ballot is determined as a result of counting procedures, it must be kept confidential and never revealed. If the secrecy of the vote of individuals or a community is a concern, measures such as counting at counting centers, rather than at individual polling stations, or mixing ballots from different polls, can be considered. Numbered ballot papers corresponding to

matching stubs with the voter details, while facilitating accountability and clear audit trails, compromise secrecy and are best avoided.

(6) *Timeliness.* Delays in completing the count and in the release of unofficial preliminary results can negatively affect the level of integrity and confidence in the voting process. The responsible electoral management body should carefully plan all stages of the counting process to facilitate the early announcement of results, or at least to realistically assess when results can be announced, taking into consideration the communications and transport infrastructure.

(7) *Accountability.* Clear responsibility and accountability for each stage of the counting process are important. At the national level, the electoral management body should be accountable. At the electoral district level, it may be a senior election officer or commission official. At polling stations, specified poll workers may be responsible for polling and counting. Clearly defined complaints and appeals processes are also crucial. Counting rules, including criteria for rejecting ballots, should be clear, known in advance, and understood by everyone involved in the election, including election officials, the general public, political parties, candidates, non-governmental organizations, and national and international electoral observers. Clear audit trails are essential in ensuring accountability.

(8) *Equity.* Equity generally means that the rules are the same for all participants in the electoral process, and that they accept these rules. The proper training and non-partisanship of counting officials and polling officials, and the presence of political party representatives, [and] national and international electoral observers will help to ensure that counting is conducted in a fair and correct manner.[6]

These guiding principles are designed to create an environment in which the final election results can be trusted. This is not to say that losing candidates and parties—as well as the voters whose favored candidate loses—will not question the results of any given election. However, such questions are more likely to be dismissed when the process is viewed as fair.

Applying Vote Counting Principles to Election Reforms Broadly

Each of the principles just outlined can be used to evaluate election reforms more broadly. The first principle, transparency, translates most directly to all election reforms. Before an election is conducted, all of the relevant actors should be able to know the rules of the game as established in the laws and regulations for that jurisdiction. Then, all important actors in the election should be able to witness the key aspects of the election process. When components of the election have a "black box" (or nontransparent) property, they should be subject to external audits. The use of postelection audits that compare a percentage of the electronically tabulated results with the results of a hand count of the ballots is one type of audit that some states have recently enacted. Election activities other than voting, such as the addition of voters to the voting rolls (or their removal), could also be subject to external audit. The use of statewide electronic voter registration systems in the United States allows audits to ensure that the lists have a high level of accuracy. In addition, the failure of many states to allow election observers into polling places inhibits the ability of third parties, such as the OSCE, from engaging in election observation and auditing activities as well.

The security principle likewise is highly transferable to all aspects of election reform. Voters should expect all critical paths in the election to be secured against tampering or unauthorized access. One example is the security of voter registration systems. Although there are clear, albeit limited, security requirements outlined in state laws and regulations for ballots and voting technologies used in elections in most states, there are no standards for securing a voter registration system, even though compromising such a system could systematically disenfranchise large numbers of voters. For example, a requirement that voter registration systems be tested before they are used might have identified the problems that occurred in the 2006 general election in Denver, Colorado, where registration problems created delays at the polls.[7] Similarly, voter authentication and chain of custody requirements could help to ensure that an election is secure and that there is no unauthorized access to ballots or the voting machines. One key aspect of security is to ensure that it is implemented equitably, so that all voters and voting technologies are subject to the same rules when appropriate.

The professionalism principle should apply to more than the counting of ballots. In addition to knowing how to do their jobs, elections officials should understand how their job performance can affect the outcome of an election. Research has shown that the voter–poll worker interaction has a critical effect on the voter's confidence that his or her vote was counted accurately.[8] Likewise, when poll workers are asked about their work experience, their perceptions of the training they received has a large effect on the quality of their work—more problems occur in precincts where the poll workers sense they were less adequately trained.[9] The training task in elections is made more difficult by outsourcing, especially in the voter registration process. For example, employees of the Department of Motor Vehicles, where persons may register to vote, may not view themselves as election officials, even though a majority of voters register to vote at the DMV.

The accuracy principle relates to many of the other principles associated with free and fair elections, since accuracy is what ensures that the election has integrity. Accuracy is important to all facets of an election, not just the counting of ballots. Election officials must be sure that the voter registry is accurate, that they accurately authenticate a voter before giving the voter a ballot, that the ballot is accurately counted, and that the aggregated count (the final result) is reported accurately.

In order to ensure that the public perceives the vote count to be credible, election officials must balance the need for accuracy with the desire to announce election results in as timely a manner as possible. The idea here is simple; the longer it takes election officials to count the ballots and report the results, the more likely it is that the public will sense some chicanery in the counting of the ballots. The timeliness principle can be applied to many election reforms, including some that have just begun to be implemented. One example is provisional ballots; any voter whom a poll worker believes to be ineligible to vote must be given a provisional, or paper, ballot to cast. Administrators then examine the provisional ballots for their validity after the election and count them accordingly. Election rules should seek to minimize the number of provisional ballots cast: the more provisional ballots that are cast by voters, the longer it will take to authenticate the provisional ballots, integrate these ballots with the ballots tabulated on election day, and achieve an accurate vote count.

Just as there need to be clear lines of accountability in the vote counting process, there should be similarly clear lines of accountability in other aspects of election administration. The individuals in charge of voter registration, the poll workers in the polling place, and the related actors in elections—such as vendors and other governmental actors such as the DMV—should also be accountable for their election-related duties. In addition, the rules of the game need to be specified and clear to everyone before the election. In many cases, this means that there should be greater voter and candidate education about the electoral process, so that the public knows how to properly hold officials accountable for their efforts. The principle of transparency is linked with all of the other principles to create a fair and open election process.

The final principle—equity—is perhaps the most important aspect of evaluating electoral reforms. Reforms should treat all types of voters similarly whenever possible. Likewise, all similar processes in the election should be equitable. Early, absentee, and election-day voters should all be treated similarly, and security concerns related to the implementation of each of these voting systems should be equitable. Likewise, the process for handling voter registration applications—regardless of the source of the registration application—should be the same for all voters. When there is a lack of equity, the rationale for any differential treatment should be clear and unambiguous.

The equity principle is exceptionally important in American elections because of the long history of inequitable elections. As Robert Dahl has noted, a nation is truly democratic when it allows all of its citizens eighteen years of age or older to cast ballots.[10] The United States has only just approached achieving this goal since the 1960s and still does not allow convicted felons to vote. Before that time, there was a history of unequal voting rights based on sociodemographic differences such as wealth, race, gender, education, and language proficiency. However, the equity principle should not be taken to mean that any reform that in practice benefits one group of voters over another is inherently problematic. For example, there is some evidence that early voting (voting by mail before election day) benefits more partisan voters and voters with higher incomes. However, early voting does not affect the distribution of all voters casting ballots in the election. It merely changes the mode of voting by voters who would have cast ballots anyway, and the overall effect is not inequitable. By contrast, there is some preliminary evidence that vote centers, which allow voters in a given election jurisdiction to cast a ballot anywhere in the jurisdiction (not just in the precinct where the voter lives and is registered), both increase turnout and bring voters who would not have otherwise voted into the electorate.[11] Vote centers benefit one group—nonvoters—more than others, but this is easily judged as a benefit to the electoral process as a whole.

Implications

Efforts to address election fraud should meet international norms for the integrity of elections. The principles of democratic elections articulated in the Copenhagen Document, the election observation principles articulated by the United Nations, and the vote counting standards articulated in the work of the ACE project provide a minimal framework for evaluating vote counting reform procedures. The former two documents provide a basis for understanding broadly the factors that are part of a legitimate election, as well as the new issues that are important for ensuring that modern elections continue to meet these standards. As election processes and procedures change with the advent of new voting technologies, new registration systems, and new voting methods (such as voting by mail or in-person early voting), there needs to be strong consideration given to how such reforms affect the fairness of the election process. Small changes can have a large impact on the tone and flavor of elections, with different effects on different groups of voters and on specific election technologies.

Reforms should create a more accurate, transparent, secure, accountable, and timely election process. As we noted previously, the United States does not perform well on the principle of transparency. Not only do many states not allow for independent election observation of voting or vote tabulation, but many states and localities are also unable to provide the public with important election data in a timely manner. Such data are critical for answering basic questions about the conduct of elections and for helping researchers and election observers identify problems. Most states also do not conduct basic election auditing, which is critical for ensuring the accuracy of the electronic tabulation that is used in almost all voting today (both electronic and paper ballots are typically electronically tabulated). Audits provide voters, candidates, and parties with confirmation that the votes were counted properly and that a systematic effort was made to identify any anomalies in the counting of ballots, the custody of ballots and voting machines, or more generally in the conduct of the election.

Given that the United States has a long history of treating classes of voters differently, changes to election laws that are perceived to favor one class of voters, such as the wealthy or nonminorities, are likely to be viewed with concern. Whenever possible, voting technologies and voting processes should be equitable across the board. In a given election, voters who vote by mail, who vote using in-person early voting, and who vote in-person on election day should all be treated as similarly as possible and subject to similar procedures. Similarly, the auditing of elections should treat all voting technologies the same way; electronic and paper-based systems should be subject to the same scrutiny and standards.

By incorporating these principles into the election process, the government can reassure voters that the electoral process is free and fair. The government should provide a framework for detecting points in the electoral process where fraud might occur and where fraud should be monitored. In addition to examining the accuracy and fairness of the vote count—multiple techniques for which are covered in this volume—fraud investigations should consider other aspects of the electoral process such as the legal framework governing the election, the professionalism of poll workers, and the transparency of the electoral process. A broad approach to fraud should focus not only on the ballot box but also on the legal and procedural techniques that have been used historically to disenfranchise voters and ensure that such techniques are not used today.

Notes

1. An expanded argument about how these international principles can be specifically applied to the issue of voter identification requirements in the United States can be found in Thad E. Hall and Tova Wang, "Show Me the ID: International Norms and Fairness in Election Reforms," *Public Integrity* (2008).

2. *Election Observation. A Decade of Monitoring Elections: The People and the Practice* (Warsaw: OSCE/ODIHR, 2005).

3. Both of the authors have conducted research and analyses of state election laws; one of the authors (Hall) conducted a fifty-state survey for the Election Assistance Commission related to vote counting and recounting. The ease with which state laws and regulations could be accessed varied widely across the states.

4. The Council of Europe, the European Commission, and OSCE/ODIHR are also endorsing organizations to the DPIEO. A copy of this report can be found at www.cartercenter.org/documents/2231.pdf.

5. See www.aceproject.org (January 2008).

6. This is quoted directly from www.aceproject.org/main/english/vc/vc20.htm.

7. "The 2006 Election," Electionline.org Briefing, electionline.org, November 2006, pp. 3, 5 (http://electionline.org/Portals/1/Publications/EB15.briefing.pdf [January 2008]).

8. See, for instance, Thad Hall, Quin Monson, and Kelly Patterson, "The Human Dimension of Elections: How Poll Workers Shape Public Confidence in Elections," manuscript, University of Utah, 2006.

9. Thad E. Hall, J. Quin Monson, and Kelly D. Patterson, "Poll Workers in American Democracy: An Early Assessment," *P.S.: Political Science and Politics* 40, no. 4 (2007): 647–54.

10. Robert Dahl, *On Democracy* (Yale University Press, 1998).

11. Robert M. Stein and Greg Vonnahme, "Election Day Vote Centers and Voter Turnout," paper presented at the 2006 Annual Meetings of the Midwest Political Science Association, Chicago, Illinois, April 20–23, 2006 (www3.brookings.edu/gs/projects/electionreform/20060418Stein.pdf [January 2008]).

three

Beyond Election Fraud: Manipulation, Violence, and Foreign Power Intervention

Gamze Çavdar

As multiparty competition has expanded to many parts of the world, the challenge of ensuring the integrity and quality of elections is no longer limited to well-established and newly emerging democracies. Elections now take place in ever more challenging environments, including territories under military occupation. These cases raise important questions about our understanding of election fraud and election integrity, as well as our understanding of the role that elections play in a community's political life. To explore these questions, this chapter analyzes the Iraqi parliamentary elections, which were held in late 2005, and the Palestinian parliamentary elections, which were held in early 2006.

These cases are important for two reasons. First, they were widely considered rare opportunities to hold meaningful elections in the Middle East, a region often characterized by highly sophisticated legal and illegal techniques of

I gratefully acknowledge the critical comments of Sue Ellen Charlton, Valerie Asetto, Ibrahim Karawan, Walter Mebane, Susan Hyde, and the members of the Workshop on Election Fraud. Abdel Rahman Abu Arafeh, director of the Jerusalem-based Arab Thought Forum, and Ismail Abu Arafeh, a Palestinian political activist, greatly contributed to this project by sharing the organization's documents and answering my questions. I also would like to extend my gratitude to former U.S. ambassador Robert Keely, who observed the Palestinian elections as part of the U.S.-based Council for the National Interest team, for kindly sharing his experience and insights.

manipulation. The Iraqi elections were meant to elect the first full-time legislature since the collapse of Saddam Hussein's rule in 2003, while the long-postponed Palestinian elections aimed at renewing the first nationally elected legislature of 1996. Examination of these cases will shed light on the extent to which these hopes have materialized.

Second, the Iraqi and Palestinian elections demonstrate the importance of understanding the broader context in which elections take place. In both cases, the amount of fraudulent activity detected was low, and the Palestinian election, in particular, was hailed as "a model for the wider Arab world."[1] But it would be a mistake to consider either election a success for democracy. In neither case did the new legislature or the government have the capacity or the authority to enforce the election outcome since both elections were held under military occupation. Moreover, both parliaments have subsequently been largely crippled. The Iraqi parliament has been deliberately incapacitated by ongoing violence, and the Palestinian parliament has been subject to international political and economic sanctions.

These two cases thus highlight the importance of distinguishing between election fraud, generally defined as illegal and intentional violations of procedures pertaining to elections, and election manipulation, which consists of actions that are intended to exercise control over the electoral system, its outcome, and its meaning. Manipulation encompasses fraud, but it moves beyond such activities to include such larger forces as political violence and foreign power intervention. When prominent, such forces are likely to limit the extent to which even clean elections contribute to establishing democracy.

Conceptual and Methodological Considerations

Elections are central to our understanding of democracy. For example, Robert Dahl's definition of a polyarchy includes five election-related criteria: the government must be controlled by elected officials; elected officials must be chosen and removed in free, fair, and frequent elections where coercion must be absent; all adults must have the right to vote and most must be able to run for offices; and citizens must have the rights of freedom of expression and association as well as alternative sources of information.[2]

Within this context, election fraud is usually defined in procedural terms. Typically, legal criteria constitute a crucial yardstick for determining what constitutes a fraudulent action. Accordingly, numerous legal attempts to manipulate the electoral process are excluded from the discussion on fraud. As Fabrice Lehoucq explains, as long as no law has been broken, "Regardless of whether peasants have been duped into voting in favor of the landlord's party or wish to avoid the reprisals associated with voting against their employer, these activities are not really fraudulent, even if they are morally reprehensible."[3]

In its narrowest form, the concept of election fraud can be understood as "the corruption of the process by which votes are cast and counted."[4] However, many analysts define fraud more broadly to encompass activities "at any stage of the electoral process, from voter registration to the final tally of the ballots."[5] As Larry Diamond puts it:

> Elections are fair when they are administered by a neutral authority; when the electoral administration is sufficiently competent and resourceful to take specific precautions against fraud in the voting and vote counting; when the police, military, and courts treat competing candidates and parties impartially throughout the process; when contenders all have access to the public media; when electoral districts and rules do not systematically disadvantage the opposition; when independent monitoring of the voting and vote-counting is allowed at all locations; when the secrecy of the ballot is protected; when virtually all adults can vote; when the procedures for organizing and counting the vote are transparent and known to all; and when there are clear and impartial procedures for resolving complaints and disputes.[6]

But even this broader definition still conceives of election fraud as deliberate violations of a set of procedures.

This approach may make sense in well-established and stable democracies, where all constituents enjoy a voice in the political system, socioeconomic inequalities are limited, and basic features of the state, such as sovereignty and legitimacy, are present.[7] However, as the Iraqi and Palestinian examples show, this procedural understanding of democracy provides only limited insight into the role that elections play in societies under military occupation.

These societies, by definition, lack sovereign and effective political institutions, the most significant of which is the state. In Iraq, for example, the neopatrimonial personalistic state created by Saddam Hussein collapsed after his overthrow.[8] Subsequently, deep ethnic and sectarian cleavages among various communities intensified the grievances resulting from the colonial British rule, and the subsequent discrimination under Saddam's regime has hindered the development of a national identity. The result is "a profound security vacuum that has engulfed the south and centre of the country" and the need to rebuild "many key institutions, especially the police and the judicial system . . . from the bottom up."[9]

In contrast, the Palestinians have a stronger sense of national identity and better established institutions. However, the Palestinian territories lack the minimum characteristics of a state, including an internationally recognized border, sovereignty, economic and political autonomy, and the provision of basic services. Although the Israeli army has occasionally withdrawn from Gaza, as it did in 2005, it retains "almost complete control over Gaza's borders, sea and air space, tax revenue, utilities, population registry, and the internal economy of Gaza."[10] In addition, the territories suffer from frequent violent clashes among internal factions.

These conditions require us to modify our understanding of electoral fraud in three important ways. First, we must realize that attempts to manipulate electoral behavior are by no means limited to procedural violations. In Iraq, during the electoral campaign and on election day, citizens' safety could not be ensured, let alone such niceties as providing media access to all competing political parties and candidates. Political violence not only undermined the safety and integrity of the process by targeting campaign workers, candidates, and monitors, but it also affected the process during which voters' preferences were shaped by significantly contributing to ethnic and sectarian hostility. Moreover, in both cases, the political pressure exerted by the occupying powers was present at every stage of the elections, including the preparation, management, and endorsement of the outcome. These factors make it clear that we must focus not only on how citizens' preferences are turned into votes but also on how those preferences are constructed and how the parameters of elections are set.

Second, we must look beyond the election process to what occurs once elections have taken place. If, for example, an election outcome has no chance of being enforced because of ongoing violence, the lack of international recognition, or both, it may not matter much that the election itself is considered "flawless" on procedural grounds. The Palestinian elections can be considered the example par excellence of this situation.

Third, any discussion of election fraud needs to be tied to the meaning of the elections. Elections should not be treated as an end in themselves. We also need to address the extent to which elections play a role in instituting, reinstating, or consolidating democracy.[11] In a society where political institutions are not functioning, the question of fraud—that is, the quality of the electoral process during which leaders are elected for nonfunctional institutions—matters very little.

Therefore, in discussing the Iraqi and Palestinian legislative elections, rather than focus on electoral fraud, I emphasize the importance of electoral manipulation. The following sections highlight the similarities and differences between the two cases. The conclusion addresses the role of elections in the process of democratization.

Legislative Elections in Iraq

After the Saddam regime fell in 2003 at the hands of the allied forces under the leadership of the United States, the first major efforts toward establishing a new and participatory regime took place in early 2005. While the occupying forces were still present and violence was still intense, the first elections for an interim parliament were held in January of 2005 and were boycotted by the Sunnis, the second largest sectarian group. The interim parliament's main task was to write a constitution and form a temporary government until the full-term parliament could be elected. After a period of intense debate, the constitution was approved in a referendum in October 2005, a vote that again did not escape the Sunni boycott. The December 2005 elections to elect the first full-time, four-year, 275-seat Iraqi parliament presented a better opportunity for "normalization," since major Sunni parties were finally persuaded to participate in the elections. Thus the legislative elections not only signified the end of the transition period but also raised hopes for a more inclusive parliament and the control of violence.

The elections of December 15, 2005, took place amid extreme tensions between ethnic and sectarian groups, each of which was concerned with playing a greater role in the formation of the new state by increasing their representation in the legislature. This concern was closely related to the vast potential power of the parliament. The new parliament was going to be equipped with the power to choose the Iraqi president and two vice presidents, amend the constitution, implement controversial laws, such as how to divide tax and oil revenues between the central government and the regions, and, far more important, set precedent in exercising the basic rules of the political process.

However, the hopes for holding democratic elections as the first steps to establishing a more inclusive parliament faced significant challenges. Widespread allegations of fraud were raised as soon as the early results began coming in. Despite the turnout rate of 70 percent and the low level of violence on election day, the credibility of the elections was questioned by tens of thousands of Iraqis who took to the streets and asked for a revote.[12] The intensity of the allegations even delayed the release of the final results until the end of

January 2006, leading to a postelection deadlock; in addition, the perception of manipulation significantly contributed to mistrust among different political groups.

The striking feature of the Iraqi case was that the complaints were not limited to a few political entities that failed to gain the majority of seats, but were voiced by many, including the winners of the elections. Almost every political party, including the Shiites and Kurds, who won first and second place, respectively, complained about alleged fraud. The United Iraqi Alliance, the religious-based Shiite group that won 128 seats, argued that it would have won at least 6 more seats if there had been no vote manipulation. Similarly, the Kurdish Alliance, which won 53 seats, argued that cheating prevented the alliance from winning at least 4 more seats. The most discontented group was the Sunnis, who claimed that, given their population, they deserved second place, and their actual number of seats should have been 55, rather than 44.

The discontent among political entities led to an alliance called Maram, an Arabic acronym for the Conference Rejecting Rigged Elections (Mutamar Rafadi Al-Intikhabat Al-Muazzawra).[13] The group, consisting of over thirty-five political entities with various political leanings, asked for the election to be repeated and for the suspension of the Iraqi electoral commission. The previous prime minister, Iyad Allawi, who led the group, argued that there was widespread fraud in vote counting (*tazwir*) and asked for help from the United Nations and Arab countries.[14] These entities, particularly the Sunnis, threatened to boycott the new government unless the elections were repeated.

The scope of these complaints was wide, ranging from a shortage of ballot papers to allegations of theft, violence, intimidation, and ballot box stuffing, as well as questions about the validity of the electoral law and accusations of improper conduct by the security officers.[15] The Turkmen Front argued that as many as 227,000 unqualified Kurds illegally voted in Kirkuk and accused the commission of overlooking the problems.[16] Some Iraqis even claimed that thousands of ballot boxes containing fraudulent ballots were intercepted near the Iranian border while being carried into Iraqi cities just before the elections.[17] Certain media outlets argued that the election results had been announced in Iran days before the preliminary results were released in Iraq, implying that the election outcome was preplanned.[18] General George Casey, the top-ranking U.S. officer in Iraq and the commander of the international forces, also joined the fray by accusing Iran of intervening in the legislative elections.[19] The ongoing violence and the threat of violence undoubtedly created an unsafe environment for the elections. Hameed Majeed Mousa, a member of the National Iraqi List, argued that great pressure was exerted on members of the list, aimed at influencing and changing their political and ideological beliefs. These pressures were topped by the assassination of five members and supporters of the National Iraqi List before the elections.[20]

Some of the most serious criticism was about the election law passed by the previous interim parliament and the voters' list originated by the election law. The law assigned a certain number of seats to each district, a total of eighteen governorates, according to the number of registered voters. The fairness and accuracy of the seat assignment was widely challenged because it was based on the less-than-reliable Food Ration list. The Iraqi Turkmen Front argued, for example, that the process of assigning seats gave disproportionate advantages to the Shiites and Kurds.[21] Similar complaints were raised by the Sunni and Assyrian communities. In sum, whether they involved some organizational shortcomings or intentional misconduct, if proven right, many of the complaints were serious enough to alter the distribution of seats in at least some provinces. Not all the criticism directed at the electoral system and the characteristics of the elections was translated into formal complaints, partly because of the lack of trust for the Iraqi Electoral Commission and partly because of the narrow criteria set for the formal complaints, which are discussed below.

In response to the formal complaints, the Independent Electoral Commission of Iraq (IECI), the main organization responsible for conducting the elections, launched an investigation and decided to delay the announcement of the final results. The commission classified the formal complaints as red and blue, red ones being the most serious ones with potential repercussions for the outcome. The month-long investigation resulted in a decision that simply confirmed the preliminary results. The commission reported that, of about 2,000 complaints, only a small number involved actual fraud.[22] And votes from only 227 of the 30,000 ballot stations were invalidated, less than 1 percent of the votes (table 3-1). The IECI examined the complaints according to narrow criteria established before the elections. The commission was only interested in discovering if the voting process was in compliance with electoral procedures and rules, and did so by investigating only the technical and legal aspects of the complaints.[23] By doing so, the commission significantly reduced the number of formal complaints filed. As a result, the minority communities' widespread dissatisfaction with issues such as the voters' list (the list of eligible voters), the electoral law, and violence was excluded from the investigation. These off-investigation issues, however, constituted a major reason why minority communities, particularly the Sunnis, argued that the elections disproportionately favored the Shiites and Kurds. The postelection

Table 3-1. Voters, Complaints, and Observers

Item	Iraqi elections[a]	Palestinian elections
Registered voters	15,568,000	1,350,000
Actual voters	10,900,000	1,042,000
Turnout rate	70 percent	77 percent
Invalid votes	139,656	29,864
Blank votes	62,836	21,687
Complaints	1,985	61
Total ballot stations	31,348	n.a.
Number of ballot stations invali-dated because of fraud	227[b]	None[c]
International observers	800[d]	1,066

Source: Independent Electoral Commission of Iraq and Palestinian Central Election Commission and the Arab Thought Forum.

n.a. = Not available.

a. These figures are based on voting in previous Iraqi locations.

b. The number of invalidated votes constituted less than 1 percent of the total.

c. Based on a report by the Arab Thought Forum.

d. For security reasons, observers were not present in every location.

demonstrations and the subsequent political crisis were closely related to the conviction of many political entities that they were left out of the political process.

The IECI's investigation and the complaints were also evaluated by the Independent Mission for Iraqi Elections (IMIE), a team that consisted of international experts. Its long-awaited report stated that the legal framework was consistent with international democratic standards.[24] The IECI admitted that many of the complaints were not examined properly by the commission and that some IECI employees were directly involved in fraudulent actions. Although the IMIE criticized the fact that no new elections were held to replace these ballots, stating their importance in a proportional system, it agreed with the IECI that the fraud was limited in scope and endorsed the election results.[25] The final results were released on January 20, 2006.

Manipulation during the Electoral Process

In addition to the fraudulent actions identified by the IECI and IMIE, the electoral process in Iraq witnessed significant irregularities and acts intended to affect the electoral process, many of which went beyond procedural violations. The most obvious was violence. In some cases, the violence was clearly intended to paralyze the entire political process. Kidnappings, assassinations, intimidation, and vandalism continued during the electoral campaign, although on election day the violence reportedly decreased. During 2005, when three elections were held, insurgents increasingly targeted politicians, their families, campaign workers, and high-level government officials. Among them were Baghdad's governor, members of parliament, and the director general of the Foreign Ministry.[26] The release of final reports prompted further attacks intended to destabilize the new government.

In other cases, the violence did not necessarily target the electoral process per se, and yet the outcome was equally damaging to the electoral process. The lack of security in Iraq reached such alarming levels that it "affected the electoral administration itself," and several field officers were killed. Owing to lack of security, 3 percent of the polling stations could not be opened or even set up; the IMIE had to be located outside Iraq; and observing teams were made up primarily of political entity observers—that is, partisans rather than independent observers. Lack of sufficient neutral observation negatively affected the quality of the elections. Security concerns and political pressure to finish the investigation in order to end the political deadlock prevented the complaints from being fully examined. It is therefore quite possible that a significant number of violations went uninvestigated.

The most obvious manifestation of nonprocedural manipulation was the impact of ongoing violence on what Fouad Ajami called "identity voting."[27] Ajami argued that "Iraq had held a census rather than an election" since "voting groups distinguished themselves by voting according to their identity: Sunnis voted for Sunnis and Shiites voted for Shiites." Ghassan al-Atiyyah, director of the Iraqi Foundation for Development and Democracy, agreed that Iraqis did not vote as Iraqis, but as Kurds, Shia, and Sunnis.[28] Indeed, in the legislative elections of December 2005 and January 2006, Shiite-, Kurdish-, and Sunni-dominated towns voted accordingly regardless of the candidates' qualities and abilities. While political violence did not create this situation, it significantly exacerbated it.

The fact that the elections took place under military occupation cannot be ignored as a minor detail. Ironically, the elections were held in Iraq mainly thanks to the occupation, but the occupying powers were involved in every step of the electoral process. Although the U.S. presence in Iraq ostensibly left the political arena to the Iraqis after the formation of the interim parliament, and its presence was limited to military issues, the prominence of U.S. strategic interests in the nature of the new regime made its presence felt in both clandestine and obvious ways during the electoral process. Adeed Dawisha and Larry Diamond have argued, for instance, that the formidable role of the United States in the institutional design exacerbated the exclusion of the Sunni communities.[29] The U.S. efforts to shape the outcome of the elections continued during the legislative elections as well. For instance, the United States insisted on the exclusion of former Baath Party members from the party lists, even after those lists were made public. The White House representative declared the elections "free and fair" even before the investigation was concluded. A representative of the United Nations in the independent higher election commission, Craig Jeans, rejected calls to conduct the elections, again before the IECI's decision. Jeans argued that the UN considered the elections to have been conducted transparently and the results credible, pointing out that there was only one complaint for every 7,000 votes.[30]

After the Election

The fact is that the small number of fraud cases detected by the IECI by no means helped to legitimize the new government, which took months to form and failed to end the political violence. Deep communal divisions and mounting sectarian and ethnic violence in postelection in Iraq not only undermined the ability of the first full-time parliament and the newly elected government but also significantly weakened any prospect of establishing democracy in Iraq. The number of deadly attacks rose immediately after the preliminary results were released in December 2005 and continued to do so steadily. The bombing of the sacred Golden Mosque, a Shiite mosque, in February 2006 resulted in what may be called a "chain reaction." In the summer of 2006, six months after the elections, Iraq witnessed some of the deadliest months on record. In the midst of this chaos, Iraq experienced a disintegration of political authority that has "neither the intention nor perhaps the capacity to forge a national compact."[31] It was estimated in 2006 that 600,000 deaths had resulted from violent causes since the invasion.[32] Although there is no agreement among experts on the exact number of deaths, all agree that violence increased steadily in 2006. A report by the United Nations in November of that year stated that October 2006 was the deadliest month since the American invasion in 2003.[33]

In today's Iraq, the divisions among Kurds, Shia, and Sunni Arabs are so deep that the unity of the country is in danger. There exists no consensus on the basic characteristics of the state as competing ideologies, including secularism, secessionism, and Shiite and Sunni Islamism, envision a different Iraq. Nor is there a commitment to nonviolence in the pursuit of them. Political actors, including political parties, are heavily armed, and political differences in the form of ethnicity, religion, and ideology are not negotiated but simply fought over. What has been going on constitutes a dangerous trend in Iraq: the shrinking domain of politics and the expanding scope of violent conflict. As the next section discusses, unfortunately, the same trend is present in the Palestinian case as well.

Palestinian Legislative Council Elections

The Palestinian Legislative Council, established by the Oslo Accords of 1993, held its elections in 1996 with a clear victory for Fatah (Harakat Al-Tahrir Al-Watani Al-Filastini, the Palestinian Liberation Movement) under the leadership of Yasser Arafat. The term of the first legislature was over in 2000. However, the volatile political situation and the violence following the collapse of the Camp David negotiations of 2000 made it impossible to hold the second legislative election. Finally, on January 25, 2006, the Palestinians went to the polls for the long-delayed election of the Palestinian Legislative Council, which put an end to Fatah domination of the legislature.[34]

The Palestinian elections differed from those of Iraq in a number of ways. First, the electoral process was better organized and monitored, thanks to a large number of international and domestic observers. There were over 1,000 international observers present during the elections, and every polling station was closely scrutinized.[35] Some observers were engaged in long-term observation lasting up to two years. The National Democratic Institute (NDI), in partnership with the Carter Center, was one of the organizations that closely followed the two-year electoral process preceding the elections. Representatives and media outlets of Arab countries also closely followed the elections. This scrutiny of the Palestinian elections was directly related to the generally low level of intrafaction and intrastate violence preceding the election and on election day itself. Equally important was a commitment to the electoral process by all the political parties. A Palestinian civil society organization called the Arab Thought Forum took an unprecedented step by outlining a voluntary code of conduct that was adopted by all political entities except the Islamic Jihad. This was done in order to avoid violence and ensure the rule of law during the electoral process.

Second, neither the existence nor the perception of fraud reached the level it did in Iraq. The incumbent Fatah, which lost the elections, showed greater willingness to accept the outcome than the losers in the Iraqi elections. Palestinian acceptance of the results was undoubtedly related to the fact that, no matter how underdeveloped Palestinian political institutions are, they are not directly run by occupying forces, which gives the population a sense of self-rule and control over the political process. In short, unlike in Iraq, although the outcome was unexpected, the electoral process went relatively smoothly and enjoyed legitimacy in the eyes of the constituency.

The conduct of those involved in the elections was generally praised by international monitors. For instance, the team of the European Union Parliament concluded that "despite some problems, there was nothing which would indicate that the final result was not the outcome chosen by the voters."[36] The Carter Center characterized the process as "competitive" and "free and fair."[37] The European Union Election Observation Mission (EU EOM) agreed with the statement.[38] The Canadian International Development Agency praised the orderliness and management of the elections.[39] Since no major violent incident occurred on election day, the voting and counting process went ahead according to the rules and regulations of the elections.[40] The elections were the best managed and organized in Palestinian political history and produced an impressively small number of fraud allegations.

Manipulation during the Electoral Process

Despite all the progress, however, the voting process was plagued by a series of manipulations. Violations were committed by both major political parties, namely Fatah and Hamas, although, the observers reported, Fatah's incumbent status gave it an advantage in mobilizing government facilities for its own political purposes. Also, in a clear violation of the code of conduct, Hamas used mosques for meetings and for propaganda purposes. A pattern of intimidation did exist against voters of opposite parties. According to the national monitoring committee set up by the Arab Thought Forum, the largest number of violations (34) took place in Bethlehem. The organization received a total of 61 complaints about 242 violations in the West Bank and Gaza.[41] These figures were considerably lower than in Iraq and did not result in the cancellation of votes or lead to any political disputes (see table 3-1).[42] The overwhelming majority of political parties voluntarily signed a code committing to follow election rules, but because it was voluntary the code could not be enforced. As a result, anyone who violated the rules went unpunished.

Israeli intervention in the Palestinian elections also took various forms. Since Hamas refuses to recognize the state of Israel and is committed to using violence, Israeli authorities took every measure possible to prevent Hamas's participation in the elections. The authorities did not give permission for the registration of an estimated 123,000 voters in East Jerusalem until January 15, ten days before the elections. This created a number of logistical problems on election day, including maintaining polling stations and ensuring the secrecy of the vote. Furthermore, Israeli checkpoints continued to pose serious obstacles to all parties on voting day as well as during the electoral campaigns.[43]

The intervention in the Palestinian elections was by no means limited to the occupying power. The United States and the European Union tried to influence the results by threatening to cut off aid if Hamas won the elections.

The Palestinian media and election monitors reported that the "United States through its intermediary USAID provided the PA (Fatah) with campaign funds."[44] In fact, fifteen candidates were reportedly in prison during the time of the elections. Fourteen of them were in an Israeli prison and one in a Palestinian one "under CIA and British Intelligence supervision. Eleven of them are affiliated with Hamas, three with Fatah, and one with the Popular Front for the Liberation of Palestine."[45] Moreover, Palestinian refugees in exile and 9,000 prisoners remained ineligible to vote.[46]

The level of politically motivated violence was significantly less in the Palestinian case, and election day passed almost without violence. However, as was acknowledged by the Canadian International Development Agency (CIDA), international observers remained concerned "about the threat that widespread possession of arms poses to the future of the democratic electoral process."[47] The threat of violence at times turned into violent confrontations within political entities, and threats of violence against the Central Election Commission undermined its independence.[48] These confrontations resulted in a death during campaigning. There were also kidnappings and threats targeting election observers.[49] The political violence and the threat of violence were by no means limited to intrafaction conflicts. Between late 2005 and mid-2006, Palestinian armed groups fired hundreds of Qassam rockets into Israel, which retaliated with 8,000 artillery shells.[50] Between January 3 and January 22, 2006, eight Palestinians died and fifty-two were wounded during the attacks.[51] As the next section discusses, since the capture of an Israeli soldier in the summer of 2006 by a group of militants including Hamas, the armed conflict with Israel has intensified.

After the Election

The fact that the Palestinian elections were conducted successfully quickly turned into a minor detail as soon as the results were announced. Contrary to the predictions of preelection and exit polls, Hamas won the most seats in the parliament and became eligible to form a majority government. The Israeli, U.S., and EU authorities immediately denounced Hamas's victory, and the Hamas-led government, formed in March 2006, lacked any capacity to enforce its mandate. The economic and political implications of the Hamas victory were devastating when international donor aid was cut off. For Israel, recognition of the Hamas-led government was simply not possible as long as the group refused to recognize the state of Israel and the agreements signed between the previous Palestinian authority and Israel. A number of Hamas members were arrested by the Israeli authorities, including cabinet members, and the new government came under intense political pressure as it was unable to pay the salaries of about 160,000 civil servants.[52] In other words, although for different reasons than in Iraq, those who were elected were also incapacitated. In late June 2006, Palestinian armed groups took an Israeli soldier hostage, further complicating the already volatile security conditions. The Israeli army reentered the Gaza Strip and armed groups fired more rockets into Israel. As Human Rights Watch reported in late 2006, "Since September 2005 alone, Palestinian armed groups have fired around 1,700 homemade rockets into Israel, injuring 36 Israeli civilians. The rocket attacks have largely been launched toward civilian areas rather than at any apparent military target, which makes them illegal under the laws of war, and criminal."[53] The implications of the hostage crisis went beyond the borders of the Palestinian territories and led to a thirty-four-day war between Hezbollah in Lebanon and the Israeli army.

The lack of commitment to nonviolence among the factions continues to undermine the prospects of establishing a democratic practice for Palestinians. The increasing unrest among the population and the discontent with the Hamas-led government led to violent clashes between the factions in October 2006. Lawlessness and vigilante violence dominated the political scene, leaving eleven Palestinians dead and more than 100 injured during the fights between the factions.[54] After Hamas fighters gained control of the Gaza Strip in mid-June 2007, President Mahmoud Abbas dissolved the government and declared a state of emergency. However, the Hamas-led forces refuse to acknowledge the dismissal and continue to exercise a de facto authority in the Gaza Strip.

Concluding Remarks

Holding elections has been so closely associated with democracy that it is often forgotten that the two are not synonymous. Much of the electoral politics literature assumes that when elections do not lead to democracy it is because they were not "free and fair." However, in many instances, the chance for democracy remains slim regardless of the quality of elections. Scholars of democratization have a long list of conditions that must be met for democracy to flourish, including the existence of effective state institutions, a minimal level of elite commitment, national unity, and a minimal level of national income. As the Iraqi and Palestinian elections suggest, in the absence of these conditions and in the presence of vigilante violence, merely holding elections, even "free and fair" ones, will not be effective. As Eva Bellin puts it, "To a large degree, order is prior to democracy. Democracy cannot thrive in chaos."[55]

Consequently, democracy promoters and political reformers need to look beyond holding elections. Instead, they should focus on establishing and facilitating the preconditions for democracy, the most significant of which is the creation of effective state institutions. Given that a majority of countries in the world today suffer from insufficient state building, the policy implications undoubtedly go beyond the Iraqi and Palestinian cases.

Notes

1. See "Statement of Preliminary Conclusions and Findings," *European Union Election Observation Mission, West Bank and Gaza*, p. 6 (http://www.elections.ps/pdf/Observer_Report_2006_EUEOM_Preliminary_Statement_English.pdf [January 2008]).

2. Robert A. Dahl, *Democracy and Its Critics* (Yale University Press, 1989), p. 233.

3. Fabrice Lehoucq, "Electoral Fraud: Causes, Types and Consequences," *Annual Review of Political Science* 6 (2003): 235.

4. Lori Minnite and David Callahan, "Securing the Vote: An Analysis of Election Fraud," *Demos* (2003): 14; Fabrice Lehoucq uses similar definitions in *Stuffing the Ballot Box: Fraud, Electoral Reform, and Democratization in Costa Rica* (Cambridge University Press, 2002).

5. Andreas Schedler, "The Menu of Manipulation," *Journal of Democracy* 13, no. 2 (2002): 44; Daniel Calingaert, "Election Rigging and How to Fight It," *Journal of Democracy* 17, no. 3 (2006): 138–51.

6. Larry Diamond, "Thinking about Hybrid Regimes," *Journal of Democracy* 13, no. 2 (2002): 29.

7. This understanding of democracy has been criticized regardless of the subject of analysis. For a Marxist critique of liberal democracy, see Michael Levin, *Marx, Engels and Liberal Democracy* (New York: St. Martin's, 1989); for a feminist critique, see Susan Moller Okin, *Justice, Gender and the Family* (New York: Basic Books, 1989); Carol Pateman, *Democracy, Feminism and Political Theory* (Stanford University Press, 1989); for the requirements of "meaningful" elections, see Said Adejumobi, "Elections in Africa: A Fading Shadow of Democracy?" *International Political Science Review* 21, no. 1 (January 2000): 59–73.

8. Mehran Kamrava, *Politics and Society in the Developing World* (London: Routledge, 1999).

9. Eva Bellin, "Iraqi Intervention and Democracy in Comparative Perspective," *Political Science Quarterly* 19, no. 4 (2004–2005): 599. See also Kamrava, *Politics and Society in the Developing World*, p. 188.

10. Human Rights Watch, "Human Rights Council Special Session on the Occupied Palestinian Territories," July 6, 2006 (http://hrw.org/english/docs/2006/07/06/isrlpa1 3698.htm [January 2008]).

11. Similar criticism has been raised about international monitors. Thomas Carothers, "The Observers Observed," *Journal of Democracy* 8, no. 3 (1997): 17–31; Henry Munson Jr., "International Election Monitoring: A Critique Based on One Monitor's Experience in Morocco," *Middle East Report*, no. 209 (Winter 1998): 37–39.

12. Participation rates in Shiite provinces were around 70 percent, in Sunni provinces a little over 70 percent, and in Kurdish provinces around 80 percent. Iraqis living abroad cast their votes in fifteen countries between December 13 and 15. In the previous referendum on the constitution in October 2005 and the elections for the interim parliament in January 2005, the turnout rates were 63 percent and 58 percent, respectively.

13. The group's formation was announced shortly after the elections were over. It was led by the previous prime minister, Iyad Allawi. See *Al-Zaman* (Iraqi edition), December 21, 2005, p. 1 (www.azzaman.com [January 2008]). (The translation of Arabic documents is by the author unless stated otherwise.)

14. See *Al-Quds Al-Arabi* (Pan-Arab Daily, London), December 22, 2005, p. 4 (www.alquds.co.uk [January 2008]).

15. See "Iraqi Election Official on Fraud Allegations, Observers, Appeals Procedure," *BBC*, December 23, 2005 (www.bbc.co.uk [January 2008]); IMIE Team Report, January 22, 2006, p. 4.

16. See Mofak Salman, "Kirkuk and Kurdish Election Fraud" (www.kerkuk.net/eng/index.asp?id=1740&katagori=1&s=detay [January 2008]). For similar claims raised by the Turkmen Front during the January 2005 elections, see www.kerkuk.net/eng/index.asp?id=406&katagori=23&s=detay (January 2008).

17. The interior minister denied that such reports were true, although similar reports appeared in Western media as well.

18. Those who complained about fraud particularly accused the United States and Iran of being responsible. See *Al-Zaman* (Iraqi daily), December 23, 2005, p. 1 (www.azzaman.com).

19. See *Al-Sabah* (Iraqi daily), December 21, 2005 (www.alsabaah.com [January 2008]).

20. See *Al-Sabah*, December 18, 2005 (translated by Ismail Abu Arafeh) (www.alsabaah.com).

21. See Nermen Al-Mufti, "Elections Again," *Al-Ahram Weekly* (Egyptian weekly), December 15–21, 2005 (http://weekly.ahram.org.eg/2005/773/re3.htm [January 2008]).

22. Hussein Al-Hindawi, the head of the IECI, said in a news conference that twenty of the complaints were serious fraud allegations. Unless there was systematic rigging in stations in a given district, the invalidation of some boxes or stations did not require a revote. See *Al-Zaman*, December 21, 2005 (www.azzaman.com).

23. The rules pertaining to filing a complaint were outlined before the elections. Accordingly, one could only file a complaint about a particular incident at a particular station.

24. "Iraqi Voting Found to Be Flawed but Mostly Fair; Sunnis Are Skeptical," *New York Times*, January 20, 2006, p. A10.

25. International Mission for Iraqi Elections (IMIE), "Final Report on the December 15, 2005, Iraqi Council of Representatives Elections," April 12, 2006 (www.imie.ca [January 2008]).

26. See Human Rights Watch, "A Face and a Name: Civilian Victims of Insurgent Groups in Iraq," October 2005 (www.hrw.org/reports/2005/iraq1005 [January 2008]).

27. Fouad Ajami, "Identity Voting in Iraq," *U.S. News and World Report*, January 9, 2006, p. 35.

28. Christian Richmond, "U.S. Institute of Peace Panel Considers Post-Election Iraq," *Washington Report on Middle East Affairs* 24, no. 3 (2005): 64.

29. Adeed Dawisha and Larry Diamond, "Iraq's Year of Voting Dangerously," *Journal of Democracy* 17, no. 2 (April 2006): 89–103.

30. See *Al-Sabah*, December 29, 2005 (translated by Ismail Abu Arafeh) (www.alsabaah.com).

31. Fareed Zakaria, "There Is One Last Thing to Try," *Newsweek*, October 23, 2006, p. 49.

32. Gilbert Burnham, Riyadh Lafta, Shannon Doocy, and Les Roberts, "Mortality after the 2003 Invasion of Iraq: A Cross-Sectional Cluster Sample Survey," *The Lancet* 368, no. 9545 (2006): 1421–28.

33. See the *New York Times*'s editorial analysis on November 22, 2006 (www.nytimes.com [January 2008]).

34. Exit polls failed to predict the winning party. An exit poll from the Palestinian Center for Policy and Survey Research, headed by Khalil Shikaki, showed Fatah winning 42 percent of the national vote and Hamas 35 percent, with a margin of sampling error of 2 percentage points. See "Exit Polls Give Fatah Narrow Win," *Haaretz* (Israeli daily), January 26, 2006 (www.haaretz.com/hasen/pages/ShArt.jhtml?itemNo=674916 [January 2008]).

35. For a complete list of the election observers see www.elections.ps.

36. See "EU Parliament-MEPs Oversee Historic Palestinian Election," January 30, 2006 (www.europa-eu-un.org/articles/en/article_5621_en.htm [January 2008]).

37. See "Preliminary Statement of the NDI/Carter Center International Observer Delegation to the Palestinian Legislative Council Elections," January 26, 2006 (www.elections.ps/pdf/NDI_PRELIMINARY_STATEMENT.pdf [January 2008]).

38. See European Union Election Observation Mission (EU EOM), "Statement of Preliminary Conclusions and Findings," January 26, 2006.

39. Two international agencies emphasized the difficulties of holding elections under occupation. For their reports, see Canadian International Development Agency (CIDA), "Final Report by the Canadian Observation Mission to West Bank and Gaza," March 2006 (www.acdi-cida.gc.ca/INET/IMAGES.NSF/vLUImages/Elections/$file/Palestine-En-2.pdf [January 2008]); and United Civilians for Peace, "Palestinian Legislative Council Elections Report," 2006 (www.elections.ps/pdf/Report_United_Civilians_for_Peace_PLC_Elections.pdf [January 2008]).

40. See Norwegian Association of NGOs for Palestine, "Elections for the Palestinian Legislative Council," January 25, 2005, p. 5 (www.elections.ps/pdf/Report_Norwegian_Association_of_NGOs_for_Palestine_PLC_elections.pdf [January 2008]).

41. For a summary of violations compiled by the Arab Thought Forum, see www.multaqa.org/etemplate.php?id=693 (January 2008).

42. The data used were limited to those gathered by the Arab Thought Forum.

43. There were 600 roadblocks set up, including twenty-seven checkpoints, on election day.

44. United Civilians for Peace, "Palestinian Legislative Council Elections Report"; see also CIDA, "Statement of Preliminary Findings and Conclusions, Palestinian Legislative Council Elections 2006" (www.acdi-cida.gc.ca/CIDAWEB/acdicida.nsf/En/EMA-218122158-PRU [January 2008]).

45. United Civilians for Peace, "Palestinian Legislative Council Elections Report," p. 9.

46. Norwegian Association of NGOs for Palestine, "Elections for the Palestinian Legislative Council," p. 3.

47. CIDA, "Statement of Preliminary Findings and Conclusions."

48. CIDA, "Final Report," pp. 2–3.

49. CIDA, "Statement of Preliminary Findings and Conclusions"; United Civilians for Peace, "Palestinian Legislative Council Elections Report," p. 4.

50. Human Rights Watch, "Human Rights Council Special Session."

51. See Palestinian Monitoring Group, "Israeli Obstructions of the Palestinian Electoral Process" (www.nad-plo.org/news-updates/PMG%20PLC%20 Elections%2023%2001%2006.pdf [December 2007]).

52. See Human Rights Watch, "Human Rights Council Special Session."

53. See Human Rights Watch, "Israel: IDF Probe No Substitute for Real Investigation," November 10, 2006 (www.hrw.org/english/docs/2006/11/10/isrlpa14550.htm [January 2008).

54. See Human Rights Watch, "Occupied Palestinian Territories: Factions Must Stop Endangering Civilians," October 6, 2006 (http://hrw.org/english/docs/2006/10/06/isrlpa14337.htm [January 2008]).

55. Eva Bellin, "Coercive Institutions and Coercive Leaders," in *Authoritarianism in the Middle East*, edited by Marsha Pripstein Posusney and Michele Penner Angrist (Boulder, Colo.: Lynne Rienner, 2005), p. 38.

part two

Measuring Election Fraud: Learning from Observational Data

four

Measuring Perceptions
of Election Threats:
Survey Data from Voters and Elites

R. Michael Alvarez and Thad E. Hall

In the United States since the 2000 election there have been concerns raised regarding electoral irregularities—either intentional election fraud or unintentional problems in the election that result in an inaccurate (and thus sometimes in the eyes of the losing side, fraudulent) outcome.[1] The ongoing debate about the security of electronic voting technologies reflects one aspect of this debate. Concerns have also been raised about fraud in absentee voting, early voting, precinct voting, and voting by military personnel and overseas civilians (UOCAVA voters named for the Uniformed and Overseas Citizens Absentee Voting Act), that are all unrelated to the type of voting technologies used.[2] Moreover, in the 2002 gubernatorial election in New Hampshire there were convictions related to jamming political party "get-out-the-vote" telephone banks.[3]

There have been numerous claims in recent years that the public does not have confidence that its vote will be counted accurately. This claim was central

We thank the Carnegie Corporation of New York, the John S. and James L. Knight Foundation, the Caltech/MIT Voting Technology Project, and the Center for Public Policy and Administration at the University of Utah for their support of this research. We also thank Doug Chapin and electionline.org, Sarah Hill, and Melissa Slemin for their help with some of the data collection and analysis reported here. Finally, we thank Morgan Llewellyn for his assistance in our research.

to the Carter-Baker Commission's report on election reform.[4] However, public data on this issue present a mixed message. For example, in previous work with Morgan Llewellyn, we found that roughly nine of ten voters reported being confident that their ballots will be counted as intended. However, we also found that confidence among African American voters dropped considerably between the 2000 and 2004 elections: around 16 percent reported a lack of confidence after the 2000 elections, but over 30 percent expressed a lack of confidence in the 2004 election cycle.[5]

In this chapter we explore the connection between voter confidence and fraud in elections. Since before the 2004 presidential election we have been conducting periodic national public opinion polls to assess Americans' perceptions of the electoral system. We have asked specific questions about voters' confidence that their individual votes will be counted accurately. More recently, we asked respondents in a national probability sample about their perceptions of security threats to the electoral process. We also conducted a pilot survey in 2005 that sought to obtain detailed threat assessment data from the "elite" population: election administrators, academics, policymakers, and advocates. Here we present data from these surveys, which provide important information on the perceptions of Americans about the security of their electoral system. Before we do so, we discuss the potential threats and risks associated with the fair conduct of elections and provide the results of a small elite survey that considers the threats and risks associated with the voting process. The potential for fraud is predicated on specific threats' coming to fruition. We consider the potential problems that can arise in elections and the likelihood that they will occur, and examine the methodological question of whether a survey-based approach can elicit useful data for threat assessment analyses.

Elections as a Threat-Probability Environment

We often discuss risks in our daily lives: What are the risks of getting cancer? Of being in an accident? Of being attacked by a shark while swimming in the ocean? In order to understand these risks one must understand four facets of risk. First, what is the threat that may be encountered (for example, being attacked by a shark)? Second, what is the level of disruption the threat would cause (since being attacked by a shark could kill you, the level of life disruption is potentially high)? Third, what is the likelihood of being eaten by a shark (lower than the risk of being crushed by a pig)? Fourth, how can one mitigate the risk (for example, by not going into the ocean in areas where sharks have been seen)? We can thus write a definition for the perceptions of risk as: Threat = (Disruption * Likelihood) – Mitigation.[6]

As this equation shows, not all threats manifest themselves equally as risks. Some threats may not produce very high levels of disruption. Some threats may be problematic but very unlikely to occur. Some threats may be problematic but easy to mitigate. However, just as not all threats are equal when considered as risks, the calculation of risk using the equation above will vary according to the decisions made by different individuals. This is especially true in areas where there are different types of people involved in the evaluation process. When the Food and Drug Administration had a panel of medical experts consider whether certain Cox-II inhibitors, such as Vioxx, should be removed from the market, there was a difference of opinion between clinicians who treat patients and researchers who study risk.[7] The clinicians understood the threat and the disruption problem, but calculated the likelihood and mitigation differently than the researchers. The clinicians thought they could effectively mitigate the risk through aggressive monitoring of patients, thus lowering the likelihood that a problem will arise. The risk researchers examined the aggregate data and made a different calculation of risk.

The issue of risk analysis varies across issue areas, as does the willingness to tolerate risk. For the public and for policymakers alike, the media often play a critical role in framing our understanding of risk. One framework for understanding how risk is interpreted examines the social amplification and attenuation of risk. This framework has multiple components: personal (how the risk is perceived to affect the individual), institutional, and social, all of which affect how risks are interpreted and addressed.[8] "Risk analysis, then, requires an approach that is capable of illuminating risk in its full complexity, [that] is sensitive to the social settings in which risk occurs, and that recognizes that social interactions may either amplify or attenuate the signals to society about the risk."[9]

Risk analysis is made difficult on an individual level by the fact that most people do not experience certain risks directly. Instead, an individual's perceptions of risk are understood and "experienced" through the media. The media's framing of an issue, the attention given, the tone of the coverage, the amount of information provided, and the symbolism used to characterize the risk shape how the public perceives a given risk. In addition, not all media discuss risk in the same way. There are obvious differences in how risk is covered by the mass media—television, radio, and print newspapers—and by the Internet or specialized professional publications. However, even in the mass media, risk is treated differently in news stories than it is in opinion pieces and on talk shows. Finally, the actual likelihood that a risk will be serious can be inversely related to the amount of media coverage the risk receives. For example, the risk of dying from radiation exposure from the sun is much higher than the risk of dying from radiation exposure from an accident at a nuclear power plant, but the latter has received more attention, historically, than the former. Similarly, the coverage of West Nile virus and the flu is inversely related to the number of deaths they cause.

Measuring Risk Assessments in Survey Research

As far as we know, there is no existing literature on the use of survey approaches for collecting information on the assessments of a population regarding threats or risks to the electoral system. But there are studies examining threat assessments of violence and violent behavior, where interview research has been employed in part to develop risk models.[10] There are also projects that aim to probe the expectations of target populations regarding propensities to engage in other types of risky behavior, for example, the likelihood that teenagers will engage in behaviors that present health risks.[11] But while survey-based methods for studying expectations of future events and behavior are used in some areas of social and policy research, we are not aware of their use in developing risk or threat assessment in the field of election administration.

In part this is due to the lack of research on election administration.[12] But that there is little research in the social sciences on survey measurement of threats to the electoral or political process is most likely due to skepticism in the social science community about how individuals think about probabilities and expectations and whether surveys can facilitate accurate assessments of probabilities and expectations. On one hand, psychologists Amos Tversky and Daniel Kahneman have shown with experimental data that subjects use shortcuts to process information and develop expectations, thus implying that individuals may not be well suited to forming expectations or probability assessments about events such as the possibility of threats to election systems in a way that is consistent with notions of rational expectations. On the other hand, there is research in political behavior showing that survey respondents are poor predictors of the likelihood of candidate victories in elections, and that the process of expectation formation in the election setting is influenced by how much the respondents like the candidates and not just by information on how well they are doing in the race. And last, as recently reviewed by

Charles Manski, the economics profession has until very recently been reluctant to turn to survey methodologies to study economic expectations.[13]

Following in the path of recent work by Manski and his collaborator Jeff Dominitz, we have experimented with different survey-based approaches, using different populations and sampling strategies, gathering data from survey respondents that might be used in threat assessment analysis for election administration. In the remainder of this chapter we discuss two of these experiments, the first seeking to gather data on the likelihood of election system threats from well-informed and highly knowledgeable populations: election officials, academics, policymakers, and election reform advocates. In the second experiment we tested a question on assessment of election system risks in a national probability telephone sample. Below we present data from the two different methods, and then in our conclusion we provide some tentative evaluations of the survey method's utility for developing threat assessments, and discuss some future research directions.[14]

Risk Assessments in Elections: Elite Perceptions

Working in conjunction with the Caltech/MIT Voting Technology Project, electionline.org, and the University of Utah's Center for Public Policy and Administration, we conducted an elite survey that examined potential risks to the conduct of a fair election. The complete survey instrument is available at www.vote.caltech.edu/media/threat_risk.pdf. The survey examined a wide array of potential threats, ranging from outright election fraud to tampering with the electoral process and unintentional problems. Specifically, the first survey examined illegal or double voting; coercion or disrupting an election; voter registration; problems with precinct voting; problems with early voting (in-person and absentee); and problems with postelection ballot processing.

For each type of threat, the respondent was asked to score on a scale from one (1) to ten (10), with one being a low score, the following:

1. What level of disruption would the event cause to an election?
2. What is the likelihood the threat would occur in the 2005 elections (if any)?
3. What is the likelihood the event could occur in the 2006 elections?
4. How would you rate the ease of mitigating the threat?

These questions require a respondent to think about risk comprehensively. For each type of threat we identified, we required respondents to think through the components of the risk in a way that allowed its potential magnitude to be determined. The survey also asked respondents to provide an overall assessment of the risk threat presented by six types of substantive problems, in an effort to assess the threat profile of the existing election process.

To implement this survey, we posted it (in "fillable" pdf format) on several websites that are frequented by academic researchers, election officials, policymakers, and election reform advocates.[15] In the end, we received only twenty-three complete survey responses; the poor response rate appears due to the complexity and length of the survey and to concerns about how the information in the survey might be used. Respondents, though, came from a variety of backgrounds: academia, election administration, policymaking, and advocacy.

Despite the low response rate to this elite survey and the nonrandom method of respondent selection, we think that the data can shed some light on elite perceptions of threats to the electoral process. The first set of questions concerned perceived threats from a wide variety of types of election fraud. Elite respondents saw what might be called "denial of service" attacks on the electoral process (disruptions of early, absentee, or precinct voting) as ones likely to cause the greatest disruption—and to be among the most difficult to mitigate. At the other end of the spectrum, our elite respondents saw illegal voting, the various types of double voting, and registration fraud as among the least disruptive types of election fraud. However, respondents perceived voting in multiple jurisdictions and registration fraud as difficult to mitigate. As to the relative likelihood of occurrence, elite respondents saw coercion as the most likely of the many types of election fraud to occur and disruptions of the process and voting in multiple precincts as the least likely.

We now turn to a second set of potential threats: efforts to tamper with the voting process itself, either early or precinct voting, or ballot transport and tabulation. Elite respondents uniformly saw these as threats likely to disrupt the process, ranking each one at 5.0 or greater on the 1-to-10-point scale. They said tampering with early voting had the greatest estimated potential of disruption (an average of 6.9), followed closely by the threat posed by tampering with precinct e-voting machines (an average of 6.8). Despite the potential for disruption, though, elite respondents saw these as having a relatively low likelihood of occurrence in the current election cycle; tampering with precinct tabulators received the highest average ranking (2.4); the rest averaged around 2 on the 1-to-10-point scale. Furthermore, none of these threats was perceived as highly difficult to mitigate: tampering with early and precinct e-voting, as

Table 4-1. Likelihood of Various Election Fraud Activities, According to Survey Respondents

Activity	Most likely					Least likely
	1	2	3	4	5	6
Illegal or double voting	2	2	1	8	3	6
Coercion or deception in voting	2	2	3	3	7	5
Voter registration	12	1	3	2	2	2
Problems with precinct voting	3	5	4	2	4	4
Problems with absentee voting	4	7	6	1	3	1
Problems with postelection affairs	3	1	3	4	4	7

Source: Responses to survey of "23 election elites" conducted by the authors.

well as ballot transport and tabulation, received average ratings of approximately 3 on our 10-point scale.

Finally, we consider a third set of potential threats: an array of unintentional problems with early and precinct voting, as well as with ballot processing. Here we find that some of these unintentional problems were perceived as somewhat of a threat for disruption, especially unintentional problems with early and precinct e-voting machines and their associated paper trails. Interestingly, some of these unintentional problems were among some of the most likely to occur in the current election cycle, especially problems with early voting and precinct paper trails, and processing of absentee and provisional ballots. Elite respondents also saw the early and precinct voting paper trail problems as more difficult to mitigate relative to the other unintentional problems we posed to them.

Another question in our elite survey that produced helpful data was the third and final question: "For each part of the electoral process in the county where you vote, please rank the relative chance that the problems (intentional or unintentional) will occur in upcoming elections in November 2006. Please label the risk that is most likely as 1, and the one that is least likely as 6." The set of problems we asked about included illegal or double voting, coercion or deception in voting, voter registration, problems with precinct voting, problems with absentee voting, and problems in postelection ballot processing and tabulation. The response counts in each of the categories are presented in table 4-1.[16] Overwhelmingly, our elite respondents saw voter registration as the most likely threat to the election process in their county (twelve of twenty-two respondents rated that as most likely). Second in terms of likelihood were problems with absentee voting, as four respondents rated it most likely to be a threat, and seven respondents rated it second most likely. Third most likely were problems with precinct voting, which three rated most likely and five rated second most likely.

We see that a survey-based approach for eliciting data from election elites regarding potential threats is a viable methodology. Of course, future efforts to gather similar data can learn important lessons from our pilot study. First, our survey instrument was lengthy and complex, even drawing complaints about length and complexity from experts in the field; thus future survey-based efforts should concentrate on gathering data in less complicated ways. Second, we were unable to obtain a large pool of survey respondents for this survey. This indicates that perhaps other efforts, including working more closely with organizations that have credibility with election administrators (in particular) might be productive, as would other methods for increasing the sample size. Third, working to obtain data that are more representative of the population of election administrators, academics, policymakers, and advocate representatives should be pursued, including both quantitative (survey) and qualitative (focus group) methods.

Risks Assessments in Elections: General Public Attitudes and Concerns

From 2004 to 2006 we conducted several surveys asking American voters about their confidence in various voting technologies. In January 2006 we asked 2,025 respondents in a national probability sample a survey question that was designed to replicate, as accurately as possible, the types of open-ended question that were included in the election threats questionnaire discussed previously.[17] The difference is that the January 2006 survey used a closed-ended question format and came at the end of a series of questions on election reforms and problems. The specific question asked of all survey respondents was: "What do you perceive as the greatest threat to the integrity of the electoral system?" Possible answers were as follows:

 a. Intentional voting fraud, such as by tampering with electronic voting machines or stuffing the ballot box,

 c. unintentional human errors by poll workers or election officials,

 d. voter registration fraud,

 e. illegal voting such as voting twice,

 f. intimidation through which voters are coerced to vote for a specific candidate or ballot measure,

g. some other problem, or

h. don't know.

Several findings are of immediate interest (see table 4-2). First, it is clear from these data that fraud is an issue that most American adults are uncertain about. In the sample, 33.8 percent of respondents did not have an answer to this question and 0.9 percent of respondents refused to answer the question. In addition, 36 percent of respondents gave the answer "some other problem." The question does attempt to force the respondent into a response about fraud; respondents not concerned about fraud are generally forced to respond "some other problem" or "don't know." That so many respondents answered "some other problem" can be interpreted as another indication of uncertainty; some or all of the survey respondents may have used this answer to avoid the perception that they were uninformed about the problem. The fact that 7 of 10 respondents may have no opinion about potential threats to the electoral system indicates that this issue may not have yet penetrated the minds of most Americans.

Second, if we examine the responses to the threats provided in the list, we see that the category "intentional voting fraud" has the highest incidence of response (12.3 percent), followed by "unintentional human errors" (6.9 percent) and "voter registration fraud" (5 percent). In addition, illegal voting—such as voting twice—and voter intimidation both were the greatest concern of between 2 percent and 3 percent of respondents. These four forms of fraud—intentional voting fraud, voter registration fraud, illegal voting, and intimidation—are forms of intentional fraud, and together approximately 22 percent of the respondents in our sample indicated that some form of intentional election fraud is a significant concern. By examining the data more closely, we can determine the subpopulations of voters who are most concerned about intentional election fraud.[18]

The subpopulations of voters that are of greatest interest initially are classified by race, partisanship, and whether the voter voted in the last election. The differences between black and white voters are of especially high interest given the amount of discrimination that has occurred against black voters in the past. In addition, the debates over election reform have traditionally had a very specific dynamic, with conservatives and Republicans being very concerned about voter registration fraud and liberals and Democrats being concerned about intimidation. The historical concern among Republicans about intentional fraud via ballot box stuffing—as was alleged in Cook County, Illinois, in 1960—has been compounded by concern among Democrats about intentional tampering with

Table 4-2. Election Fraud Concerns, by Party, Race, and Voter Participation in 2004

Type of fraud	Aggregate		Party affiliation			Race		Voted in 2004	
	Frequency	Percent	Republican	Democrat	Independent	White	Black	Yes	No
Voter registration fraud	100	5.0	6.9	3.8	4.9	5.6	5.2	5.2	4.3
Illegal voting	62	3.1	3.5	3.0	2.9	3.1	0.5	3.1	2.4
Intentional voting fraud	249	12.3	11.2	15.1	10.7	12.8	13.5	12.8	10.7
Unintentional human errors	140	6.9	7.3	6.9	6.1	8.1	5.2	7.3	5.7
Intimidation	43	2.1	2.4	1.7	2.3	2.0	4.7	2.8	0.1
Some other problem	731	36.1	36.6	33.4	39.8	37.8	31.6	38.1	30.4
Don't know	683	33.8	31.1	35.8	32.6	29.9	39.4	29.9	45.9
Refused to answer	17	0.9	1.0	0.3	0.7	0.9	0.0	0.8	0.5

Source: Survey of 2,025 respondents conducted January 18–24, 2006, by ICR for the authors.

electronic voting machines to steal elections for the Republicans. Finally, we examine the differences between individuals who voted in 2004 and those who did not vote. If the nonvoters have very high levels of concern about fraud, it could influence their decision to vote and keep them from participating in the electoral process.

When we examine differences between white and black respondents, we find that both groups have similar general concerns about election fraud. Nearly 10 percent more black respondents (almost four of ten blacks in our sample) had no opinion about fraud concerns relative to whites (29.9 percent of white respondents expressed no opinion). But approximately 70 percent of both populations did not select a specific fraud concern: 77 percent of white respondents and 75 percent of black respondents did not select an intentional fraud concern from the list offered. There are important differences between blacks and whites regarding the type of intentional election fraud that concerns them most. Black respondents were slightly more likely to be concerned about intentional voting fraud, registration fraud, and voter intimidation. By contrast, whites are more concerned about illegal voting.

Given the problems that have faced black voters throughout history, these findings are not surprising. Even in 2000 there were concerns about voter registration fraud—as exemplified in claims that black voters were systematically purged from the rolls. Such concerns came to the fore again in 2004, with claims that the voter registration forms of Democrats in Nevada were not being submitted to the state correctly. Recent work by Alvarez, Hall, and Llewellyn found that black voters have less confidence than whites that their vote will be counted accurately. so we are not surprised that the minority voters have a specific concern focused on fraud that can be perpetrated against voters—such as intimidation or registration fraud.[19]

When we examine fraud concerns among Democrats, Independents, and Republicans, we find that some of the anecdotal findings about fraud hold true, but some do not. Specifically, Republicans are much more concerned than Democrats about voter registration fraud. However, Democrats and Republicans are equally concerned about voter intimidation, just as they are equally concerned about illegal voting. One area where there is a large gap among partisans is in the area of concern about intentional voting fraud. Democrats are 4 percentage points more likely than Republicans or Independents to be concerned about intentional election fraud. Given the close and contentious nature of both the 2000 and 2004 presidential elections and how liberal interest groups have used concerns about the security of electronic voting as an issue, it is not surprising that Democrats have this concern.

When we compare individuals who voted in 2004 with individuals who did not vote, we find that there are interesting differences as well. Not surprisingly, those who did not vote were more likely to have no opinion about threats to the electoral system (45.9 percent for voters relative to 29.9 percent for nonvoters). Nonvoters were less likely to be concerned about both intentional and unintentional forms of fraud. Nonvoters are especially not concerned about intimidation and coercion. In total, these findings are important because they strongly suggest that nonvoters are not being kept from the polls because of a concern about election fraud or that they will be cheated or coerced in their vote.

In addition to the groups of greatest interest shown in table 4-2, we examined perceptions of fraud in different demographic groups, and here we find some interesting variations but also much agreement across groups. For example, men are slightly more concerned than women about voter registration fraud (6 percent to 4 percent), and women are more likely to answer "don't know" (37 to 31 percent) than "some other problem" (34 percent female, 38 percent male). Concerns about election fraud vary little across age cohorts, although young people (aged 18–27) are more likely to answer "don't know" than "some other problem." There is a similar pattern of answers in the income data, with lower-income individuals more likely to answer "don't know" than to provide another response. One interesting variation was among individuals with some college education but not a college degree. They were 5 percentage points more likely to be concerned about intentional voter fraud—such as tampering with electronic voting machines or stuffing ballot boxes—than either (a) individuals with a high school education or less or (b) individuals with a college degree or advanced degree.

Confidence and Threats to the System

There has been much concern among voters in recent years that their vote be counted accurately. Given the level of concern about voting technology nationally, we are interested in seeing whether people who are not confident that their votes are counted accurately have broader concerns about election fraud. The descriptive analysis examining views of fraud and a lack of confidence in vote count accuracy are shown in table 4-3.

First, we present a simple analysis of whether people who lack confidence that their votes are counted accurately are concerned about fraud generally. Here, we find that individuals who lack confidence in vote counting are 4.4 percentage points more likely to think there is intentional election fraud than indi-

Table 4-3. Voter Confidence in the Accuracy of Ballot Counting Related to Specific Fraud Concerns

Percent

Type of fraud	Confidence in counting ballots			
	Confident	Not confident	No answer/ No opinion	Total
Intentional fraud	23.5	27.9	18.5	23.9
Unintentional fraud	76.5	72.1	81.5	76.1
Voter registration fraud	5.8	1.7	0.0	5.2
Illegal voting	3.4	1.6	.9	3.1
Intentional voting fraud	11.7	20.3	15.3	12.8
Unintentional human errors	7.7	5.4	2.1	7.3
Intimidation	2.6	4.2	2.3	2.8
Some other problem	38.1	38.6	27.1	38.1
Don't know	30.0	27.9	52.3	29.9
Refused to answer	.8	.3	0.0	.8

Source: Survey of 2,025 respondents conducted January 18–24, 2006, by ICR for the authors.

viduals who are confident that their vote was counted accurately. The respondents who are not confident are also almost 10 percentage points more likely to be concerned about intentional fraud than individuals who have no opinion about whether their votes were counted accurately. When we consider the specific election fraud concerns of individuals who are not confident that their votes were counted accurately, we find that they are more concerned than other respondents about intentional voting fraud and intimidation. Interestingly, people who lack confidence that their vote will be counted accurately are less concerned, on average, about nonvoting-related fraud such as voter registration fraud. They are also less concerned about actual vote fraud—such as illegal voting—and about unintentional human errors as a source of fraud problems.

Conclusions

The results from these survey experiments illustrate three important issues regarding how we can study and prevent election fraud. First, the data from the national survey show that Americans are poorly informed and relatively uncertain about election fraud. Among those who are concerned about election fraud, the concern centers on intentional voting fraud, where illegal ballots are cast in the election. The data also suggest a "sore loser" effect from the 2000 and 2004 elections, as Democrats are more likely to be concerned about illegal voting than Republicans are.[20] Fortunately, we do not see fraud as being a greater concern among nonvoters or nonregistered voters; thus concerns about fraud do not seem to be keeping people away from the polls. We also see that some individuals are just more worried than others about fraud in general. For example, respondents who lack confidence that their votes will be counted accurately are more concerned about intentional fraud than individuals who are confident that their votes will be counted accurately.

When we think about how national population survey data on threats to the electoral system can be used in threat assessment analysis, we have two different reactions. On the one hand, because voters seem generally uninformed about election fraud and their perceptions seem systematically affected by their political orientations, caution is necessary in the use of this sort of data in threat assessment analysis. But on the other hand, as the general population is one of the ultimate consumers of election administration services, it is important to understand the public's concerns and level of knowledge, and to incorporate their concerns into fraud and threat prevention. To the extent that perceptions of threat and fraud influence public confidence in the integrity of the electoral process, studying the public's perceptions is important.

Second, concerns about threats to the electoral process—especially threats alleged to be associated with electronic voting systems—have played a large role in recent discussions about the American electoral process. In order to deal effectively with these concerns, election officials and researchers should undertake more research (like that represented in other chapters in this book) to understand scientifically the actual threats to voting systems. However, election officials and researchers also need to understand the perceptions of key stakeholders (voters, elites, politicians, advocates, and others) about these same threats. Only by understanding the real threats, and their perceived risk, can policymakers develop and implement useful communication strategies for informing the stakeholders about the real nature of election risks, and for informing the stakeholders about the steps being taken to mitigate or eliminate those risks. Such communication strategies will prove crucial for ensuring that voter and stakeholder confidence in the integrity of the American electoral process is maximized.[21]

Third, a different set of implications arise from our study of the elite-level survey results. Substantively, when we examine the opinion of individuals about specific fraud risks and the ability to mitigate these risks, we find that the threats to elections that are the most highly disruptive are also among the easiest to mitigate. This is similar to the problems faced on the Internet; denial-of-service attacks are problematic but can be mitigated with effective deterrence and prevention.[22] However, there is a more basic reason to survey informed individuals about the likelihood that various threats to elections will occur. Basic theories of economics and psychology tell us that markets—

be they stock markets, betting parlors, or in this case, decision or prediction markets—are highly effective at predicting the future. There is a wealth of literature discussing the efficiency of betting markets: such markets take advantage of collective knowledge and the aggregation of information to produce effective estimations of outcomes. Other types of markets, like the Iowa Electronic Market and the Hollywood Stock Exchange, have proven highly effective at predicting nonmarket outcomes (like presidential elections and weekend box office grosses for movies) that other methods sometimes have difficulty forecasting with accuracy.[23]

Using such markets to predict problems with elections could be controversial; witness the concerns raised about the Policy Analysis Market that the Defense Department attempted to develop in 2002–03 to help predict changes in the conditions that are conducive to a terrorist incident.[24] However, such approaches can be used to identify potential threats and determine where resources should be focused to develop a more secure election system. A prediction market for forecasting election problems could be operated at the state or local level, aggregating the knowledge of poll workers, poll watchers from political parties and interest groups, habitual voters, and other interested players in the election process. Given the wide variations in state election laws and their local implementation, such work could be highly effective in improving our perceptions of the actual threats that exist in the election process.

But using prediction markets to aggregate information might prove difficult or problematic in forecasting election problems, because well-informed elites might fear that revealing information about potential threats to election systems could be used strategically against them. As we noted in our discussion of the elite survey, the low response rate, especially from election officials, might reflect such concerns. If so, potential survey respondents would need to be assured that any data they provided would be confidential and used judiciously.

Notes

1. For examples of this literature, see Tracy Campbell, *Deliver the Vote* (New York: Carroll and Graf, 2005); John Fund, *Stealing Elections* (New York: Encounter Books, 2004); Andrew Gumbel, *Steal This Vote* (New York: Nation Books, 2005).

2. Caltech/MIT Voting Technology Project, "Voting: What Is, What Could Be," 2001 (http://votingtechnologyproject.org).

3. As reported in the *Boston Globe*: "The episode began with a political dirty trick engineered by New Hampshire Republicans on Nov. 5, 2002. Republican John E.

Sununu, then a House member, was locked in a tight Senate race against Democrat Jeanne Shaheen, then the governor, in a contest some observers thought could determine control of the Senate. In an effort to disrupt Democrats' get-out-the-vote efforts, officials with the state Republican Party hired a telemarketing company to tie up the hotlines that had been set up by Democrats and a firefighters' union to help get voters to the polls. For about ninety minutes, computer-dialed calls tied up the hotlines, until the scheme was halted by state Republican officials who grew concerned about its legality. Sununu won the race by about 20,000 votes on a day in which Republicans swept the major races in New Hampshire and much of the nation. The case has yielded three convictions so far, including those of the RNC's New England regional political director for the 2002 elections, James Tobin, and the then–executive director of the state Republican Party, Charles McGee. The third person convicted was Allen Raymond, a former Virginia telemarketing executive who was hired by the New Hampshire Republicans." Rick Klein, *Boston Globe*, April 13, 2006 (www.boston.com/news/nation/articles/2006/04/13/white_house_pressed_on_nh_tactic [January 2008]).

4. Commission on Federal Election Reform, "Building Confidence in U.S. Elections," 2005 (www.american.edu/ia/cfer [January 2008]).

5. See R. Michael Alvarez, Thad E. Hall, and Morgan Llewellyn, "Are Americans Confident Their Ballots Are Counted?" *Journal of Politics* (forthcoming); and Richard Hasen, "Beyond the Margin of Litigation: Reforming the U.S. Election Administration to Avoid Electoral Meltdown," *Washington & Lee Law Review* 62 (2005): 937.

6. This is similar to the analytical approach to defining the perception of risk offered by Peter S. Adler and Jeremy L. Kranowitz, "A Primer on Perceptions of Risk, Risk Communication and Building Trust" (www.keystone.org/spp/published_works.html [January 2008]).

7. See the website that the FDA has established regarding the Arthritis Drugs Advisory Committee's work (http://www.fda.gov/ohrms/dockets/ac/cder05.html#Arthritis Drugspercent20 [January 2008]).

8. Marc Siegel, *False Alarm* (New York: Wiley, 2005); Nick Pidgeon, Roger Kasperson, and Paul Slovic, *The Social Amplification of Risk* (Cambridge University Press, 2003); Roger E. Kasperson and Jeanne X. Kasperson, "The Social Amplification and Attenuation of Risk," *Annals of the American Academy of Political and Social Science* 545 (1996): 95–105.

9. Kasperson and Kasperson, "The Social Amplification and Attenuation of Risk."

10. Randy Borum, Robert Fein, Bryan Vossekuil, and John Berglund, "Threat Assessment: Defining an Approach for Evaluating Risk of Targeted Violence," *Behavioral Sciences and the Law* 17 (1999): 323–37; Marisa Reddy, Randy Borum, John Berglund, Bryan Vossekuil, Robert Fein, and William Modzeleski, "Evaluating Risk for Targeted Violence in Schools: Comparing Risk Assessment, Threat Assessment, and Other Approaches," *Psychology in the Schools* 38 (2001): 157–72.

11. One long-standing project in this area is the "Youth Risk Behavior Surveillance System" (YRBSS), which uses surveys of teenagers every two years, with national,

state, and local samples, to collect data on health risk behaviors. For details, see www. cdc.gov/HealthyYouth/yrbs/overview.htm (January 2008).

12. R. Michael Alvarez and Thad E. Hall, "Controlling Democracy: The Principal-Agent Problems in Election Administration," *Policy Studies Journal* 34, no. 4 (2006): 491–510.

13. Amos Tversky and Daniel Kahneman, "Judgment under Uncertainty: Heuristics and Biases," *Science* 185 (1974): 1124–31; Paul R. Abramson, John H. Aldrich, Phil Paolino, and David W. Rohde, "Sophisticated Voting in the 1988 Presidential Primaries," *American Political Science Review* 86 (1992): 55–69; Larry M. Bartels, "Expectations and Preferences in Presidential Nominating Campaigns," *American Political Science Review* 79 (1985): 804–15. Larry M. Bartels, *Presidential Primaries and the Dynamics of Public Choice* (Princeton University Press, 1988); Charles F. Manski, "Measuring Expectations," *Econometrica* 72 (2004): 1329–76.

14. Jeff Dominitz and Charles F. Manski, "Using Expectations Data to Study Subjective Income Expectations," *Journal of the American Statistical Association* 92 (1997): 855–67; Jeff Dominitz and Charles F. Manski, "Perceptions of Economic Uncertainty: Evidence from the Survey of Economic Expectations," *Public Opinion Quarterly* 61 (1997): 261–87.

15. The websites used were the Caltech/MIT Voting Technology Project website (http://votingtechnologyproject.org); our weblog (http://electionupdates.caltech.edu); Electionline (electionline.org); and the University of Utah's Center for Public Policy and Administration (www.cppa.utah.edu). Notices of the survey's availability were sent out, and electionline.org profiled this project in its newsletter. We advertised the survey in a number of conference and workshop presentations and had paper copies available for potential respondents. The survey became available on October 20, 2005; most responses were received in late 2005, though the final response was received on May 18, 2006. Unfortunately, because of the extremely small number of respondents, confidentiality concerns prevent us from providing any detailed analysis of the profile of the respondents to the survey. We return to this point in the conclusion. We heard, third-hand, that some in the community of election officials expressed concern about how the data from this survey effort might be used.

16. There are only twenty-two responses to this question; one of the survey respondents did not answer the question.

17. The survey was in the field from January 18 to 24, 2006. Interviewing was done by professional telephone interviewers from International Communications Research (ICR). We used ICR's "national telephone omnibus survey," which is a national telephone probability sample, collected twice a week. The question on election threats came at the end of a series of questions on election confidence, election reforms, and voting technologies. The data we present here are weighted using the population weights provided by ICR with the data. Data from this survey are available on the website.

18. Given that relatively few respondents provided a substantive answer to this question, we have few data that we can use for multivariate statistical analysis. Thus

here we focus on the simple bivariate correlations and leave more detailed multivariate statistical studies for future research.

19. Alvarez and others, "Are Americans Confident Their Ballots Are Counted?"

20. An analysis of the 2006 elections shows that Democrats were more confident after winning in the 2006 elections than they were before the 2006 elections, suggesting that winning is an important factor in determining confidence.

21. Adler and Kranowitz, "A Primer on Perceptions of Risk," provide a useful discussion of how understanding how stakeholders perceive risk as important for developing effective communication strategies in the area of environmental risk. Looking to other models in other policymaking areas, and studying best practices from other policy domains, will provide much light on how similar communication strategies can be developed in the realm of election administration.

22. The authors have both been to the location where the major Internet domains are managed. All we can say about the experience (we signed nondisclosure agreements to get in the door) is that it is incredibly impressive to see how the management process works and how attacks to the system are addressed.

23. Joyce Berg, Forrest Nelson, and Thomas Rietz, "Accuracy and Forecast Standard Error of Prediction Markets," 2003 (www.biz.uiowa.edu/iem/archive/forecasting.pdf [January 2008]); Charles R. Plott, "Markets as Information Gathering Tools," *Southern Economic Journal* 67, no. 1 (2000): 1–15.

24. For further information about this project see http://hanson.gmu.edu/policy analysismarket.html (January 2008).

five

Caught in the Act:
Recent Federal Election Fraud Cases

Delia Bailey

Since the 2000 election, election fraud has entered into discussions of election reform at an increasing rate—be these discussions within the academic community, among politicians, in the mainstream media, or in the blogosphere. Yet there is little empirical research on the extent and nature of recent election fraud in the United States. In this chapter, I seek to address this issue by examining election fraud cases that were prosecuted under federal law from 2000 to 2005. This analysis provides new information about the frequency, nature, and targets (federal or local races) of election fraud in the United States. In addition, the details of these cases shed some light on the motivations of fraud perpetrators and suggest avenues for future research.

When Is Fraud Likely to Occur?

If we assume that individuals are rational, the decision to commit fraud is based on a cost-benefit analysis. In order for fraud to be worthwhile, its expected benefit must exceed its expected cost. The benefits of fraud are relatively easy to identify. For example, if you are a real estate developer, by successfully rigging an election for the city council you might tip key zoning decisions your way. Calculating the cost of fraud is more complex. The would-be perpetrator must consider not only the cost of carrying out the fraud (for example, the cost of buying enough votes to steal the election), but also the probability of getting caught and the punishment she would face if convicted.[1] The probability of getting caught is a function of a number of factors, including the competence of the individual committing the fraud and the competitiveness of the election, which affects, for example, the extent of media coverage. The cost of punishment is primarily a function of the type of crime being committed and whether it is punishable under federal law.

The outcome of this calculus is likely to vary across federal, state, and local elections. Although fraud in all three types of elections typically carries the same penalties (since state and local elections are often covered by federal election law), the other costs and benefits involved often differ. Notably, the cost of acquiring enough votes to swing an election is likely to be lower in state and local elections than in federal races. State and local contests are also likely to be more competitive—a circumstance that facilitates fraud—because the barriers to entry are lower, the quality of candidates is less variable, the campaigns cost less, and the expectation that the candidates will have held previous office decreases. In addition, media scrutiny and polling data that might tip people to fraud are likely to be less pervasive than in federal races, reducing the likelihood of detection.

The benefit side of the equation also makes local and state election fraud a more attractive prospect. For example, "purchasing" one seat on a small city council could result in a profitable zoning law for the perpetrator or changes in the distribution of municipal contracts and business. In contrast, purchasing a seat in Congress gets the buyer one vote in 435 in a body where seniority is the key currency and bicameralism ensures that legislative initiatives can be stymied.[2]

Consequently, we should expect election fraud cases involving federal races to be relatively rare. Federal fraud cases more broadly (including cases involving state and local races) should also be rarer than cases brought under state or local law, given that federal sentencing is often stricter and federal prosecutorial resources are often greater than their state and local counterparts. (This second hypothesis will not be tested here.)

Federal Election Fraud: 2000 to 2005

The federal criminal cases included in this analysis were located through a LexisNexis search.[3] Each case identified in this analysis was read and categorized as either a criminal case prosecuting some form of election fraud or merely another form of criminal case containing the search term in the text of the opinion. One concern in using a dynamic database such as LexisNexis is that the search is necessarily limited and will certainly exclude some cases. However, because there is no reason to think that election fraud cases occur at a systematically higher or lower rate than the other types of cases that make it into LexisNexis, this method is likely to give a representative selection of recent cases in the United States.

The searches produced only nine election fraud cases from 2000 to 2005.[4] A larger number of cases involved the rhetorical invocation of fraud but not actual fraud prosecutions. For example, in *Sandusky County Democratic Party v. J. Kenneth Blackwell*, the court ruled that if a voter casts a provisional ballot in a precinct other than the one where he or she resides, that ballot does not count as a legal vote under the Help America Vote Act. In explaining its decision, the court argued that the precinct system makes "it easier for election officials to monitor votes and prevent election fraud."[5] However, no fraud was being prosecuted in this case.

Most of the nine fraud prosecutions involved a relatively small number of votes. Of the nine cases, one involves noncitizen voting; four involve vote-buying schemes; two involve destroying and fabricating physical evidence, such as absentee ballots; and two concern constitutional violations and equal protection claims.

The nine cases in this analysis represent both criminal prosecutions brought forth by the U.S. Department of Justice and cases brought forth by other plaintiffs alleging violations of rights under federal election fraud code. Although there are only nine cases, several involved the prosecution of multiple individuals. If we examine only the cases brought by the U.S. Department of Justice, we find that ninety-five individuals were charged with election fraud during this time and fifty-five were convicted. The charges against eight individuals were dismissed by the government, and five defendants were acquitted. Of the ninety-five persons charged with some form of election fraud, one was charged with ineligible voting, nineteen were charged with noncitizen voting, seventeen were charged with registration fraud, one was charged with ballot forgery, forty-seven were charged with vote buying, five were charged with double voting, two were charged with voter intimidation, and three were charged with civil rights violations.

In the following section, I summarize each of the nine cases, although four cases are consolidated because the fraud in each case occurred in the same election. The two important things to note are: (1) the most serious fraud cases occurred in local races, where the benefits of fraud were presumably highest; and (2) the number of votes involved in schemes that *could have* affected federal elections is very low.

McDonald v. Gonzales

Ellen Valle McDonald v. *Alberto Gonzales* was argued before the United States Court of Appeals for the Ninth Circuit in February 2005.[6] McDonald was requesting a review of a prior order by the Board of Immigration Appeals to remove her from the United States under 8 U.S.C. §1227(a) (6) (A) for voting in a manner that violates Hawaii law. McDonald is a native Filipino living in Hawaii with her husband and child, who are both U.S. citizens. McDonald applied for a Hawaii driver's license and under the Motor Voter procedures also registered to vote. On the voter registration form, McDonald checked the box indicating that she was a U.S. citizen, as "at the time [she] wasn't sure if [she was] a citizen" and attributed part of this confusion to being told by friends that by marrying a U.S. citizen she became one automatically.

Upon receiving a voter registration postcard in the mail, McDonald's husband advised her to "not take any chances" and send the form back indicating that she was not a U.S. citizen. Subsequently McDonald received a Notice of Voter Registration and Address Confirmation in the mail and took this to mean the government was allowing her to vote even though she had reported not being a citizen. McDonald voted in the 1996 primary and general elections and said she did so because she believed it to be her "civic duty." Then, in the process of applying for naturalization in 1997, McDonald volunteered to the INS agent that she had voted in the previous election. At this point the agent terminated the interview and halted her naturalization proceedings.

Current INS policy states that "if . . . the election law penalized the act of voting only upon an additional finding that the individual acted 'knowingly' or 'willfully,' adjudicating officers cannot conclude that the applicant voted unlawfully until they assess the circumstances surrounding the voting, the applicant's credibility, and the documentary evidence." As Hawaii law states that a person commits a felony by "knowingly voting when the person is not entitled to vote" (H.R.S. §19-3.5(2)), the court determined that the government must show a knowing and willful violation by McDonald and that they failed this burden. Therefore her petition for review was granted, and the court expressed its hope that her removal proceedings would be terminated.

United States v. Madden, United States v. Slone, United States v. Smith and Newsome

There are four cases related to indictments for violating the federal vote-buying statute by paying people to vote in the 1998 Knott County, Kentucky, local primary election.[7] The first case, *United States* v. *Patrick Wayne Madden*, was argued before the United States Court of Appeals for the Sixth Circuit in March 2005. The case is an appeal of the conviction and sentencing of Madden for his violation of the federal vote-buying statute, 42 U.S.C. §1973i(c). Madden was indicted on charges of vote buying for paying three people to vote for a candidate in the Knott County election. He was charged at the federal level because the ballot included candidates for the U.S. Senate, even though Madden did not offer any voters money for their votes in the Senate race. The court determined that the earlier court erred in its sentencing, but upheld the conviction.

In the second case, Phillip Slone was convicted of conspiring to knowingly and willfully pay voters and was convicted of paying, offering to pay, and causing others to pay voters in the same election in Knott County.[8] Testimony established that the conspiracy was based on a plan to recruit students at a nearby college to register out-of-county students to vote by absentee ballot with the promise of payment if they voted. Several local races on the ballot were of interest, particularly one involving the defendant's brother for the office of county attorney.

A description of the payment plan noted that, after the students voted, the defendants were to take them to Slone's Market and, upon presenting "I voted" stickers with the purchase of a peach Mr. Fizz soda, the students were to be paid $25 to $30 by someone in the store. The defendant was convicted and sentenced to three years' probation, one month in a halfway house, and five months in home detention, and he was fined $1,000. In a subsequent case, Slone pled guilty to seven counts of vote buying in a federal election. He pled guilty to the charge that he offered to pay seven voters $50 each for their votes in "a judge race" in the 1998 primary election in Knott County. He was convicted of the charge. The appeals court affirmed the defendant's conviction and sentencing.

United States v. Willard Smith and Donnie Newsome was filed at the United States Court of Appeals for the Sixth Circuit in July 2005. It is an appeal of the conviction and sentencing of Smith and Newsome for vote buying and conspiracy to buy votes in violation of 18 U.S.C. §§2, 371 and 42 U.S.C. §1973i(c). Donnie Newsome, who at the time was a Kentucky state representative, decided to run for Knott County judge executive in the 1998 primary election. Newsome asked an individual to purchase votes for him and two other candidates in the election. In return for his assistance, Newsome promised that, if he won, he would hire the individual for a position in the Knott County Fiscal Court. Newsome also hired another individual to assist in the vote buying, promising that if elected he would have the county pave the road leading to the hollow where the individual lived. Together with these two individuals—Keith

Pigman and Newton Johnson—Willard Smith worked to buy votes for Newsome. Several witnesses, including Pigman and Johnson, testified that they sold their votes directly to Newsome and his associates, or directly assisted in the vote-buying scheme.

Jackie Darrell Slone and his cousin Denzil Slone both testified that Smith and Pigman approached them on the street and offered them $50 apiece for their votes. Jackie Darrell and Denzil agreed, and Pigman accompanied them into the courthouse to fill out absentee ballots. The cousins told the clerk that each was illiterate and needed Pigman to accompany them into the voting booth. Once inside the booth, Pigman voted each man's ballot for him. Similarly, Johnson testified that he was enlisted to procure the votes of his sister, two nieces, and nephew-in-law. Johnson drove these four relatives to the courthouse so that they could vote by absentee ballot, for which each was paid $50. In addition, Smith's first cousin, Mary Baum, testified that Smith brought her to the courthouse to vote via absentee ballot and gave her $60 after she had voted. Another man, Ralph Hicks Jr., testified that he and his brother were walking past the courthouse before election day when Smith called out to them and asked them to come over. Smith then offered Hicks and his brother $50 each to fill out an absentee ballot and vote for Newsome, which they agreed to do. Finally, Donald Ray Thomas testified that Newsome personally paid him $100 after he voted by absentee ballot in the 1998 primary election.

In addition to paying people to vote by absentee ballot, on the actual primary day Newsome instructed Johnson to drive people to the polls. After Johnson brought them to the polls to vote, Smith, who was stationed at a polling place, paid them for their votes. Johnson testified that he believed Smith had around $5,000 to pass out on election day and that the money ran out before the day was over. Johnson also testified that Newsome had other individuals scattered at other polling places passing out money for votes. In addition, Kali Holbrook and Smith's nephew, Paul Shannon Johnson, testified that when they went to vote on election day Smith and Pigman approached them and offered to give them each $10 and beer to vote for Newsome. However, Holbrook and Paul Shannon declined, as each had already been paid $50 to vote for Newsome's opponent, incumbent Knott County judge executive Homer Sawyer. The defendant's convictions were affirmed upon appeal. The case was remanded upon appeal for resentencing.

Hileman v. Maze

The case of *Susan C. Hileman* v. *Louis Maze* was argued before the United States Court of Appeals for the Seventh Circuit in May 2003.[9] The case is an appeal of the decision that Hileman's claim that Maze violated her rights under the Fourth, Fifth, and Fourteenth Amendments to an election free from fraud, under 42 U.S.C. §1983, had reached its statute of limitations. In March 2000, Susan Hileman entered the Democratic primary as the incumbent circuit clerk of Alexander County, Illinois. Five days before the primary, a police raid confiscated 681 absentee ballots for the upcoming primary from the home, office, and truck of County Clerk Louis Maze. Along with the ballots was evidence suggesting that Maze was opening the absentee ballots and replacing ballots in favor of Hileman with ballots cast in favor of her opponent, McGinness, and then regluing the envelopes shut. For "mysterious reasons," the ballots were returned to Maze on the day of the primary. The ballots were then distributed to the appropriate precincts and counted with the other ballots in the election.

Hileman lost the primary election to McGinness by 210 votes, 1,299 to 1,089. Hileman then filed a suit, *Susan C. Hileman v. Sharon McGinness, and Louis Maze* (2000) to contest the election. The results of the primary were declared invalid and McGinness was removed from office. A new election was held, but Hileman did not run in it. Instead on March 20, 2002, she filed suit against a number of defendants, including Louis Maze, alleging that her rights under the Fourth, Fifth, and Fourteenth Amendments had been violated. In a prior hearing, the court determined that the statute of limitations on Hileman's claim had expired, with the reasoning that her claims accrued from the date the ballots were seized, March 16, 2000, rather than the date of the primary, March 21, 2000. The appeals court overturned this ruling with the reasoning that her claims accrued on the date of the primary and remanded the case for further proceedings.

United States v. Smith and Tyree

The case of *United States v. Frank Smith and Connie Tyree* was decided by the United States Court of Appeals for the Eleventh Circuit in October 2000.[10] The case appeals the conviction and sentencing of Smith and Tyree on thirteen federal criminal counts relating to violating absentee voter laws under 18 U.S.C. §2, 18 U.S.C. §371, 42 U.S.C. §1973i(c), and 42 U.S.C. §1973i(e). In the 1994 general election in Greene County, Alabama, Frank Smith and Connie Tyree voted more than once and voted the absentee ballots of seven other residents without the knowledge and consent of those voters. Smith and Tyree also gave false information on the application for absentee ballots for those seven voters. In addition they were charged with aiding and abetting each other and others in the offense of obtaining and casting fraudulent absentee ballots. After a seven-day trial in 1997, a jury convicted Smith and Tyree of all charges. This case came about in October 2000 as an appeal of the previous conviction. The court upheld all of Smith's convictions and all but one of Tyree's convictions. The court ordered that Tyree be resentenced.

Luther et al. v. Fong Eu and Shelley

The case of *Gary Brian Luther, Darrell Edwards, James Snider, and Samuel Dubyak* v. *March Fong Eu and Kevin Shelley* was decided by the United States District Court for the Northern District of California in January 2005.[11] The case challenges the constitutionality of the passage of Proposition 7 in the 1978 California election under 42 U.S.C. §1983. The plaintiffs in this case allege that March Fong Eu, the California secretary of state in 1978, placed an inaccurate version of Proposition 7 on the ballot and otherwise "failed to satisfy state election requirements." The plaintiffs alleged that the California secretary of state violated the Equal Protection Clause of the Fourteenth Amendment by perpetrating fraud and deceit upon the voters. Specifically, the financial impact of Proposition 7 was described in the voters' pamphlet as an "indeterminable future increase in state costs" even though the documents that authorized the proposition to be on the ballot described the fiscal impact as an "indeterminable *but potentially significant* future increase in state costs" (emphasis added). Given that the election was in 1978 and the plaintiffs did not bring charges until 2004, the statute of limitations had clearly expired and the court dismissed all claims.

Schuler v. Board of Education

The case of *Donna Schuler, Board Member, Central Islip Union Free School District, et al.* v. *Board of Education of the Central Islip Union Free School District* was decided by the United States District Court for the Eastern District of New York in February 2000.[12] The plaintiffs in this case were taxpayers and property owners within the Central Islip Union Free School District (CIUFSD) who were unhappy with the state of public education in general and the treatment of minority and disabled children in particular; they alleged many claims against the defendants, namely the Board of Education of CIUFSD and related actors. Among the claims, the plaintiffs alleged that various acts of misconduct surrounding CIUFSD elections in 1996 and 1997 "rose to a level of federal constitutional violation."

The misconduct was alleged in three parts. First, members of the Civil Service Employment Association (CSEA) of the CIUFSD posted fliers throughout the school district intended "to create confusion in the minds of potential voters." Patrick O'Brien was an incumbent running for reelection to the school board; the fliers posted by the CSEA displayed a picture of another man named Pat O'Brien, with text stating that Pat O'Brien was not running for the school board and voters should not vote for him. Second, the plaintiffs alleged that CSEA sent letters to the homes of special education students requesting that students vote for specific candidates. Third, the plaintiffs alleged several examples of miscounting and other irregularities such as persons without proper identification being allowed to vote. Because the first two claims were committed by CSEA and its employees, and not federal employees, the court determined that they had no standing under federal election code. The court determined that there was no evidence that the state employees acted willfully in any miscounting or allowing persons without identification to vote and therefore dismissed all claims under "federal election law."

Conclusion

Both the LexisNexis search of criminal case law from 2000 to 2005 and the examination of prosecution statistics from the Department of Justice indicate that election fraud prosecutions at the federal level in the United States are quite rare. Moreover, actual cases of election fraud explicitly intended to affect the outcome of a federal election are almost nonexistent. Although federal races may be affected by fraud in certain schemes, such as cases involving illegal absentee voting, the actual targets of the fraud are almost always state or local races.

A further conclusion to draw from the data is that most of the fraud cases were related to registration fraud, noncitizen voting, and vote-buying schemes. Although vote-buying schemes are reprehensible, it is difficult to imagine that large-scale enterprises of this nature would go undetected. It is also clear that buying a large number of ballots is relatively difficult. Therefore, at least at the federal level, efforts to prevent election fraud should probably focus on voter registration.

Notes

1. For simplicity I assume that the potential perpetrator of fraud has no other way to achieve her goal. In real life, of course, she might consider additional options, such as bribing an existing council member.

2. Note that recent scandals in Congress related to quid pro quos, such as the case of Representative Randy Cunningham, were cases of bribery, not election fraud.

3. The LexisNexis sources for the federal criminal case law at the time of the search included selected criminal material from cases of the United States Supreme Court; the United States Courts of Appeal; the United States District Courts; the United States Bankruptcy Courts; and specialty courts, including: the U.S. Court of Federal Claims, Courts of Military Appeals and Military Review, the U S. Court of International Trade, the U.S. Tax Court, Tax Court Memos, and the U.S. Court of Veterans Appeals. The searches were conducted between August 26, 2005, and September 6, 2005. As a result, the 2005 calendar year search is incomplete. The search terms used were: "vote buying" OR "vote-buying"; (absentee OR registration) AND fraud; (election OR electoral) AND (fraud* OR corrupt*); (vote* OR voting) AND fraud; (offense* OR fraud* OR tamper* OR stuff* OR handl* OR print* OR secrecy OR secret) AND ballot; "voter intimidation"; and "voter registration."

4. There were 1,802 hits, of which forty were election fraud cases but only nine were unique cases. Because LexisNexis Academic is a dynamic database, even in its historical documents, replicating this analysis on a different date would likely result in slightly different numbers.

5. *Sandusky County Democratic Party* v. *J. Kenneth Blackwell*, 387 F.3d 565 (2004).

6. *McDonald* v. *Gonzales*, 400 F.3d 684 (2005). Alberto Gonzales is substituted for his predecessor, John Ashcroft, as attorney general of the United States.

7. *United States* v. *Madden*, 403 F.3d 347 (2005); *United States* v. *Slone*, 411 F.3d 643 (2005); *United States* v. *Slone*, 43 Fed. Appx. 738 (2002); *United States* v. *Smith and Newsome*, 139 Fed. Appx. 681 (2005).

8. The search produced the two cases of *United States* v. *Slone*. Each was an appeal of specific parts of the sentencing of one initial federal case against Phillip Slone.

9. *Hileman* v. *McGinness*, 316 Ill. App. 3d 868 (2000); *Hileman* v. *Maze*, 367 F.3d 694 (2004).

10. *United States* v. *Frank Smith and Connie Tyree*, 231 F.3d 800 (2000).

11. *Luther* v. *March Fong Eu and Kevin Shelley*, U.S. Dist LEXIS 10437 (2005).

12. *Schuler* v. *Board of Education*, U.S. Dist LEXIS 1006 (2000).

six

Correlates of Fraud: Studying State Election Fraud Allegations

R. Michael Alvarez and Frederick J. Boehmke

Maintaining the integrity of the electoral process is a fundamental goal of election administrators in democracies around the world. If questions arise about the integrity of an election, the legitimacy of the subsequent governing regime can—and often is—undermined. Thus election administrators have developed systems to monitor and protect the integrity of the democratic electoral process. Despite these protections, claims about significant election

We wish to thank Alex Chang for his assistance with data collection. We also thank John Mott-Smith and Gillian Underwood, and the California Secretary of State's Office for providing us with access to the data we use in this paper; Richard Ciaramella and the staff of the Election Fraud Investigation Unit provided detailed comments on earlier versions of this research. We thank Kathy Rogers and the Georgia Secretary of State's Office for providing us with data as well. Melanie Goodrich, Thad Hall, Rick Hasen, Mary Sikora, Conny McCormack, Betsy Sinclair, Hans von Spakovsky, Charles Stewart, and Ray Wolfinger all provided helpful discussions and detailed comments about earlier versions of this research. An earlier version of this chapter was presented at the 2004 annual meeting of the Midwest Political Science Association, and we thank Michael McDonald and panel participants for their helpful comments. Our research was supported by grants from the Carnegie Corporation of New York and the John S. and James L. Knight Foundation to the Caltech/MIT Voting Technology Project; the conclusions reached in this chapter reflect the views of the authors and not necessarily the Caltech/MIT Voting Technology Project.

fraud arise frequently, even in long-established democratic nations like the United States. Allegations of election fraud in the United States have a long history, dating back to the founding of the republic. But while there are often allegations of election fraud, there is little empirical evidence about how frequently election fraud occurs, how many votes it potentially influences, and where in the electoral process fraudulent activities occur. In this chapter we offer preliminary analyses of two novel databases in an effort to help fill this gap. In recent decades, California and Georgia have collected information on election fraud allegations by the year, county, and substantive nature of the allegation. We discuss how this type of data might be used in future academic research and in other ways to help deter and prevent election fraud.

Election Fraud in California and Georgia

Our research began with a database we obtained from the California secretary of state's Election Fraud Investigation Unit (EFIU).[1] It provides information on all electoral fraud cases referred to the Office of the Secretary of State from 1994 to 2003, including the nature of each allegation and the final action taken. It also lists the county and year in which each case originated, allowing us to link allegations of fraud to county characteristics. However, this database does not contain information on federal or local cases, or on cases that were unresolved at the time we received the data.[2]

We also obtained a similar database from the Georgia Office of the Secretary of State, running from 1999 through 2003, and organized at the county level. For each case, the Georgia database provides a detailed description of the substance of the allegation and an estimate of the potential number of ballots affected by the malfeasance. Together, these two databases provide us with rich variation in time, context, and geography.

Unfortunately, for the purposes of this chapter, we can only briefly compare the election fraud incidence rates between the states. We leave for future work detailed multivariate statistical analysis of these data. Below we begin by looking at the distribution of allegations made by aggregated substantive area and by year, for each state. We then turn to a correlational analysis that examines the bivariate correlations between fraud allegations at the county level and various demographic and political attributes of each county. We follow the analysis with a spatial study of the fraud allegation data from each state. We conclude by talking about what county-by-county election fraud data can yield for academic and policy discussions about studying, detecting, and preventing election fraud.

Table 6-1. California Election Fraud Complaints, 1994–2003

Year	Voting	Registration	Absentee voter	Miscellaneous	Total
1994	26	64	6	53	149
1995	17	152	0	32	201
1996	45	97	2	58	202
1997	63	69	1	53	186
1998	13	185	2	45	542
1999	5	33	1	27	66
2000	13	52	1	27	93
2001	33	24	0	15	72
2002	25	27	0	15	67
2003	0	0	0	4	4
Total	240	703	13	329	1,285

Data on Fraud Allegations

Table 6-1 provides summary data on election fraud allegations, by year, in California. We separate the cases into four categories: voting fraud, registration fraud, absentee fraud, and miscellaneous fraud. Voting fraud cases involved allegations of the following: consideration for voting, corruption of voters, double voting, fraudulent voting, intimidation of voters, noncitizen voting, payment for voting, tampering with voting devices, or violations of ballot secrecy. Voter registration fraud involved allegations of altering voter registration party affiliation, charging fees for registration, fraudulent voter registration, holding the voter registration card more than three days, noncitizen registration, false residency claims, or voter registration after deadlines. Absentee voting fraud involved the violation of absentee voting requirements, fraudulent absentee voting, or the nonreturn of an absentee ballot application. All other types of cases are included in the miscellaneous category.[3]

Table 6-1 shows that from 1994 through 2003, 1,285 cases were opened and resolved in California. The category of election fraud with the highest incidence is voter registration fraud, with 703 cases opened and resolved in the period 1994–2003. Voting fraud is the second most common (240 opened and resolved cases), followed by absentee voting fraud (thirteen cases opened and resolved). The number of cases fell over time, especially after 1998—probably because more of the recent cases remained unresolved in 2003, the final year in our database.

Fraudulent voter registration is the allegation with the highest incidence, with 469 cases opened and resolved. (These cases constitute the bulk of the

Table 6-2. Georgia Election Fraud Complaints, by Category and Year, 1999–2003

Category	1999	2000	2001	2002	2003	Total
Absentee	21	44	8	11	16	100
Registration	4	2	1	2	0	9
Miscellaneous	2	4	1	0	0	7
Voting	3	2	0	3	0	8
Election	4	7	1	19	23	54
Administration	32	12	0	30	15	89
Candidate	0	2	0	1	3	6
Total	66	73	11	66	57	273

703 reported cases of voter registration fraud.) It is followed by corruption of voters and noncitizen registration, both with 153 allegations; falsified petitions (109 allegations); and fraudulent voting (96 allegations).

Table 6-2 provides similar statistics from Georgia for the period 1999–2003. The categories here are slightly different because of differences in the two states' election codes. In particular, the Georgia data include cases in three additional categories: election, candidate, and administration fraud. Administration fraud involves allegations that proper election procedures were not followed; election fraud allegations are similar but involve improper procedures on election day; and candidate fraud allegations involve charges that candidates violated campaign procedures.[4]

In Georgia, unlike in California, registration, voting, and miscellaneous fraud constitute a small proportion of total cases. Even considering the fact that we have new categories to consider, the total number of allegations in these three categories was only 24. On the other hand, absentee fraud cases increased from barely one a year in California to twenty per year in Georgia. This makes it the largest category in Georgia, ahead of administration fraud, of which there were 89 allegations. Behind these two is election fraud, with 54 cases; the smallest category is candidate fraud, with only 6 allegations.

Within the category of absentee fraud, 4 out of every 5 allegations involve some form of absentee ballot mishandling, either on its own (55 cases) or in combination with some other allegation (24). Of the 55 cases in the former category, 21 include information on the number of ballots affected. These numbers total to 441, for an average of 21 ballots per allegation; 2 of these cases each involved 85 ballots.

In the administration fraud category, half of the cases involve a challenge to a candidate's qualifications. Other allegations in this category include the following subcategories: "Voter Registrar Did Not Attend Training," "Wrong Voter Registration Directions Published in Newspaper," and "Candidate's

Name Printed Incorrectly on Ballots." Some of these allegations are unlikely to be representative of fraud per se, but some—such as "Ballot Counting Misconduct" and "Alleging That Votes Weren't Tabulated in Public"—certainly suggest the potential for fraud. At this point, we are not in a position to know whether election violations involve attempts to fraudulently manipulate the results and when they are simply mistakes in procedure.

In addition to providing the first comparison of different categories of fraud allegations within states, our data also afford the first opportunity to consider geographic variation in total allegations. Figures 6-1 and 6-2 show the number of fraud allegations per county as well as the number of allegations per 10,000 people in California and Georgia, respectively.

The map at the top in figure 6-1 depicts fraud allegations across California, showing that there are more allegations in more populous counties. Further, fraud allegations are concentrated in southern California counties, though there are similar concentrations near the Bay Area and in the middle of the Central Valley. The map at the bottom in figure 6-1 shows that these findings are partly driven by the large populations in these counties. When fraud allegations per capita are mapped, a somewhat different pattern emerges, with smaller northern counties exhibiting more fraud allegations per capita and the southern counties exhibiting relatively fewer. In fact, total violations and violations per capita have a correlation of –0.03, suggesting almost no relationship between the two.

Similar results obtain in figure 6-2, which displays the same results for Georgia. The map at the top shows a concentration of high-allegation counties around Atlanta, with 23 cases in Fulton County, 9 cases in DeKalb, and 6 cases in Clayton and Cobb counties. There is a also a chain of 10 high-fraud counties that starts near Augusta in Richmond County and continues southwest to Coffee and Bacon counties; these counties account for 56 fraud cases. At the other end of the spectrum, there were 66 counties, or 40 percent of all counties, with no fraud allegations over this time period; about 20 percent have one or two allegations. When allegations per capita are considered, the concentration shifts somewhat from the Atlanta area to the Macon area, particularly the area between Macon and Columbus on the western edge.

After looking at the geographic distribution of election fraud allegations in both California and Georgia, we see clearly that the number and rate of fraud allegations within the two states differs. Using these data, we next consider whether any particular county-level characteristics have a clear correlation with election fraud allegations. It is to this task that we turn in the next section.

Figure 6-1. Total Electoral Fraud Violations in California, per County, 1994–99

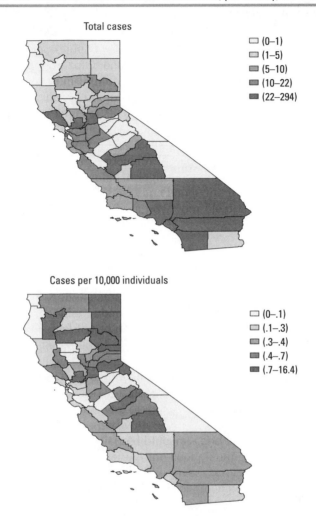

Total cases

- ☐ (0–1)
- ☐ (1–5)
- ☐ (5–10)
- ☐ (10–22)
- ☐ (22–294)

Cases per 10,000 individuals

- ☐ (0–.1)
- ☐ (.1–.3)
- ☐ (.3–.4)
- ☐ (.4–.7)
- ☐ (.7–16.4)

The Correlates of Fraud

In exploring possible explanations for the variation in fraud allegations from county to county, we focus on variables suggested by existing research on election fraud. The potential correlates of election fraud include political competition, economic factors, partisanship, and such demographic variables as urbanization.[5]

Figure 6-2. Total Electoral Fraud Violations in Georgia, per County, 1994–2003

Total cases

☐ (0)
◻ (0–1)
▨ (1–2)
■ (2–23)

Cases per 10,000 individuals

☐ (0)
◻ (0–.2)
▨ (.2–1.1)
■ (1.1–9.6)

Perhaps the most critical variable to focus on is the opportunity for fraud to influence electoral outcomes. Specifically, the potential benefits from fraud are much greater when only a handful of votes can change the outcome of an election. Thus we expect that fraud is most likely to occur in highly competitive races with small margins of victory.

Unfortunately, we cannot link our fraud allegations to specific races, which makes it more difficult to assess the effect of competitiveness on the occurrence of fraud. Of course, many fraud cases are not associated with specific races, or the nature of the allegation is such that it would be impossible to know if any specific race motivated the actions. (This would be true, for example, of many allegations of voter registration fraud.) Because we have county-level data, however, we can study the correlation between local competitiveness and fraud allegations. We hypothesize that counties that are more competitive exhibit a greater number of fraud cases.

To test this hypothesis, we include a measure of competitiveness using data from gubernatorial elections. In California we used data from the 1994 and 1998 elections to calculate the absolute margin of victory in each county in these two elections; then we combined these values into one variable based on the most proximate election for each year. Thus competitiveness for 1994–96 is constructed from the 1994 gubernatorial election results, and for 1997–99 from the 1998 election. In Georgia, we used the results from the 1998 gubernatorial race for the years 1999–2000 and the 2002 results for 2001–03. We also used these data to construct measures of county-level partisanship by matching results to years in the same way. Although our competitiveness measure may miss out on election-to-election incentives for committing fraud, we feel it is an appropriate measure since it would be impossible to measure vote margin in all races in each county.

In addition to competitiveness, we consider demographic measures, economic performance, population size and density, education, age, and partisanship. To account for the effect of county demographic factors, we consider measures of a county's *total population, population density,* the percentage of the population that is *African American,* the percentage that is *Hispanic,* the percentage that has completed a *high school education,* and the *median age.* We expect that counties with larger, denser populations experience greater levels of fraud. The relationship with other variables may be different for different types of fraud. For example, we might expect registration fraud but not absentee fraud to increase with the percentage of the population that is Hispanic. More education and an older population should produce lower levels of voting and registration fraud, but may increase levels of absentee fraud.

We also consider a number of economic factors, including the *percent unemployed* and *per capita personal income.*[6] We expect fewer fraud allegations when economic performance is good. We are able to obtain two unique variables for the state of California concerning county election expenditures: *election operating expenses* and *election capital expenditures.* These variables capture county investment in staffing and monitoring elections and updating

Table 6-3. Pairwise Correlations between California Fraud Allegations and County Variables, 1993–99

Variable	Total	Voter	Registration	Absentee	Miscellaneous
Percent white	−0.25	−0.21	−0.18	−0.12	−0.28
Percent African American	0.34	0.26	0.26	0.14	0.33
Percent Hispanic	0.19	0.12	0.14	0.15	0.23
Percent high school graduates	−0.12	−0.06	−0.09	−0.09	−0.17
Percent unemployed	−0.11	−0.11	−0.08	0.00	−0.11
Per capita income	0.12	0.13	0.09	0.05	0.10
Total population	0.68	0.48	0.54	0.40	0.68
Population density	0.40	0.31	0.29	0.24	0.44
Median age	−0.20	−0.13	−0.14	−0.11	−0.25
Democratic vote	0.11	0.07	0.09	0.02	0.09
Vote margin	0.02	−0.01	0.03	0.05	−0.03
Time	−0.03	−0.05	−0.01	−0.08	−0.03
Election operating expenses	0.67	0.48	0.52	0.40	0.68
Election capital expenses	0.07	0.06	0.03	−0.02	0.15
Election operating expenses per capita	−0.23	−0.17	−0.18	−0.11	−0.26
Election capital expenses per capita	−0.08	−0.05	−0.06	−0.05	−0.08

Sources: California spending and demographics are from the (now defunct) California Institute of County Governments' website. Political variables are from 1994 and 1998 gubernatorial races, downloaded from the California secretary of state's website.

election machines, respectively, and we expect that they will be related to observed levels of alleged fraud. We consider these variables measured both in total and on a per capita basis. Finally, we consider the correlation between election fraud cases and time by including a linear time trend variable in our correlation analysis. This variable helps us determine whether various reforms in California between 1993 and 1999 have resulted in greater amounts of fraud, or at least in more allegations of fraud.

Tables 6-3 (California) and 6-4 (Georgia) present the results of our correlation analysis. In California, we see that four variables have relatively strong and positive correlations with the total number of election fraud allegations in each county: total population, election operating expenses, population density, and the percentage of the county's population that is African American. That is, election fraud allegations increase as each of these variables increases. On the other hand, some of the variables are surprising in the weakness of the estimated correlations, especially the estimated competitiveness of the county (as measured by the vote margin variable).

In California, the main substantive type of election fraud reported was voter registration fraud. In this category, we see results that, not surprisingly, parallel those just discussed for total fraud: strong positive correlations

Table 6-4. Pairwise Correlations between Georgia Fraud Allegations and County Variables, 1999–2003

Item	Total	Absentee	Registration	Miscellaneous	Voting	Election	Administration	Candidate
Percent white	-0.13	-0.08	-0.04	-0.02	-0.05	-0.09	-0.08	-0.04
Percent African American	0.12	0.09	0.03	0.01	0.05	0.07	0.06	0.04
Percent Native American	-0.05	-0.06	-0.03	-0.01	0.00	-0.01	-0.01	-0.04
Percent Asian	0.16	-0.05	0.14	-0.02	0.06	0.16	0.18	0.08
Percent unemployed	0.06	0.05	-0.01	-0.01	0.03	0.04	0.03	-0.01
Percent high school graduates	0.09	-0.07	0.07	0.00	0.05	0.09	0.14	0.06
Total population	0.34	-0.02	0.20	0.00	0.15	0.23	0.39	0.11
Per capita income	0.15	-0.04	0.11	-0.02	0.09	0.10	0.21	0.07
Population density	0.27	-0.05	0.16	0.00	0.13	0.24	0.31	0.12
Median age	-0.02	0.06	-0.02	-0.04	0.02	-0.07	-0.05	-0.02
Vote margin	-0.11	-0.11	-0.02	0.00	-0.05	-0.04	-0.04	-0.01
Democratic vote	0.08	0.11	0.00	0.01	0.02	0.02	0.01	-0.01
Time	0.02	-0.07	-0.07	-0.08	-0.03	0.15	0.04	0.05

Sources: Georgia demographics from 2000 Census data. Political variables from 1998 and 2002 gubernatorial races, downloaded from the Georgia secretary of state's website.

between the total number of fraud allegations and total population, election operating expenses, population density, and percentage of the county population that is African American. We also see a weak correlation between competitiveness and fraud allegations.

The results for Georgia also show strong and positive correlations between total cases and total population and population density. Positive but smaller correlations are found with percentage African American, percentage Asian, and per capita income. Moderate and negative correlations are found with percentage white and gubernatorial vote margin. Unlike the California data, the Georgia data indicate that less competitive counties (albeit with a simple measure of competitiveness) have fewer fraud allegations.

In looking at specific types of election fraud in Georgia, we see a strong correlation between total county population and allegations pertaining to registration, election, administrative, and voting fraud. We also find that the number of administrative fraud cases has relatively strong relationships with percentage Asian, percentage high school graduates, and per capita income. Absentee fraud exhibits a positive correlation with Democratic vote share and a negative correlation with vote margin.

Conclusion

A few interesting observations follow from our investigation of these data. First, studying reported fraud allegations across time and space offers a new opportunity to understand electoral fraud. By comparing the number and type of allegations across geographic units, we are able to learn about the factors associated with higher allegation rates. For example, we find that racial and economic characteristics of a population have relatively strong relationships with allegations. We hope to build on these findings in future work.

Second, the nature of the allegations in our databases offers a sense of what kinds of fraud cases are brought forward in different places and circumstances. In California, voter registration cases constitute over half of all cases, whereas registration fraud is barely 3 percent of cases in Georgia. Absentee fraud cases, on the other hand, are much more prevalent in Georgia and almost nonexistent in California.

These differences underscore one of the limitations of our analysis. Currently, we only have information on legal cases involving allegations of fraud. We have no doubt that variation in cases across time, counties, and states depends on both the rate at which fraud and violations occur, but also on the priorities of local and state election officials. We suspect that differences in emphasis may be responsible, at least in part, for the different types of cases we find in different states. For example, the data we received from Georgia included an entire file devoted only to absentee fraud cases, suggesting that it may have been a higher priority there than in California. We suspect that variations in the number of fraud cases therefore depend both on the political priorities of government officials and on the behavior of individuals seeking to manipulate elections. Future studies of fraud should keep this in mind, and may benefit from a detailed understanding of the priorities of enforcement officials in the government.

But no matter how we analyze the pattern of reported fraud cases across time and space in the future, the most important conclusion we draw from our work is that data like these are critical for future research on election fraud, forensic analysis of elections, and the development of threat assessments. We thus call upon election administrators at the state and federal level to develop guidelines for the reporting of election fraud cases. Reports should include the number of cases opened, the type of election code violation that is alleged, the geographic location of each allegation, details about the potential number of votes affected, and information about how the allegations were resolved. Were the U.S. Election Assistance Commission to issue guidance for the collection and reporting of these data, and to assist states in their efforts to collect and publicize them, both research and public understanding of election threats would be improved.

Notes

1. Our use of these data distinguishes our research from most of the previous research on election fraud. Fabrice Lehoucq, "Electoral Fraud: Causes, Types, and Consequences," *Annual Review of Political Science* 6 (2003): 233–56, notes that there are six different methodological approaches to studying election fraud: collect survey data from voters or political agents; undertake qualitative studies and use in-depth interviews of political participants; study memoirs of political agents; analyze reports of fraud from political agents (typically parties) that are filed with appropriate authorities; study media reports of fraud; and use data collected by nonpartisan electoral observers. The data we have appear to cut across two of Lehoucq's categories, as we are studying a database of reported allegations of election fraud, but they are not necessarily allegations with a political motivation, as the allegations in our database can come from a wide variety of sources, including as far as we can determine any source, political or nonpolitical.

2. Another database we received for California breaks allegations of fraud down by type and year but not by county; this database covers all cases opened between 1994

and 2002, including all completed and pending cases over the same time period, and indicates that our data do not omit any cases filed before 2000. Given that this second database does not have geographic variation, we focus our attention here on the more extensive database, which gives data for closed cases, by time, over time, and by county.

3. There was a long list of other types of miscellaneous fraud, including: alteration of election returns, electioneering, failure to file nomination papers, failure to maintain records on paid personnel, false declarations of candidacy, falsified petitions, fictitious name on nomination paper, mishandling of ballots, mass mailing of penal provisions, misleading voters, misuse of information, misuse of signatures on petition, misuse of voter rolls, neglect of official duties, printing of simulated sample ballots, suppression of nomination papers, threats to circulator, vandalism of political signs, and other unspecified violations.

4. In addition to the cases reported in the table, the data we received from the Office of the Secretary of State included sixty-nine cases listed as "Monitor," which are as-yet-unspecified allegations that were being monitored for potential future allegations. Since we do not know the nature of the fraud involved in these cases, we cannot include them in this table.

5. M. L. Anderson, *Practicing Democracy: Elections and Political Culture in Imperial Germany* (Princeton University Press, 2000); J. I. Dominguez and J. A. McCann, *Democratizing Mexico: Public Opinion and Electoral Choices* (Johns Hopkins University Press, 1996).

6. We obtained time-varying measures of these variables for California; for Georgia we use time-invariant data from the 2000 Census.

seven

Fraud or Failure?
What Incident Reports Reveal about
Election Anomalies and Irregularities

*D. Roderick Kiewiet, Thad E. Hall, R. Michael Alvarez,
and Jonathan N. Katz*

When things go wrong in elections involving direct-recording electronic (DRE) voting technology, these episodes are viewed by many as proof of the vulnerability, or at least the unreliability, of these systems. Claims by election officials that such problems are "par for the course" in elections or symptomatic of "growing pains" associated with implementing a new technology ring false to many Americans who expect elections to be run without error every time. To date, however, each side in the debate has been able to rely on only limited data and scant research. DRE technology has only recently been introduced on a large scale in the United States, so there is little systematic information regarding the difficulties encountered in its implementation.

In this chapter, we examine a novel and potentially very useful source of data concerning the frequency and severity of different types of problems encountered by voters and precinct workers in a DRE environment. The data consist of incident reports collected by poll workers during the May 2, 2006, primary election in Cuyahoga County, Ohio. This election marked the first use of DRE technology in this jurisdiction. Voters cast their ballots on Diebold

We thank Stephen Hertzberg of the Election Science Institute and the Cuyahoga County (Ohio) Board of Elections for their assistance in collecting the data we analyze in this chapter. We would also like to thank Fred Boehmke, Candice Hoke, Peter Ordeshook, and Kathy Rogers for their helpful comments.

AccuVote-TSx voting machines—touch-screen machines equipped with printers to produce the voter-verified paper audit trail (VVPAT) mandated by Ohio election law. Since most voters were unfamiliar with this technology, the Cuyahoga County Board of Elections took the prudent and useful measure of providing poll workers at each precinct with incident report forms to record and to describe difficulties they encountered in conducting the balloting.

The incident report forms were not elaborate. Other than asking for average and longest voter wait times, they were essentially blank pieces of paper on which poll workers wrote accounts of the problems they encountered. These verbatim reports were entered into an electronic database and then coded into categories.[1] Poll workers may have been given some direction as to what constituted an "incident" that was worth reporting or what did not, but given the large number and wide variety of incidents that were reported, it appears that what to report was left largely to the poll workers' discretion.

In addition to being a valuable source of information concerning election administration, we think that these data can be used to identify avenues that might be pursued by those seeking to commit vote fraud, or, perhaps more plausibly, to undermine public confidence in the results of an election. The incident reports can also be used to identify scenarios in which administrative snafus might be created or exploited to produce long waiting times at the polls and thus discourage voters from voting. If those who are discouraged from voting have different candidate and issue preferences from those who persist, such "denial-of-service" attacks are tantamount to fraud and could conceivably alter the outcome of an election. These tactics and scenarios are not hypothetical; Pakistan's Benazir Bhutto had prepared a report before her death stating that the Pakistani intelligence services planned to create a conflict at polling stations during upcoming elections, even conflict by killing people, to stop voting for several hours.[2]

Our analyses of these data and discussion of the results are in no way intended to suggest that any of the scenarios discussed below actually occurred in Cuyahoga County in May 2006 or in any other election. However, in an era when large numbers of citizens remain very concerned about the security and accuracy of DRE voting technologies, addressing the problems that we identify would be beneficial in assuring voters that their votes are being counted fairly and accurately. We begin our analysis with a discussion of the vulnerabilities of electronic voting, then turn to a detailed analysis of the precinct incident report data from the May 2006 Cuyahoga primary. We conclude with a discussion of the utility of these data for studying election fraud and anomalies, as well as for the development of threat assessment models.

Vote Fraud in a DRE Environment

Conventionally, vote fraud is seen to be the wrongful altering of vote totals in an election or engaging in efforts to systematically disenfranchise voters in an election to alter the outcome.[3] Since the widespread introduction of DRE voting technology, a number of computer scientists have been particularly concerned about the possibility that someone could hack into these systems and insert "malicious code" to alter vote totals and thus produce fraudulent election results. This might be accomplished by writing vote-altering programs onto a "home-brewed" access card. Uploaded when the card is inserted into a DRE machine, the malicious code, or "malware," alters or overrides vote-counting programs on the DRE device.[4] Uploading malware onto DRE machines via memory cards might also accomplish the purpose of creating fraudulent results.[5]

Manufacturers of DRE voting machines, and election officials who deploy DREs, have incorporated many security features into the technology and the procedures used to implement DRE voting, including audit logs, tamper-evident seals on such critical peripherals as memory cards and printer canisters, cryptography, password protection, and "digital signatures" on access cards and memory cards that the DRE machine must recognize as valid before the machine can be put into balloting mode.[6] They are adamant that hacks on their machines have been confined to unrealistic laboratory demonstrations and that there is not a single instance in which a vote-altering program infiltrated a DRE machine in an actual election.[7] DRE technology critics point out that the absence of evidence is not evidence of absence and that vote-altering programs can be written to delete themselves (rendering them undetectable) once they have done their damage.[8]

Rather than revisit the debate over technical issues of DRE security, let us first take a step back and consider a simple question: why would someone want to commit fraud? The answer to this question would seem to be glaringly obvious; the fraudulent altering of vote totals is intended to determine the outcome of an election. As others have noted, however, the cost-benefit calculus associated with such fraud is highly problematic.[9] In even extremely close elections, to achieve a realistic chance of affecting the outcome of the election would require altering a candidate's vote totals by hundreds of votes in a state legislative race and by tens of thousands in a U.S. Senate race. This calculus is especially difficult to attempt because the person wanting to affect the outcome of the election does not know what the result will be ahead of time—hence, how many votes have to be stolen to win—or whether the opposition in the election is also engaging in some effort to affect the outcome of the election. Because the typical DRE voting machine will log at most 150 or so votes on an election day, large numbers of them would need to be exploited to potentially affect a statewide or even countywide race. Such alterations of vote totals would produce results incongruous enough to raise questions and trigger investigations. Several chapters in this volume discuss the techniques that can be used to identify such incongruous patterns in election results. Even if the likelihood of detection is not great and the punishments imposed not severe, breaching DRE machine security systems in order to affect the outcome of an election presents a dauntingly high risk-to-reward ratio.

Of course, the motive for tampering with a DRE voting system may not be to alter vote totals. Hackers might seek to attack a DRE machine for the same reason that they have hacked computer systems and Internet sites since the dawn of the Computer Age: to simply demonstrate that they are able to do it. Because such an attack would be most accurately characterized as an act of electronic vandalism, the perpetrator would not attempt to keep the attack secret. He or she would strive instead to make sure that the hack was easily recognizable, for example, by assigning all votes to the most obscure candidate in the contest (or perhaps to George Washington), and by then contacting major news outlets to boast about the accomplishment. Such fraud would not be committed to affect an election outcome, but rather to increase concerns about the viability of electronic voting systems, or to create bad publicity about a particular vendor, or just to get the hacker some publicity.

But home-brewed access cards or memory cards carrying malware, which require considerable knowledge and expertise to create, are not the only source of potential vote fraud in a DRE environment. What is almost always overlooked in scenarios of DRE vote fraud are "low-tech" attacks that can be undertaken to create problems at polling places and thus alter election results. Fraud of this nature does not involve breaching security features of the DRE machines—indeed, this approach might well exploit the proper working of their security features. Low-tech election fraud would undermine the proper working of the voting system by creating problems that appear to be the result of unintentional mistakes, administrative snafus, and acts of God. Not a single line of code on a single machine need be compromised, and every DRE machine would function exactly as it is supposed to. Every vote would be counted, and the votes would be perfectly tabulated. Although many of the attacks we outline below have analogies in the world of paper balloting, the complexity of electronic voting may create an environment where such attacks might be more effective.

In a low-tech fraud scenario, the attacker would seek to trigger problems that reduce the rate of voting on DRE machines and so increase the amount of time voters must wait before voting. Significantly increasing the length of waiting times reliably lowers turnout. Some voters who are in line give up and go home, what operations researchers call "reneging."[10] Perpetrators of such attacks could greatly amplify the damage they have created by alerting television and radio news stations to the long lines present at certain voting centers. This information would persuade many others to "balk" and not even go to the polling place. These attacks are equivalent to denial-of-service attacks on Internet sites, which is one objection that has been lodged against Internet voting.[11] Targeting precincts where voters are extremely likely to vote for a particular party or candidate would thus reduce the number of votes cast for that party or candidate, ideally by enough to alter the outcome of the election.[12] Efforts like these have been undertaken in recent, and historical, elections, though to our knowledge the efforts to inhibit voter participation have not involved the exploitation (or attempted exploitation) of DREs.[13]

Attacks of this nature pose a serious problem for what might be called the "forensic analysis" of election administration—using data from an election to find anomalies and potentially pinpoint election fraud. The problem is that, if we see anomalies, we may not be able to determine whether they were the consequence of unintentional, nondeliberate actions or of deliberate actions with malicious intentions. If we cannot separate the two, how should we react when a forensic analysis shows evidence of an anomaly? We believe that precinct incident reports potentially provide one method by which to better understand balloting anomalies.

Incident Reports Concerning DRE Security

We received incident reports concerning the May 2 election from 1,216 of the 1,435 precincts in Cuyahoga County. Of those precincts, 1,108 (nearly 90 percent) reported at least one incident. A total of 6,285 incidents were coded from the reports. Figure 7-1 shows the distribution of incidents reported by poll workers across precincts. Most of the precincts reported four incidents or fewer, but some reported ten or more. Over 90 percent of the incidents reported clearly referred to a problem, but some did not. For example, one report stated that "supplies arrived from the Board of Elections." A few incidents were actually positive comments, such as "voters like the new machines," or "poll worker X doing a particularly good job."

Figure 7-1. Incidents Reported by Precinct, Cuyahoga County, Ohio, 2006

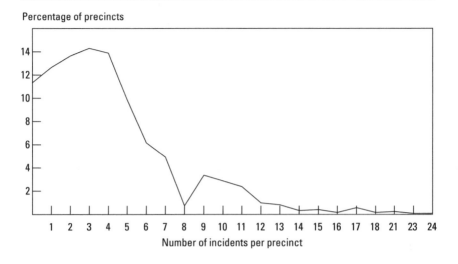

Percentage of precincts

Number of incidents per precinct

Because incident reports were made voluntarily, we cannot say for sure why some precincts reported more problems than others. More incident reports are surely indicative of more problems, but they may also reflect the industriousness of the poll worker responsible for writing the reports. It is possible that some precincts encountered so many problems during the day that they did not have time to record all of them on the incident report form. In short, it is likely that there was underreporting of significant problems in some precincts and overreporting of minor problems in others. As long as such biases are randomly distributed, the incident report data are still quite useful for our purposes.

The data show, for example, that in Cuyahoga County on May 2, 2006, the basic security features of DRE voting machines were sometimes compromised. Figure 7-2 charts the percentage of precincts that reported at least one incident of a particular type. It shows that in over 15 percent of the precincts that filled out an incident report there was a problem involving tamper-evident seals. In this election, poll workers installed the memory cards at the voting sites. Memory cards, printer canisters, and other needed supplies were delivered to the voting centers in sealed plastic bags, and many of the incident reports indicated that seals on these bags were broken, missing, or had not stuck. In other cases they indicated that not enough seals had been sent to secure the DRE devices once the memory cards and printer canisters were installed. Other reports indicated that these seals either tore easily or did not stick once placed on the device.

Figure 7-2. Frequency of Different Incident Types Reported, Cuyahoga County, Ohio, 2006

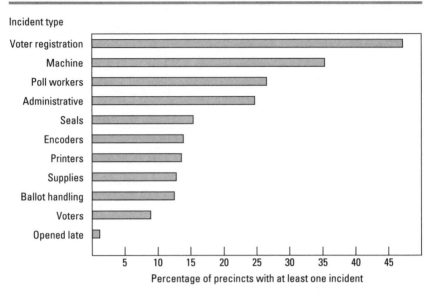

Incident type

Percentage of precincts with at least one incident

We cannot tell what poll workers did when they encountered problems with the tamper-evident seals. We surmise that the machines in question were nevertheless put into service. Nothing from the incident reports suggests otherwise, and the impression we have garnered from reading the reports is that poll workers felt considerable pressure, although not necessarily formal pressure from the central election office, to keep as many DRE machines operating as possible.

The data presented in figure 7-2 also show that nearly 10 percent of the precincts encountered difficulties that directly involved the memory cards. These problems had a variety of manifestations. A few reports simply stated that they had received "bad" memory cards, that the memory cards did not work, or that data would not download to the memory cards. Poll workers also wrote in the incident reports that the Board of Elections had not sent them enough memory cards or that they had received too many. Some of the incident reports indicated that new memory cards were sent out and that they were installed after the nonfunctioning cards were removed.

Almost two-thirds of the incidents in this category did not involve the functioning of the memory cards per se, but rather reflected confusion over their proper installation. At some point in the day, poll workers in many precincts discovered directions indicating that specific (numbered) memory cards were to be installed in specific DRE machines. By this time they had already installed the memory cards, resulting in large numbers of mismatches. Only two of the reports indicated that the DRE machines were taken out of service to match the right card with the right machine, and several other reports simply listed the new machine-card pairings. Most such reports, however, did not indicate exactly what the poll workers had done in this situation.

In our opinion, problems involving tamper-evident seals and memory cards could largely be avoided by adopting the practices mandated in California and other states.[14] Interestingly, the Cuyahoga County Board of Elections adopted what turned out to be problematic procedures for reasons of security. Their concern was that DRE machines were sent out to some voting site many days before the election and that not all of these sites could be adequately locked and secured. It is reasonable to conclude that security procedures involving memory cards in this election left much to be desired.

What about the encoded access cards, which are the other major peripheral device that could be exploited to infiltrate malware into a DRE voting system? The data in figure 7-2 indicate that nearly 14 percent of all precincts in our database reported problems with encoders. This category includes both incidents involving the machines used to encode access cards and the access cards themselves. Almost all of these reports stated simply that a particular encoding machine or a particular card was not working properly. Although poll workers can ensure that memory cards have not been tampered with and that the machines in which they have been installed are secure, it is hard to see how poll workers could determine whether a "home-brewed" access card has been inserted into a DRE machine. For this reason, incident reports about encoders and access cards are not likely to be informative as to whether these devices have been used in an attempt to hack into a DRE voting machine. As we shall see, however, problems involving encoders and access cards may be symptomatic of a different sort of attack on a DRE voting system.

In response to concerns that electronic voting machines are potentially vulnerable to hackers, Ohio and twenty-four other states have mandated that DRE machines be equipped with printers to produce a voter-verified paper audit trail—a paper printout of the ballot cast via the touch-screen—that voters can check before casting their vote.[15] If fraud is suspected, the DRE machine archive and memory card can be compared to the physical record of the VVPAT, which presumably cannot be altered by vote-altering software.

The incident reports of May 2 do not paint a pretty picture of the precincts' experiences with the VVPAT printers. Nearly 14 percent of the precincts filing an incident report indicated that they had had one or more problems with the printers. According to these reports, in some printers the paper roll failed to advance. It is not possible to tell how many ballots were printed on top of each other in such cases. Ideally, a voter would notice and report a printer failure as soon as it occurred, but not all voters actually inspect the VVPAT record before casting their ballot. In other instances the paper kept advancing after the voter had voted, and in others the paper roll became torn. A few of the incident reports indicated that the printers were not printing because they had run out of ink. The printers involved actually use heat-sensitive paper instead of ink, so this reported problem could obviously not have been the cause of failure. It is our suspicion that in at least some of these cases nothing printed because the paper canisters had been installed backward, as was noted in other reports. Equally problematic, the seal problems associated with the voting machines also occurred with the VVPAT printers. Thus the chain of custody of some of the printers was as problematic as the chain of custody of the voting machines. Given the legal status of the VVPAT in Ohio, stealing the VVPAT tape is equivalent to stealing ballots from the ballot box.

It is possible that VVPAT printing technology is not generally as unreliable as it was on May 2 in Cuyahoga County, but there have been reports of printer failure in several other jurisdictions. In the June 2006 primary election in Orange County, Calfornia, in seven of eight precincts visited by the authors, at least one DRE voting machine had been taken out of service because the VVPAT device had jammed. One of these precincts had two VVPAT devices fail on election day.[16] In the case of printer failure it is a simple matter to recreate a new paper record of the votes cast on a DRE machine by printing out the contents of the machine's data archive. But doing so undermines the rationale for requiring the VVPAT in the first place. Failure to create an accurate VVPAT record also represents more than the failure of a desired security feature, as many states stipulate that the VVPAT paper records are to be considered the official ballot in case of a recount or contested election.

Low-Tech Vote Fraud

To date, debate over the security of DRE voting machines has been dominated by the concern that votes can be altered if hackers insert malware into one or more machines. The incident report data discussed so far show that poll workers in Cuyahoga County identified hundreds of cases in which at least one of the primary security features in the DRE system had been compromised. Even if incidents involving DRE security potentially affected only a small number of votes, they can nevertheless significantly undermine public confidence in the accuracy of election results.

What we found particularly striking about the incident report data, however, are the many possibilities suggested by these data for the perpetration of what might be best described as low-tech fraud. Attacks of this nature would take advantage of the principal-agent relationships that exist in elections; it is very difficult for election officials to effectively monitor and supervise the polling places that they operate. Instead, they must delegate authority and power to poll workers and to the owners of polling locations on election day.[17] These attacks do not require an attacker to overcome the DRE security systems to alter votes but rather to disrupt the DRE system and so impede the ability of voters to cast their votes. These might be more accurately referred to as social engineering attacks. Their purpose is to create a denial of service—not to change votes, but to prevent them from being cast.

Looking again at figure 7-2, we see that one of the largest categories of incident reports, involving fully one-quarter of the precincts that filed a report, fell under the rubric "administrative." These included, among other things, incidents involving the polling place itself. Polling places are located in many different facilities, such as schools, community centers, and other buildings, and poll workers must rely on those in charge of these sites to open the polls on election day. According to twenty-five incident reports, on May 2 in Cuyahoga County poll workers were unable to enter the polling place on time because no one had come to unlock the doors. This led to several voting centers opening late, as keys needed to be located and building supervisors needed to be found. Any attack that would affect the opening of a polling place has the capacity to cause problems throughout the day, especially if a line forms that is difficult to ease.

This type of problem could be readily exploited. It would require identifying the owners or building supervisors who have the keys to unlock the voting site early on election day and misinforming them as to when they are supposed to unlock the facility. For example, they might be told to open the building at 7:30 a.m. instead of 5:30 a.m. Also, an attacker might simply jam the lock to the room where voting is to take place.

A similar "social engineering" attack could be made on poll workers. As figure 7-2 also shows, over 25 percent of precincts were missing at least one poll worker. Several precincts were missing more than one poll worker. If even a small number of poll workers were told by someone impersonating a county election official that they needed to arrive at the polls late, this could cause difficulties in opening and initially operating the polls, when a relatively large number of voters come to cast ballots.

Over one-third of the precincts filing incident reports reported problems with the DRE machines themselves; these problems were coded in the "machines" category. Most were simply reports that one or more machines were not working, could not be booted up, or had quit working. Many of these reports, however, point to attacks that can be made on machines that do not involve hacking. As indicated previously, the goal would not be to alter votes, but to take the machine out of service. One such attack could be on the power supply. In the May 2 primary, poll workers in two voting centers indicated that their DRE machines had lost power because they had overloaded a circuit and thus tripped a circuit breaker. Eight other precincts reported that machines had been running on batteries and eventually powered off. Four other power-related problems were also reported, such as surge protectors that could not handle the number of machines assigned to the voting center. Even assuming that no ballot data were lost or misrecorded when sudden power outages occurred, returning these machines to functioning status takes time and would necessarily delay voting.

Another way to create a bottleneck at the polls is to attack the voter access cards. In order to vote on the DRE machine used in this election (the Diebold AccuVote-TSx), one needed to have a valid access card, which must be encoded anew for each voter. These cards, moreover, must be preprogrammed at a central location to embed the digital signature security feature. In Cuyahoga County on May 2, the incident reports included 198 problems, occurring in 15 percent of precincts, with access cards or encoders that in some cases created delays in voting. Specific problems included having too few access cards, voters walking off with access cards instead of returning them to poll workers, cards becoming stuck in the DRE machines, voters leaving the cards in the DRE machine, voters inserting the cards into the machine backwards or upside down, cards that could not be encoded or re-encoded, cards that during the course of the day became dirty and greasy (and thus unusable), encoders that did not work, and encoders that ran out of battery power and stopped functioning.

It takes little imagination to see how the need for voter access cards could be exploited to stall voting. After voting, a perpetrator could use an emery board or similar abrasive device to scuff the magnetic strip on the card and thus render it unusable. Smearing grease, dirt, or grime on the card, which some voters did unintentionally on May 2, would also make it impossible to reprogram the card. Simply having some voters pocket the access cards right before a high-volume period on election day (say, in the early evening) could cause considerable confusion in a polling place and could generate long lines. Unless election officials programmed many more cards than they did in recent elections, putting even a few voter access cards out of commission at a precinct could dramatically slow the rate of voting.

Printer problems could also be created and exploited to slow down voting. The incident reports documented episodes in which voters pried open the magnifying plastic cover and tore the printer tape. They did this because they were under the mistaken impression that the VVPAT was equivalent to an ATM receipt that they could take with them. Feeding false information to voters to the effect that the VVPAT actually is equivalent to a receipt and that they have the right to take it with them could dramatically exacerbate this problem. Poll workers might be able to get machines that are damaged in this fashion back on line, but the potential for significant delay is present. In addition, if the printer can be jammed—for example, by introducing a paper clip or similar item into the canister—it can also create damage to ballots, as well as take the voting machine out of service until the jam is fixed.

Finally, we can readily imagine denial-of-service attacks associated with the voter registration rolls. As we see in figure 7-2, incidents involving voter registration were reported by nearly half the precincts that filed reports. These included voters who are not listed in the poll book, voters with misspelled names, voters whose signatures were inconsistent with the recorded signature, voters who had moved and had new addresses, and notes that certain voters who appeared on the rolls were deceased. In the debate over voting today, most attention has been paid to the security of electronic voting machines, but very little attention has been paid to the security of voter registration databases. Given that these systems list voters by precinct, and often by party, it would be quite easy for a hacker with access to the voter registration database to target voters for deletion from the rolls. Voter registration problems are by far the most common form of voting problem in the United States, according to both these data and the report of the Caltech/MIT Voting Technology Project, "Voting: What Is, What Could Be."[18] Problems with a voter registration system would cascade through precincts and create delays when voters could not be authenticated and then have to cast a provisional ballot. Such an attack would create lines and would also likely create a hostile environment in the polling place.

Denial of Service: Random or Disproportionate in Impact?

The incident report data we have analyzed show that there are literally dozens of reasons why a DRE machine can fall out of service on election day. If the many reasons we have identified are the product of unintentional errors, inadequate training of poll workers, uninformed voters, poor machine design, or simple machine failure, we would expect to see no pattern in the occurrence of such problems. But what if, as a result of such problems, DRE machines fell out of service, thus producing longer voter wait times, are not randomly distributed across precincts? The greater the extent to which problems creating denial of service are concentrated in particular types of precincts—for example, heavily Democratic or heavily Republican ones—the greater the likelihood that they could affect the outcome of an election. Previous research on the 2004 presidential election in Ohio indicates that John Kerry may have lost thousands of votes because inadequate numbers of voting machines were assigned to urban, heavily Democratic precincts, leading in some cases to extremely long wait times that must have discouraged some voters from voting.[19] All indications are that these problems occurred because turnout in these precincts ran much higher than had been anticipated. But a disproportionate impact of denial-of-service incidents does increase the probability, in our opinion, that the problems could be the result of concerted, purposeful action.

For this reason we analyzed the incident report data to determine whether certain types of incidents occurred more frequently in certain types of precincts. This was done by correlating the occurrence of the various categories of incidents displayed in figure 7-2 with the partisan breakdown of the vote for governor in each precinct. The latter figure was derived by adding up the votes for all Democratic candidates and all Republican candidates, respectively, and then calculating the Democratic percentage of the two-party vote.

For the most part, correlations between incident types and the partisan breakdown of the vote in each precinct were low.[20] But there were some exceptions, and these are presented in table 7-1. For purposes of illustration we have grouped precincts into three types: (1) heavily Democratic, where over 75 percent of the voters voted for a Democratic candidate for governor; (2) Democratic, where the percent voting for Democratic candidates was between 50 and 75 percent; and (3) Republican, where more than 50 percent voted for Republican candidates.

As the entries in table 7-1 show, Democratic precincts were more likely to report higher frequencies of problems involving poll workers. Although a few

Table 7-1. Incident Frequency and Party Breakdown of Precinct Vote in 2006 Elections, Cuyahoga County, Ohio

Percent (except where noted)

Type of incident	Precinct vote		
	Heavily Democratic	Democratic	Republican
Voter registration	32.9	50.9	64.2
Poll worker	26.8	30.9	16.7
Encoders	8.0	16.7	17.9
Long waiting time	4.0	6.8	7.3
Number of incidents reported	426	544	246

of the reports in this category were negative comments about specific individuals, the overwhelming majority of them were reports that one or more poll workers had not shown up, either to set up on Monday evening or to work at the election on Tuesday. Republican precincts, in contrast, were more likely to report incidents involving voter registration errors and encoder/access cards. The last row of percentages in table 7-1 also shows that over 7 percent of the majority-Republican precincts, but only 4 percent of the heavily Democratic precincts, reported long waiting times. Precincts were considered to have experienced long waiting times if this was mentioned specifically in the incident report or if they had noted a figure of thirty minutes or more in the "longest waiting time" entry.

There is absolutely no reason to think that the results reported in table 7-1 reflect a purposeful effort to disenfranchise Republican voters. First and foremost, there would have been absolutely no reason to have attempted a denial-of-service attack. This election was essentially two independent primary elections; the Republican candidates were not running against Democratic candidates. Like most primaries, the May 2 election was a low-turnout affair, which further undercuts the motivation for carrying out such an attack. As for voter registration problems in particular, it is most likely the case that poll workers in highly Republican precincts were simply more fastidious in noting misspellings and address changes.

In general elections, where the two parties are competing head-to-head for votes, however, the patterns of data evident in table 7-1 might raise suspicions of wrongdoing. In such an election, precinct incident reports could probably best be used in conjunction with other types of forensic analyses to determine whether anomalies observed in election data are due to intentional and deliberate fraud or are just the result of mistakes. For example, assume that an analysis of precinct election returns indicates that in a particular precinct there is a substantial "error term"—a significant deviation from what a sophisticated statistical model, based on data from other precincts and on the past history of elections, predicts should have happened in that precinct. Also assume that in their incident reports poll workers noted significant problems with the voting equipment that forced them to restart a number of voting machines during the course of election day. In this case, the presence of the incident reports might provide documentation that the problems seen in the statistical analysis were the result of problems with the voting system and poll workers' efforts to rectify those problems.

Improving Incident Reports

This study is the first to systematically analyze incident reports filed by poll workers "on the ground" on election day. Such reports necessarily focus attention on what went wrong during an election instead of what went right. It is understandable that election officials would be hesitant to collect such written records, which, in Cuyahoga County and most other jurisdictions, are considered to be public documents. The incident reports could receive intense media scrutiny, especially in the event of a contested election. Some incident reports we examined were rather defamatory in nature. In some cases the person filling out the report charged that one or more co-workers were lazy, incompetent, abusive, and argumentative with the voters, and in one instance, a drug abuser.[21]

Assuming that election officials can be given some leeway to edit or redact certain reports filed by poll workers, routinely collecting such data could certainly aid in improving election administration, and, as we have argued here, in detecting and deterring vote fraud. In implementing an incident report system, there are several measures that could be taken to improve upon what was done in Cuyahoga County. First, poll workers should be given complete and clear instructions as to which sort of incidents should be reported and which should not. Above all, they should be instructed to be particularly vigilant in noting any problems involving DRE security, chain of custody issues, and any problems that take DRE machines out of service.

Such reports would also be far more informative if workers included more specific information about what the problem was, when it occurred, and how—or whether—it was resolved. For example, many incident reports indicated that a voting machine was not working properly, but that the election day technician (EDT) was able to get it running again. What was not reported in most cases was why the machine stopped running, how the EDT got the machine running again, how long it took for the EDT to get the voting machine running again, and whether prescribed (as opposed to unorthodox and problematic) actions were taken to fix the machine.

Effective incident reporting should also enable election officials to track problems and their potential consequences. By including the identification number of a voting machine that was involved in an incident—be it a machine failure, printer failure, or issue involving the card—an incident report would enable an election official to subsequently examine that machine in order to establish the cause of the problem and whether the incident affected the vote tabulation process. Finally, incident report data should be incorporated into an audit procedure for all aspects of election administration. Poll workers and election judges could then be interviewed to determine why some precincts reported so many incidents. Appropriate steps could then be taken to ensure that any issues identified are resolved before the next election in that precinct.

Notes

1. The forms from each precinct were obtained by the Election Science Institute and then provided to the data entry firm Superdata, which created an electronic record of each unique incident. These reports were then coded by the authors.

2. This information is from "Sources: Bhutto was to give U.S. lawmakers vote-rigging report" (www.cnn.com/2008/WORLD/asiapcf/01/01/pakistan.voterigging/index.html [January 2008]).

3. See the chapter by Hall and Wang in this volume regarding international standards for what constitutes a "free and fair" election.

4. Harri Hursti, "Diebold TSx Evaluation: Critical Security Issues with Diebold TSx," May 2006 (www.bbvdocs.org/reports/BBVreportIIunredacted.pdf [January 2008]).

5. Tadayoshi Kohno, Adam Stubblefield, Aviel D. Rubin, and Dan S. Wallach, "Analysis of an Electronic Voting System," IEEE Symposium on Security and Privacy, May 2004; Ariel J. Feldman, J. Alex Halderman, and Edward W. Felten, "Security Analysis of the Diebold AccuVote-TS Voting Machine," September 2006 (http://itpolicy.princeton.edu/voting/ts-paper.pdf [January 2008]).

6. For one example of the procedural security that has been developed and implemented by an election official, see the paper by Travis County (Texas) clerk Dana De-Beauvoir, "Method for Developing Security Procedures in a DRE Environment"

(www.co.travis.tx.us/county_clerk/election/pdfs/NIST_paper_051005.pdf [January 2008]).

7. See, for example, the response by Diebold to the ESI report that is available at http://bocc.cuyahogacounty.us (January 2008).

8. Diebold Election Systems, "Checks and Balances in Elections Equipment and Procedures Prevent Alleged Fraud Scenarios," 2003; Ariel Feldman, J. Alex Halderman, and Edward Felten, "Security Analysis of the Diebold AccuVote-TS Voting Machine," Center for Information Technology Policy, Princeton University, 2006; David Wagner, David Jefferson, and Matt Bishop, "Security Analysis of the Diebold AccuBasic Interpreter," Report of the Voting Systems Technology Assessment Advisory Board, 2006.

9. Consistent with this argument is the fact that vote fraud cases are extremely rare and that many of the schemes that are carried out are very poorly considered. See Delia Bailey's chapter in this volume. For arguments about why leaders in less democratic countries may have the incentive to commit obvious and easily documented election fraud, see Alberto Simpser, "Making Votes Not Count (Ph.D. dissertation, Stanford University, 2005).

10. Alexander Belenke and Richard Larson, "To Queue or Not to Queue?" *OR/MS Today*, 2006 (www.lionhrtpub.com/orms/orms-6-06/queues.html [January 2008]).

11. For a more general discussion of these types of attacks, see R. Michael Alvarez, "Precinct Voting Denial of Service," October 2005 (http://vote.caltech.edu/media/documents/wps/vtp_wp39.pdf [January 2008]).

12. Benjamin Highton, "Long Lines, Voting Machine Availability, and Turnout: The Case of Franklin County, Ohio, in the 2004 Presidential Election," PSOnline 65 no. 8 (2006). Walter Mebane, "Voting Machine Allocation in Franklin County, Ohio, 2004: Response to the U.S. Department of Justice Letter of June 29, 2005," Cornell University, 2006.

13. For example, in October 2006 reports surfaced in Orange County, California, that as many as 14,000 Latino voters in a congressional district there were the targets of a potential vote-suppression campaign involving a letter they received that made claims about immigrants and voting rights (http://electionupdates.caltech.edu/2006/10/more-on-latino-voter-intimidation.html [January 2008]).

14. Elaborated in an October 30, 2006, Factsheet issued by California Secretary of State Bruce McPherson, California's certification of all DRE systems requires the following: "For those systems with removable memory cards, each voting system's memory card is serialized and inserted into the system in the presence of at least two elections officials at the county level, and a tamper evident seal with a serial number on it is applied to the protective case covering the memory card. The tamper evident seals with serial numbers will indicate if the system's internal mechanisms have been exposed at any point leading up to election day. The county must maintain a written log recording which memory cards and tamper evident seals, along with serial numbers are assigned to each machine. Additionally, the county must maintain a written log that

accurately records the chain of custody of each memory card and unit from the point of programming the memory card for use in the election through the time of completion of the official canvass. . . . Prior to a system being used on election day, a review of the system and the tamper evident seals is conducted by at least two election officials at the county level. If any of the seals are broken or have been tampered with, the system must be removed and a complete inspection of the system must be conducted. Additionally, a full report must be done and submitted to the Secretary of State's office" (www.ss.ca.gov/elections/voting_systems/e_voting_factsheet.pdf [January 2008]).

15. "Election Reform Briefing 12: Recounts: From Punch Cards to Paper Trails," October 2005 (http://electionline.org/Portals/1/Publications/ERIPBrief12.SB370 updated.pdf [January 2008]).

16. Thad Hall and Mike Alvarez, "ElectionUpdates' Observations on the June 6 California Primary," June 2006 (http://electionline.org/Portals/1/docs/Alvarez.hall. report.6.06.pdf [January 2008]).

17. For a discussion of this, see R. Michael Alvarez and Thad E. Hall, "Controlling Democracy: The Principal-Agent Problems in Election Administration," *Policy Studies Journal* 34, no. 4 (2006): 491–510; and R. Michael Alvarez and Thad E. Hall, *Point, Click, and Vote: The Future of Internet Voting* (Brookings, 2004).

18. Caltech/MIT Voting Technology Project, "Voting: What Is, What Could Be," July 2001 (http://vote.caltech.edu/reports/2001report.htm [January 2008]).

19. Highton, "Long Lines"; Mebane, "Voting Machine Allocation."

20. Low in this case is defined as a correlation score resulting in a Pearson $r < .1$.

21. The actual text of this report was "NAME DELETED, presiding judge left the premises—using crack. She is not allowed in building—substance abuser. Management has told her to stay out."

eight

Identifying and Preventing Signature Fraud on Ballot Measure Petitions

Todd Donovan and Daniel A. Smith

Most studies of election fraud focus on what happens once voters try to cast their ballots. However, important forms of fraud can also occur before election day. In this chapter, we focus on one such form of fraud: the forging of signatures in order to place an initiative or referendum on a statewide ballot. After providing some background on the business of signature gathering and assessing the incentives for fraud, we analyze the incidence of signature fraud for measures on the ballot in Washington State between 1990 and 2006. We also examine in detail the validity of the more than 265,000 signatures submitted for a 2006 initiative, I-917, which narrowly failed to qualify for the ballot. We conclude by discussing some of the difficulties in monitoring and regulating the signature collection process.

The Purpose of Signature Collection and Qualification

One of the principal reasons proponents of ballot measures are required to collect signatures in every state that permits direct democracy is to demonstrate that the proposed measure has some threshold level of public support. This threshold is typically a specified percentage of the statewide votes cast in a previous election. In the state of Washington, in order to place a measure on the 2006 ballot, its proponents had to collect roughly 225,000 valid signatures within six months. Collecting this many signatures is very labor-intensive. As a result, the vast majority of ballot measures that are filed with the Office of the Secretary of State in Washington and in other states never collect sufficient signatures to qualify for a public vote—whether because the issues are of limited interest to the public or because their backers lack the resources and broad base of committed volunteers that are needed to circulate petitions.[1] Nonetheless, compared to other states, Washington has a record of relatively frequent ballot measure qualification. From 1996 to 2002, only three other states (Oregon, California, and Colorado) had more initiatives qualify for their state ballots by petition.

The Signature-Gathering Industry and Incentives for Fraud

Increasingly, groups proposing ballot measures hire people to circulate their petitions. In some recent election cycles in Washington, Oregon, and California, every initiative to reach the ballot did so by using paid petition circulators, who are typically compensated by signature-gathering firms only for valid signatures.[2] As a result, the cost of putting an initiative on the ballot has climbed. Washington Public Disclosure Commission records reveal that expenses for initiative qualification for a single proposal can now exceed $700,000.[3] The cost is usually higher in larger states such as California and Florida.

The relationship between a ballot measure campaign and the individuals who circulate petitions is often indirect. Many measure proponents hire political consultants who subcontract their signature qualification work to a petition management firm or firms. These firms, including Arno, NVO, PCI Consultants (also known as Progressive Campaigns, Inc.), National Petition Management (formerly American Petition Management), and Citizen Solutions, have expertise in administering petition efforts for multiple campaigns in multiple states simultaneously.

A petition management firm typically subcontracts the work it receives to crew chiefs in various states, who in turn hire and manage the individuals who actually circulate the petition sheets. The individual "street-level" petition circulators migrate from state to state in search of work over the course of a campaign season, and in any single state they may simultaneously circulate petitions for several different ballot issue campaigns. Petition circulators are usually paid for each valid signature, unless state law stipulates an hourly wage or salary. The average "cost per signature" for a campaign (which ranges from $0.75 to $2.00 and even higher) can include fees paid to the petition management firm, to regional coordinators, to locally subcontracted crew chiefs, and to the individual circulator. Individual petition circulators earn more by generating more signatures, by carrying petitions for several measures at the same time, and by holding onto signatures to sell to crew chiefs when the signatures fetch the highest price (that is, as the deadline to file approaches). The largest proportion of the cost per signature goes to the individual circulating the petition.[4]

Unlike volunteers, professional signature collectors may have a financial incentive to generate signatures by any means. According to a survey of county-level supervisors of elections in Florida, campaigns using paid signature gatherers submitted much higher rates of invalid signatures than campaigns using volunteers.[5] Since there can be such distance between the ballot measure sponsor and the person actually collecting the signatures that appear on petitions, well-intentioned campaigns seeking to file legitimate signatures on qualification petitions must depend on the integrity of transient individuals who are paid per signature and who often work with little supervision.

Signature Fraud in Ballot Measure Qualification Petitions

Petition management firms have been at the center of numerous scandals involving fraudulent signatures.[6] Paid signature gatherers in Florida were found to have filed fraudulent signatures that included names copied from phone books in 1994 and names of deceased people in 1995. One Florida initiative committee delivered 10,087 signatures to county officials, of which only 697 were valid.[7]

More recently, California-based PCI Consultants was accused of fraudulently securing signatures on behalf of casino proponents in the District of Columbia. The District of Columbia Board of Elections and Ethics rejected the proposed measure (Initiative 68) after signatures were submitted, finding that petition fraud "polluted" the signature-gathering process so much that thousands of signatures had to be rejected. Among the irregularities, petition crews hired by one subcontractor failed to sign, or falsely signed, the affidavit required by the D.C. Code swearing that the signature gatherer was in the presence of each person signing, and that "according to the best information available to the circulator, each signature is the genuine signature of the person it purports to be." The D.C. Board was able to use information from the affidavits to subpoena signature gatherers, who admitted to falsely signing affidavits on petitions they did not circulate, and implicated others involved in petition fraud that included forging names on petition sheets.[8]

Thousands of fraudulent signatures were also reported to have been found on petitions filed in Massachusetts to qualify a same-sex marriage measure in that state. The Massachusetts legislature held hearings to document examples of petition fraud associated with work conducted in Massachusetts by California-based Arno Political Consultants in 2005 during the campaign, and the Massachusetts attorney general subsequently conducted a criminal investigation.

Similarly, in October 2006, three statewide initiatives that had been certified for the November 2006 Montana ballot (Initiatives 97, 98, and 154) were ruled invalid just two weeks before the November 2006 election because of pervasive fraud in signature collection by paid petition circulators. Media reports and facts documented in a state District Court decision (facts that were also cited when the District Court ruling was affirmed by a unanimous State Supreme Court) indicate that a Montana initiative campaign hired multiple firms, including Nevada-based National Voter Outreach (NVO), to conduct petition management.[9] Individual petition circulators were found to have tricked voters into signing petitions for multiple ballot measures, falsely swearing in signature certifications to facts they had no personal knowledge about, and giving false addresses in sworn affidavits.[10] NVO has conducted petition signature gathering in dozens of states, including Oklahoma, where it is facing another voter fraud lawsuit. In 2007, the president of NVO, Susan Johnson, was one of three individuals indicted by an Oklahoma grand jury for knowingly hiring out-of-state paid petition gatherers to come to the state temporarily to collect signatures. According to state law, petition gatherers must be over the age of 18 and bona fide residents of the state. Johnson was charged with conspiring to defraud the state, along with Rich Carpenter, the sponsor of a 2006 statewide tax limitation measure, and Paul Jacob, an adviser to the campaign.[11]

In an effort to curb fraud, many states have adopted laws regulating the signature-gathering process. Many states require petitions to be notarized, petition circulators to be registered voters in or residents of the state in which they petition, and deputized voter registrars to observe and verify the act of signing petitions. Other states require paid petition circulators to wear badges informing citizens if they are being paid and volunteers to sign affidavits saying they are not being paid. Some require signature gatherers to swear they are not paying people to sign their petitions. A few states even prohibit per-signature payment for signatures. Most states now require a person gathering signatures to attest that he or she witnessed each signing.[12]

Rates of Invalid Signatures on Ballot Measure Petition Sheets

Although the anecdotes above provide examples of petition fraud, it is difficult to demonstrate empirically how widespread petition fraud may be in a state. In their chapter in this volume, Michael Alvarez and Fred Boehmke indicate that "falsified petitions" was the fourth most common allegation of electoral fraud in California (after fraudulent registration, double voting, and noncitizens being registered). One falsified petition, however, can contain many fictitious names. To get a better sense of the potential for petition fraud in the collection of signatures to qualify a ballot measure, we collected data on the rates at which signatures were rejected in Washington State for being invalid. When petitions are submitted to the secretary of state's office, a sample of signatures (from 2 to 5 percent, depending on the number of signatures submitted) is hand-checked against public records of names, addresses, and signatures of registered voters. The primary reasons for excluding individual signatures are: the name of the person signing is not found (because, for example, he or she is not registered to vote), the signature on the petition does not match the registration signature on file, and the name of the person who signed appears more than once on the petition (it is a duplicate).

Table 8-1 illustrates rates of signature invalidity in Washington since 1990. On average across the ballot measures, 18.9 percent of signatures were ruled invalid, mostly because the names on the petitions could not be found among the lists of registered voters. There is no correlation between measures that have higher rates of invalidity owing to nonexistent names (unregistered voters) and those that have higher invalid rates because the same names appear on petitions multiple times. Much of signature invalidity likely comes from unregistered citizens (or even noncitizens) who naively sign petitions, from signature collectors who fail to ensure that only registered voters sign petitions, and from citizens who forget they have already signed a petition. Nonetheless, it is possible that a greater proportion of the fictitious names submitted corresponds to greater "not found" rates, and that a higher incidence of the use of fictitious names corresponds to greater invalid rates due to duplication.

We suggest above that paid petitioners may have greater incentives to commit fraud. This hypothesis is difficult to test with the data in table 8-1, because few ballot issues qualify for the ballot in Washington, California, or other large

Table 8-1. Invalid Signatures on Ballot Measure Petitions: Washington, 1990–2006

Ballot measure	Topic	Total signatures submitted	Percent not found[a]	Percent duplicates	Total percent invalid	Total signatures required	Signatures over (ratio)
2006							
I-917	$30 car tabs	265,935	13.6	4.0	17.6	224,880	1.35
I-920	Repeal estate tax	395,219	12.7	2.7	15.4	224,880	2.00
I-933	Property rights	317,353	12.2	5.0	17.3	224,880	1.60
I-937	Clean energy	337,804	12.0	12.3	24.3	224,880	1.71
2005							
I-330	Medical malpractice	319,146	16.4	2.7	19.1	197,734	1.61
I-336	Medical malpractice	300,776	19.7	6.4	26.1	197,734	1.52
I-900	Performance audits	311,858	12.2	4.5	16.7	224,880	1.58
I-901	Smoking ban	321,615	12.4	5.0	17.4	224,880	1.63
I-912	Repeal gas tax	400,996	13.1	0.8	13.9	224,880	2.03
2004							
I-297	Nuclear waste	280,382	16.5	7.2	23.7	197,734	1.42
R-55	No charter schools	153,718	11.7	0.0	11.7	98,867	1.55
I-892	Gambling/property tax	274,293	18.4	3.2	21.6	197,734	1.39
I-872	Top-two primary	308,402	13.0	3.1	16.2	197,734	1.56
I-884	Sales tax / education	321,932	18.6	3.7	22.4	197,734	1.63
2003							
I-841	Repeal ergonomics	258,411	15.2	4.8	20.1	197,734	1.31
2002							
I-776	$30 car tabs	260,898	16.8	3.8	20.6	197,734	1.32
I-790	Firefighters	345,543	21.0	3.2	24.3	197,734	1.75
R-53	Repeal L&I tax	151,239	22.6	0.7	23.3	197,734	1.53
2001							
I-747	Property tax limit	290,704	14.6	2.7	17.3	197,734	1.47
I-773	Tobacco tax/health care	275,081	18.6	2.6	21.2	197,734	1.39
I-775	Home health care	304,327	18.3	2.2	20.5	197,734	1.54
2000							
I-713	Animal trap ban	261,268	14.9	6.4	21.3	179,248	1.46
I-722	Property tax limit	272,678	14.3	4.6	18.9	179,248	1.52
I-728	School class size	297,199	15.7	2.2	17.8	179,248	1.66
I-729	Yes charter schools	306,361	19.2	2.1	21.3	179,248	1.71
I-732	Teacher COLA	298,722	10.2	0.7	10.9	179,248	1.67
I-745	Transport / roads	274,490	18.5	2.1	20.6	179,248	1.53
1999							
I-695	$30 car tabs	514,141	19.3	3.6	22.9	179,248	2.87
I-696	Fishing regulations	234,750	15.1	2.4	17.5	179,248	1.31
1998							
I-688	Minimum wage	288,357	16.6	2.4	19.0	179,248	1.61
I-692	Medical marijuana	260,335	22.4	1.4	23.8	179,248	1.45
I-694	Abortion	216,716	9.7	0.9	10.5	179,248	1.21

(continued)

Table 8-1. Invalid Signatures on Ballot Measure Petitions: Washington, 1990–2006 (continued)

Ballot measure	Topic	Total signatures submitted	Not found[a]	Percent duplicates	Total percent invalid	Total signatures required	Signatures over (ratio)
1997							
I-678	Dental hygienists	272,764	15.0	1.8	16.8	179,248	1.52
I-677	Gay rights	229,793	13.5	4.6	18.1	179,248	1.28
I-676	Gun locks	239,805	14.2	3.1	17.2	179,248	1.34
I-673	Health insurance	241,508	14.1	5.0	19.1	179,248	1.35
1996							
I-671	Tribal gaming	290,996	24.7	1.9	26.6	181,667	1.60
I-670	Term limit notice	232,522	16.0	0.5	16.5	181,667	1.28
I-655	Bear baiting	228,148	15.1	4.8	20.0	181,667	1.26
1995							
I-651	Tribal gambling	267,401	24.9	2.6	27.5	181,667	1.47
I-640	Fishing regulations	258,995	16.5	3.1	19.6	181,667	1.43
1994							
I-607	Denturists	241,228	11.3	1.4	12.7	181,667	1.33
1993							
I-602	TELs	440,160	12.8	1.2	13.9	181,667	2.42
I-601	TELs	249,707	9.1	3.4	12.5	181,667	1.37
I-593	Three strikes	290,613	9.1	2.2	11.3	181,667	1.60
1992							
I-582	Campaign finance	151,601	10.7	9.0	19.7	150,001	1.01
I-573	Term limits	206,685	15.7	1.8	17.5	150,001	1.38
1990							
I-559	Property taxes	276,653	11.9	3.7	15.6	150,001	1.84
I-553	Term limits	254,263	14.5	2.4	16.9	150,001	1.70
I-547	Growth management	229,489	17.6	4.3	21.9	150,001	1.53
I-534	Explicit material	180,373	19.4	3.6	23.0	150,001	1.20

a. Includes missing and no match.

states through the exclusive use of volunteer petitioners. A comparison of the campaigns behind the measures with the highest and lowest invalid rates in table 8-1 suggests that purely volunteer efforts (for example, I-912, 14 percent invalid), and well-financed campaigns that pay per hour rather than per signature (for example, I-732, 11 percent) had some of the lowest invalid rates. That said, the most expensive ballot qualification campaign in state history had one of the lowest invalid rates since 1990. The "Yes on Initiative 920" campaign of 2006 spent $790,000 on signature gathering (with 15 percent of the signatures subsequently stricken for being invalid) to qualify a proposal to repeal the estate tax (voters later rejected the proposal). Campaigns for gambling measures that paid per signature collected among the highest percentage of invalid signatures (I-671, 27 percent invalid; I-651, 27 percent; and I-892, 22 percent). Yet, ranking right up with these were campaigns that relied exclusively on volunteers (for example, I-695, 23 percent invalid) or heavily on volunteers (I-937, 24 percent invalid; I-790, 24 percent). In short, there is no clear pattern demonstrating that paying for signatures increases invalid rates.

Searching for Signature Petition Fraud in Washington: Initiative 917

Identifying who might commit fraud is difficult when the data do not identify which petitions were submitted by volunteers and which were submitted by people being paid per signature. To examine rates of invalidity in greater detail, and to determine the effects of requiring that circulators sign a declaration attesting to the validity of signatures on each petition sheet, we focus on the disposition of all signatures submitted for a single 2006 initiative in Washington State.

Initiative 917 (I-917), a statutory initiative that would have reduced the fees on licensing motor vehicles, provides a fairly representative example of petitioning practices in Washington. Roughly $360,000 was spent on signatures for the I-917 qualification campaign, and petition sheets were circulated by volunteers and paid petitioners (with most signatures likely collected by paid petitioners).[13] It is also an interesting case because 2006 was the first year petitioners were required to sign an affidavit on each petition sheet (although the secretary of state did not enforce this requirement).[14] This allows us to test if invalid rates were higher (or lower) on petitions with signed affidavits than on unsigned ones. Furthermore, although the affidavits do not provide direct evidence of whether a petitioner was paid or a volunteer, they do offer indirect evidence. Some petition sheet affidavits were "signed" with an ink-stamp of the name of known professional signature gatherers, while most other petition affidavits were hand-signed.

Raw data on the disposition of all individual signatures gathered for Initiative 917 in Washington were purchased from the Office of the Secretary of State as part of a lawsuit to challenge their validity. According to data furnished by the secretary of state, the proponents of I-917, SAVEOUR30TABS. COM, submitted 17,028 petition sheets with more than 265,000 signatures by the July 7, 2006, deadline.[15] According to state law, 224,880 valid signatures were needed to certify the measure for the general election ballot. The Office of the Secretary of State, in accordance with state law, conducted a random check of 4 percent of the submitted signatures for the initiative. The random check suggested an invalid rate of 18 percent among all of the submitted signatures, which was higher than the 15 percent rate required to qualify the measure. The secretary of state then proceeded to conduct a signature check of 100 percent of the signatures submitted by Permanent Offense, the sponsors of SAVEOUR30TABS.COM. The Office of the Secretary of State determined that 218,786 (82.3 percent) of all signatures were valid and 47,149 (17.7 percent) were invalid.[16] This was slightly lower than the average invalid signature rate of petitions submitted between 1990 and 2006 (18.9 percent). However, the percentage of duplicate signatures on I-917 petitions (4.0 percent) was higher than the historical average (3.3 percent). On the other hand, 13.6 percent of the signatures submitted for I-917 were declared to be invalid because the information filled out on the petition was not found in the state's voter registration database, the signature in the secretary of state's official voter file was missing, or the signature on the petition did not match the signature on file with the secretary of state. The invalid rate for signatures submitted for I-917 for these reasons was lower than the historical average (15.5 percent).

Table 8-2 lists the number of signatures that were submitted for I-917 according to whether they were found on petitions with signed affidavits or not, and table 8-3 lists the rate at which signatures were declared invalid across the different categories of petitions. Some 13,882 petition sheets (81.5 percent of the total) were submitted with either an ink-stamped or hand-signed affidavit on the backside. Among those petitions with a completed affidavit, 17.9 percent (41,444) of the 231,742 submitted signatures were determined by the secretary of state's office to be invalid. (See table 8-2.) In contrast, only 16.7 percent (5,704) of the 34,193 signatures on petitions with no completed affidavit on the backside were rejected as invalid. Although the differences are substantively small, there is a statistically significant difference [$\chi^2(1) = 29.510, p < .001$] between the rate of invalid signatures on petitions with no signed affidavit and on those with a declaration. Of the petitions with an ink-stamped affidavit on the backside (containing 24,092 signatures), 16.1 percent of the signatures were rejected as invalid. In contrast, 18.1 percent of the signatures on petitions with affidavits hand-signed by the petitioners (containing 207,650 signatures) were rejected as invalid. Again, the difference is small but statistically significant [$\chi^2 (1) = 55.520, p < .001$]. If ink-stamped petitions are assumed to come from paid circulators, it suggests this class of paid circulators (those who are willing to

Table 8-2. Signatures Submitted for I-917, by Type of Petition

Type of petition	Number of petitions
Petitions with signed affidavit	231,742
Hand-signed	207,650
Ink-stamped	24,092
Petitions with no signed affidavit	34,193
Total signatures submitted	265,935

identify themselves and who collect or purchase so many that they must use a stamp) was less likely to have their signatures invalidated.

Nonetheless, some of the better-known individuals who were compensated for circulating I-917 petitions submitted a substantial number of invalid signatures. Of the 6,272 signatures submitted on petitions with the "signed" declaration of L. Jack Fagan (he typically used an ink-stamp for his "signature"), 17.1 percent were found to be invalid. Fagan and his son, Mike Fagan, both received "compensation from voluntary donations" to a "stand-alone campaign account"—Help Us Help Taxpayers—for their work gathering signatures for Permanent Offense.[17] For his part, Mike Fagan submitted 14,880 signatures (most of which were "signed" with an ink stamp), 15.9 percent of which were rejected as invalid.

Together, Mike Fagan and L. Jack Fagan also submitted five petitions with at least thirteen invalid names (of a possible total of twenty signatures). (Table 8-4 lists eighteen petition sheets with at least eleven invalid signatures.) One of Mike Fagan's petitions with an ink-stamped affidavit, with most of the signatures coming from Adams County, had eleven of the twenty signatures declared invalid because they were not found. Another one of Mike Fagan's ink-stamped petitions, which appears to have been circulated in

Table 8-3. Percentage of Invalid Signatures for I-917, by Type of Petition

	Type of petition					
Reason invalid	With signed affidavit	Hand-signed	Ink-stamped	No affidavit	Total	1990–2000 historical average
Not found (including missing and no match)	14.1	14.3	12.0	11.6	13.8	15.5
Duplicate	3.9	3.8	4.2	5.1	4.0	3.3
Total[a]	17.9	18.1	16.1	16.7	17.7	18.9

a. Totals do not reflect sum of items because of rounding.

Table 8-4. I-917 Petitions with a High Incidence of Invalid Signatures

Secretary of state volume number	Petition page number	Number of invalid signatures	Total number of signatures on petition	Invalid signatures on petition (percent)	Name of signature gatherer on affidavit
1	13	11	20	55.0	Theola Gress
54	25	11	20	55.0	Fred Kidney
63	24	15	17	88.2	None
86	24	12	20	60.0	None
104	24	13	20	65.0	William Fischer
125	25	13	20	65.0	Alvin A. Anders
142	18	13	20	65.0	Theola Gress
236	2	13	20	65.0	Mike Fagan stamp
347	4	13	20	65.0	L. Jack Fagan stamp
383	10	13	20	65.0	Mike Fagan stamp
393	16	13	17	76.5	None
459	6	14	19	73.7	None
493	9	14	20	70.0	Mike Fagan stamp
499	7	14	20	70.0	L. Jack Fagan stamp
499	9	14	20	70.0	Terry Redick
535	17	13	20	65.0	Terry Redick
587	22	13	20	65.0	William Richardson
669	17	14	20	70.0	D. Michael Johnson

Snohomish County, had six valid names, two duplicate names, and twelve names that were not found in the state's voter registration database. It is clear that several of the names on Fagan's petition were intentionally fictitious, including Patrick Patrick, Mike Mike, Charlie Charlie, and Jason Jason.

Petitions with hand-signed and stamped affidavits on the back (including those signed by the Fagans) were more likely than petitions without a signed declaration to have signatures "not found" in the state's voter registration database (including signatures of individuals not found in the database and signatures that did not match those in the database). The average "not found" invalid rate for petitions with signed declarations was 14.1 percent, compared to 11.6 percent for petitions without a signed affidavit. In contrast, petitions with a signed affidavit had a lower duplicate invalid rate (3.9 percent) than petitions without an affidavit (5.1 percent).

The Office of the Secretary of State documented that over 300 individuals signed I-917 petitions at least three times. We are in no position to say whether individuals who signed multiple petitions did so intentionally or unwittingly. Two individuals signed their names and provided their address on at least six different I-917 petitions. For instance, one individual with a Centralia address signed six petitions that were circulated by paid petition gatherers. Several other individuals signed at least four separate I-917 petitions; some of the petitions had backside affidavits stamped with Mike Fagan's signature.

Rates of signature invalidity on petition sheets with unsigned affidavits appear to have been geographically concentrated. In seven counties—Douglas, Grant, Kitsap, Lewis, Skamania, Stevens, and Yakima—the duplicate invalid signature rate on petitions with no petitioner declaration signature exceeded 7.0 percent. In only one county (Lewis, 9.9 percent) did the duplicate invalid signature rate exceed 7.0 percent on petitions with petitioner declaration signatures. Unfortunately, it is impossible to determine the geographic distribution of petitions with "not found" invalid rates, as the secretary of state's office does not enter any contextual data when signature checkers cannot find a name or an address in the state's voter registration database.

The Deterrent Effect of Requiring Affidavits from Petition Circulators

At first blush, the Washington law requiring petitioners to swear to the integrity of the signatures they collect seems to be a reasonable policy that offers the state the ability to maintain the integrity of the signature petition process. The policy provides information about the individual most immediately responsible for, and knowledgeable of, the names that appear on petitions that are submitted to the state. Absent information about the identity of the person who had original custody of the signatures, investigations into signature fraud would likely need to rely on holding campaign organizers, petition crew chiefs, or petition management firms responsible for observed fraud. As of 2006, however, the secretary of state was not required to reject petitions where circulators failed to swear an affidavit. The lack of any enforcement or deterrent effect—no one has been successfully prosecuted despite the fact that signature fraud is a class C felony—may explain why we find only subtle differences in invalid rates between petitions with signed affidavits and those without.

The use of signed affidavits on signature petition sheets could act to deter some measure of signature fraud, but this is likely to work only if signatures on sheets that lack affidavits or have false affidavits are worth less than those that have valid affidavits. If signature gatherers and crew chiefs know that the state can link individual petitions to specific individuals responsible for the petitions, they would have an incentive to be more attentive to the quality of signatures on the petition sheets that they sell to petition management firms. If paid petitions that lack valid affidavits are rejected, crew chiefs and petition management firms would likely become more attentive to the quality of signatures that they purchase from the individuals they contract with. Signatures are a valuable commodity in initiative politics. If campaigns face greater risks when submitting petitions that lack valid affidavits from circulators, the petitions with fraudulent signatures should be worth less than those with valid signatures. Proposed legislation in 2007 would require the secretary of state's office to reject all signatures on petitions without a signed affidavit from the circulator.

If, however, signature gatherers are aware that it is difficult (or impossible) for the state to determine who applied fraudulent signatures to specific petition sheets, they may have limited reason to be deterred from fraud because they cannot be linked to any fraudulent signatures. Likewise, if affidavits are required on petition sheets but the state nonetheless counts toward qualification signatures on petition sheets that lack signed affidavits, the deterrent effect may not hold, since signature gatherers will know that they can still sell petition sheets that fail to include a signed affidavit.

Conclusion

Surveys of statewide public opinion in Washington State reveal that direct democracy is an extremely well-regarded institution. However, there is evidence that public confidence in the process has eroded in recent years. In 1990, more than 80 percent of respondents believed that statewide initiative elections were a good thing for the state.[18] In 2007, this share had fallen to 70 percent. While 95 percent of respondents agreed that the initiative process "allows concerned groups to put things before the voters," 82 percent believed—in the most common complaint—that initiative campaigns are too expensive and misleading.

Our data suggest that the voters have grounds for their concern about the integrity of initiative campaigns. They also indicate that Washington's initial experiment at requiring petitioners to sign affidavits has had little impact on the rate of signature invalidity. More far-reaching reforms are necessary if public confidence in this important democratic institution is to be maintained.

Notes

1. David McCuan and others, "California's Political Warriors: Campaign Professionals and the Initiative Process," in *Citizens as Legislators: Direct Democracy in the*

United States, edited by Shaun Bowler, Todd Donovan, and Caroline J. Tolbert (Ohio State University Press, 1998).

2. Shaun Bowler and Todd Donovan, "The Initiative Process," in *Politics in the American States: A Comparative Analysis*, edited by Virginia Gray and Russell Hanson (Washington: CQ Press, 2004); Todd Donovan, Shaun Bowler, and David McCuan, "Political Consultants and the Initiative Industrial Complex," in *Dangerous Democracy: The Battle over Ballot Initiatives in America*, edited by Larry Sabato, Bruce Larson, and Howard Ernst (Lanham, Md.: Rowman and Littlefield, 2001); Daniel A. Smith, "Initiatives and Referendums: The Effects of Direct Democracy on Candidate Elections," in *The Electoral Challenge: Theory Meets Practice*, edited by Stephen Craig (Washington: CQ Press, 2006).

3. PDC records show that $790,000 was paid by the Committee to Abolish the Estate Tax to Citizen Solutions of Lacey, Washington, for signature collection to qualify Initiative 920 for the November 2006 ballot.

4. Donovan, Bowler, and McCuan, "Political Consultants and the Initiative Industrial Complex;" David Magleby, *Direct Legislation: Voting on Ballot Propositions in the United States* (Johns Hopkins University Press, 1984); Peter Schrag, *Paradise Lost: California's Experience, America's Future* (University of California Press, 1998).

5. P. K. Jameson and Marsha Hosack, "Citizen Initiative in Florida: An Analysis of Florida's Constitutional Initiative Process, Issues, and Statutory Initiative Alternatives," *Florida State University Law Review* 23 (1996): 417–61.

6. Fraudulent signatures are hardly a new problem. Reports of fraud are as old as the process of direct democracy in the American states. In one infamous example from 1912, an Oregon court found that 60 percent of signatures on a popular referendum petition were forged or fraudulent. In 1913, seven measures were removed from the Oklahoma ballot owing to a high proportion of fraudulent signatures, and systematic petition fraud was found in other states during this era, including California and Ohio.

7. Florida State Commission on Government Reform and Oversight, "A Review of the Citizen Initiative Method of Proposing Amendments to the Florida Constitution," Tallahassee, 1995; Jameson and Hosack, "Citizen Initiative in Florida."

8. D.C. Code 1-1001.16 (h) 2001. These facts are detailed in the District of Columbia Court of Appeals decision upholding the board's actions, September 28, 2004, No. 04-AA-957, *Citizens Committee for the D.C. Video Lottery Terminal Initiative* v. *District of Columbia Board of Elections and Ethics*.

9. These facts are detailed in the September 13, 2006, decision of Judge Dirk Sandef, District Court of the Eighth Judicial District, Cascade County, *Montanans for Justice et al.* v. *State of Montana et al.*, CDV No. 06-1162(d), and *Montanans for Justice et al.* v. *State of Montana et al.*, No. DA 06-0634, 2006 MT 277 (October 26, 2006).

10. Quoted in Matt Appuzo, "Fight against 'Judicial Activism' to Continue despite Election Setbacks," Associated Press, November 11, 2006; and in Mike Dennison, "State High Court Rules Out Initiatives," *Billings Gazette*, October 27, 2006.

11. Nolan Clay, "Grand Jury Indicts Three over Signature Gathering," *The Oklahoman,* October 3, 2007.

12. Richard Ellis, *Democratic Delusions: The Initiative Process in America* (University Press of Kansas, 2002); Caroline Tolbert, Dan Lowenstein, and Todd Donovan, "Election Law and Rules for Using Initiatives," in *Citizens as Legislators,* edited by Bowler, Donovan, and Tolbert; M. Dane Waters, *The Initiative and Referendum Almanac* (Carolina Academic Press, 2003).

13. The campaign reported spending $363,000 on signatures. It submitted 266,000. If all of the signatures were paid for, the cost would have been $1.36 per signature.

14. In 2005, the Washington State legislature passed a law requiring signature gatherers for initiatives and popular referendums to sign a declaration on the back of each petition swearing or affirming under penalty of law that they "circulated this sheet of the foregoing petition" and that every person signing the petition "knowingly and without any compensation or promise of compensation willingly signed his or her true name and that the information provided therewith is true and correct." Furthermore, by signing the affidavit, the petitioner acknowledges that forgery of signatures on a petition "constitutes a class C felony." However, on May 31, 2006, the Washington attorney general issued an advisory opinion stating that declared affidavits by petition gatherers did not have to be signed. In its interpretation of the attorney general's opinion, the secretary of state determined he would reject petitions that did not contain the printed declaration but would accept those that had the declaration statement but no accompanying signature.

15. Both authors served as expert witnesses in the lawsuit, *The Washington State Patrol Troopers Association et al.* v. *The State of Washington.* The 100 percent signature check validation data and I-917 scanned petition images were furnished by the Washington State Office of the Secretary of State. We thank Kristeen Hanselman for furnishing us with the data. The signature check validation data contained 677 MS Excel files for the 677 volumes of petitions. Each volume in turn contained up to twenty-six petition pages, and each petition page contained up to twenty signatures. Examining the scanned petition images, we coded three new variables, adding them to the original I-917 MS Excel dataset: (1) whether or not there was a declaration signature on the back of each petition (coded 1 if there was a signature and coded 0 if there was no signature); (2) in cases where there was a "declaration signature" by the petitioner, whether it was "signed" with an ink stamp by the petitioner (coded 1), or if it was hand-signed by the petitioner (coded 0); and (3) if the petitioner's signature (either ink-stamped or hand-signed) on the back of each petition matched the name of known petition gatherers (specifically, L. Jack Fagan, Mike Fagan, Roy Ruffino, and Tim Eyman), if it was signed by another petition gatherer, or if the signature was illegible.

16. A discrepancy exists in the raw data for the number of signatures furnished to us by the Office of the Secretary of State (265,935 signatures), the number of submitted signatures initially reported by that office on July 7, 2006 (266,006), and the totals reported by the Office of the Secretary of State in a September 12, 2006, news release

(266,035). In the September news release, entitled "Initiative 917 does not qualify for ballot," the Office of the Secretary of State reported that the 100 percent check results indicated that of the 266,035 signatures submitted, 219,175 were approved and 46,859 were rejected (an invalidation rate of 17.6 percent). It is unclear why the data received from the Office of the Secretary of State had 100 fewer signatures than reported in the news release, but there are no statistically significant differences between the two totals. To be consistent, we use the raw data provided to us by the Office of the Secretary of State.

17. See "You Did It!" (www.permanent-offense.org, 2007 [January 2008]).

18. Data from the authors' poll of Washington voters, conducted by Applied Research Northwest (1999), and from The Washington Poll, conducted by Pacific Market Research (2006).

part three

Detecting Election Fraud: Techniques and Consequences

nine

The Case of the 2002 General Election

R. Michael Alvarez and Jonathan N. Katz

By its very nature, election fraud—which we define as efforts to use illegal means to alter election outcomes—should be difficult to detect. After all, given that documented evidence of election fraud is highly likely to result in legal action and criminal penalties, agents committing fraud have very strong incentives to cover their tracks. Perhaps the reason we do not observe widespread empirical evidence of election fraud in the United States is that the perpetrators cover their tracks sufficiently to make it difficult to observe and prosecute.

But decades of theoretical and empirical social science research have shown that elections in the United States are highly predictable.[1] Based on a handful of variables, including the state of the national economy, incumbency, and partisanship, we can predict most election outcomes with a high degree of accuracy well before the election occurs. This large body of social science research has two important implications for the study of election fraud. One implication is that because election outcomes are so highly predictable, perhaps election fraud is not widespread in the United States. But the other implication is that unpredictable election outcomes might signal the occurrence of election fraud.

An excellent opportunity to use the theoretical and statistical tools of social science to study election fraud arose in the 2002 general election in Georgia.

We thank Lexi Shankster for her assistance in collecting some of the data used in this chapter.

There, two incumbent Democrats lost their seats in closely contested races: U.S. Senator Max Cleland lost to Republican Saxby Chambliss (45.9 percent to 52.8 percent), while Governor Roy Barnes lost to Republican Sonny Perdue (46.3 percent to 51.4 percent). Not only were the two races close and won by Republicans, but this election was the first large-scale trial of electronic "touch-screen" voting machines in Georgia, a state that in the wake of the 2000 election dispute replaced old punch-card and optical scanning voting devices with the same touch-screen voting system in every precinct.

Allegations that these two races might have been marred by manipulation of the new touch-screen voting system have swirled in the wake of a study of what is reputed to be some of the source code that is used to run certain operations of Georgia's touch-screen voting devices.[2] And the controversy only intensified when the chairman and chief executive of Diebold, the corporation that produced the voting machines used in Georgia, was quoted in a Republican fundraising letter as saying that he was "committed to helping Ohio deliver its electoral votes to the president next year."[3] But was there actually a priori evidence of election fraud in Georgia? In this chapter, we seek to answer this question by combining the statistical approach of outlier detection with the wealth of theoretical and empirical research in political science on elections.

Past Research on Election Fraud

There has been relatively little empirical analysis of election fraud in the social science research literature. There is an extensive literature on the history of election fraud in the United States, including research on fraud during the "Gilded Age" of the late 1800s; much of this literature tries to estimate the extent of election fraud.[4] Other historical studies of American election fraud focus on specific components of the election process and on different geographic locations, such as early twentieth-century Pittsburgh,[5] nineteenth-century New York,[6] Texas,[7] South Carolina,[8] and Mississippi.[9] George Miller examined fraud allegations in his 1948 book on absentee voting, and others have studied allegations of fraudulent voter registration.[10] There is a chapter on election fraud covering the contemporary period in Larry Sabato and Glenn Simpson's 1996 book, *Dirty Little Secrets*.[11]

Outside the United States, scholars have studied election fraud in what Fabrice Lehoucq calls "pre-reform political systems."[12] These are nations that do not meet the minimal requirements for a functioning democracy and thus have electoral administration systems that appear to allow for much more rampant election fraud. Examples include Costa Rica, Imperial Germany, Argentina, and Brazil. The general conclusion of this literature is that political agents attempt to illegally manipulate election outcomes in many different ways; however there is little evidence that these manipulations are decisive in determining electoral winners or losers.[13]

Since 2000, some attention has been paid to alleged electoral irregularities in the 2000 American presidential election (especially in Florida), sparking renewed interest in studying electoral irregularities and fraud. A number of studies have used sophisticated statistical or econometric techniques to try to model election regularities—and to then identify election irregularities, or "outliers."[14] Detected outliers from a precinct-by-precinct or county-by-county analysis can be further examined to determine if they provide a priori evidence of fraud. In this chapter, we build on this work.

Detecting Electoral Fraud with a Model of Elections

The most often discussed approach in the statistical detection of fraud is some sort of outlier analysis. That is, the analyst suspects that some jurisdictions, ballot boxes, or electronic voting machines have been compromised. Although the individual votes usually are not observed, the vote tallies by jurisdiction are observed.[15] Under relatively mild assumptions, all "nearby" jurisdictions— perhaps within the state or region—should have a similar statistical distribution of votes.[16] These nearby jurisdictions can then serve as a benchmark by which to measure the suspect ones.

A simple example is a polling place with multiple machines. Under the assumption that voters are directed to voting machines randomly, all of the machine tallies should be similar, but not necessarily identical, to each other. Formally, we can ask if the distribution of vote tallies across the machines is consistent with a null hypothesis of a common distribution. Numerous tests, parametric and nonparametric, are valid in such a situation, depending on the amount of data available. If the observed vote distributions differ, this could be circumstantial evidence that there was a problem. This type of analysis has been done for some data from Florida counties, though because such finely grained data are hard to come by, this approach is still not common in the study of election outliers.[17]

However, this analysis assumes that we think at least some of the observed jurisdictions or machines have not been compromised. Although this may be a plausible assumption in some circumstances, it may not always be valid. In Georgia in 2002, concern focused on the statewide adoption of Diebold voting machines. There was widespread concern, at least among Democrats, that Diebold, whose senior management had strong ties to the White House and the Republican Party, might tamper with its machines to favor Republican candidates.[18]

In cases such as this, we have no contemporaneous benchmark with which to compare suspect election results. Therefore we focus here on the use of historical data, multiple elections, and political science theory about elections to study whether or not a priori the results of the 2002 elections seem to be inconsistent with historical data from Georgia. The problem with using historical data is that election results can vary for systematic reasons other than fraud, such as whether an incumbent is running. However, we can fit a statistical forecasting model to the data to control for the systematic variations. We are then in a position to test whether a particular election outcome is out of line with our forecasts. If the election result is systematically different from our forecast, this would be circumstantial evidence that there may have been a problem in need of further investigation.

We follow the work of Andrew Gelman and Gary King in developing our forecasting model.[19] The basic idea is to relate fixed characteristics of electoral units, in this case counties, to election outcomes, using a linear regression model. These fixed characteristics may include demographics, as well as past political measures. The forecasts then account both for estimation uncertainty, since we do not know the exact relationship between our predictors and the election results, and for the systematic variation inherent in an election. If a large number of jurisdictions fall outside the confidence region for our forecast, that would be evidence of a potential problem worth further investigation.

The Case of Georgia

In 2002, all 159 counties in Georgia switched to a Diebold electronic voting system. We wanted to know if these 2002 elections differed systematically from earlier elections held using different voting technologies. We focus our analysis on the Senate and gubernatorial races, the top two races on the ballot. By examining statewide elections, we were able to use data from all of the counties in Georgia. Also, by focusing on two races rather than just one, we hoped to reach stronger inferences about potential manipulation and fraud.

As a first look before fitting the model, we compared the 2000 presidential vote with the 2002 elections (see figure 9-1). The individual dots are the

Figure 9-1. Regression of 2002 Gubernatorial Vote on 2000 Presidential Vote
in Georgia[a]

Vote for governor 2002

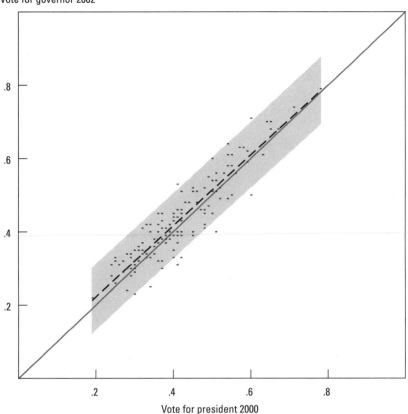

Vote for president 2000

a. The dots represent the vote share in the individual counties. The dashed line is the regression of the gubernatorial vote on the presidential vote, and the shaded region is the 95 percent confidence interval for the regression.

counties. More of the points are above the solid forty-five-degree line than
below it, implying that the vote in most counties was slightly more Democratic in the 2002 race than in the earlier presidential one, although not
enough for the Democrats to win the race. If the presidential vote perfectly
predicted voting in the 2002 election, we would expect to see the points fall
mostly along the line. They are actually not far from it. The dashed line in the
figure is the regression line that best fits these data points, and the shaded
region is the 95 percent confidence interval for this regression line. As we can

Figure 9-2. Regression of 2002 Senate Vote on 2000 Presidential Vote in Georgia[a]

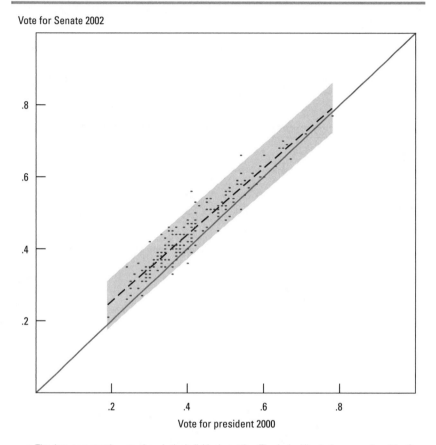

Vote for Senate 2002

Vote for president 2000

a. The dots represent the vote share in the individual counties. The dashed line is the regression of the Senate vote on the presidential vote, and the shaded region is the 95 percent confidence interval for the regression.

see, we cannot reject the hypothesis that the regression line is the same as this forty-five-degree line.

Figure 9-2 shows a similar graph for the 2002 Senate race. Here, too, we see a slight move in the Democratic direction. But once again, when we fit the regression line we cannot reject the hypothesis that each county's 2002 Senate vote tracks its 2000 presidential vote. But these two simple graphs are not the whole story. First, while the 2000 presidential vote may provide some indication of a county's political leanings, there is no strong reason to believe that it should be perfectly correlated with votes in subsequent elections. Instead one might expect differences between the two, perhaps caused by the well-known difference in turnout between presidential and midterm elections.[20] Second, and more important, examining correlations between only two elections fails to account for the known systematic variation among elections.

As a way around these problems we need to fit an actual forecasting model.[21] As predictors in our model we use the previous vote for president in the county, as well as the percentage of the county population that is non-white. We keep our model relatively sparse because we lack many of the sorts of variables that political scientists might use in such a forecasting model. Nonetheless, these two variables predict election outcomes fairly well. This procedure, unlike the earlier graphical analysis, allows the relationship between presidential vote and the results of a subsequent midterm election to differ from unity. We do not particularly care about the coefficients on these variables. All we want to ensure is that we have picked up the systematic variation in elections in the counties. Thus, unlike many other situations in which social scientists would use a multivariate statistical model, we do not care here about getting the "true" model, only a good forecast.

Once we have selected our model, we fit it to past elections. In this case, we fit the model to the 1998 races for governor and Senate, using the 1996 presidential vote as a predictor. Once we have estimated this relationship and have assumed it is constant over our study period, we can forecast the 2002 election. We can than construct our forecast confidence interval and ask if the predicted election results differed from the actual results. (For brevity, the details of our forecast model have been omitted from this discussion.)

The results of our analysis of the governor's race can be found in figure 9-3. Along the vertical axis are the 159 counties. The bar represents the 95 percent forecast confidence interval for that county given the estimates from the 1998 election. The dots represent the actual election results. If our forecast model worked properly, then about 95 percent of the actual election results—that is, all but about seven observations—should have fallen within these bounds. As one can see, our model did not work particularly well, since many of the points are outside the confidence bounds. In fact, in forty-two of the counties, the Democratic share of the vote fell below the low point of the confidence bounds, and none fell above. This suggests that the 2002 election looks systematically different from past elections, with the Democratic candidate doing worse than our forecasting model expected. This could have been caused by fraud, as was suggested by many, or by some sort of structural change in the electorate between the elections.

Figure 9-3. Forecast Errors and Actual Election Results from the 2002 Gubernatorial Election in Georgia[a]

County

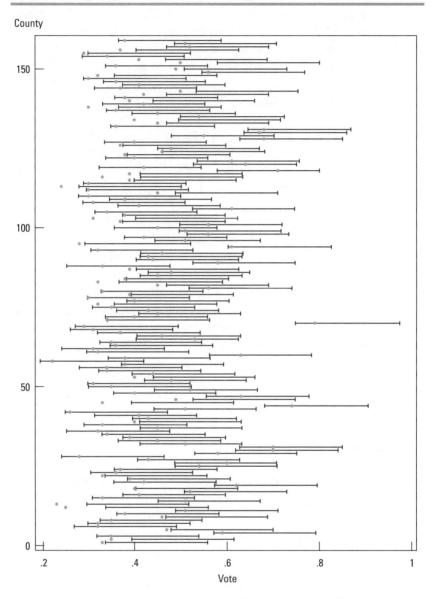

a. The dots represent the actual Democratic share of the vote in election, and the bars are the 95 percent confidence intervals for the forecast model using presidential vote and percentage nonwhite in the county, fitted on the previous pair of elections.

Our analysis of the Senate race can be found in figure 9-4. The setup is exactly the same as for the previous graph. Again, the forecasting model does not come very close to predicting the actual results, although it does better than in the governor's race. The election results were outside the confidence region in thirty-four counties. But in this case the errors were in the opposite direction. That is, the Democratic candidate did better in all instances than the forecasting model had predicted.

The evidence from the governor's race is worrisome when presented in isolation. However, since the forecast errors in the Senate race were always in the pro-Democratic direction, our inference is that concern is unlikely to be warranted. In order for there to be grounds to believe that this evidence indicates tampering with the voting devices used in Georgia, we would need to assume that the voting system vendor (Diebold) or someone else with access to the voting machines would want to rig the gubernatorial election to favor the Republican and the Senate race to favor the Democrat. Given the implausibility of this assumption, we infer that it is unlikely that these results provide a priori evidence of systematic fraud in Georgia's 2002 races. In the end, our analysis supports the conclusion reached by other observers of the 2002 election in Georgia: a combination of poor tactical choices by the Democratic candidates for Senate and governor and a strong pro-Republican tide helped swing the elections to Republicans Saxby Chambliss and Sonny Perdue.[22]

Conclusion

Election fraud is difficult to study and hard to prove. Our analysis here is intended to focus on one example where allegations have been made that voting machine tampering may have created a systematic advantage for one party in all of the electoral races. We find little support for this hypothesis, based on the use of historical election return data, at the county level, and the sort of political forecasting models that have received widespread attention in the academic literature.

It is our belief that the combination of modern statistical techniques and decades of academic research on electoral behavior and election outcomes has much to offer election officials and others interested in studying election data for anomalies and evidence of tampering. The techniques we have applied here are powerful yet simple, and could be used by election officials, policymakers, and others in the future. These tools could be built into simple-to-use software packages that could become part of software suites offered to election officials for postelection auditing. Or, election officials could collaborate with

Figure 9-4. Forecast Errors and Actual Election Results from the 2002 Senate Election in Georgia[a]

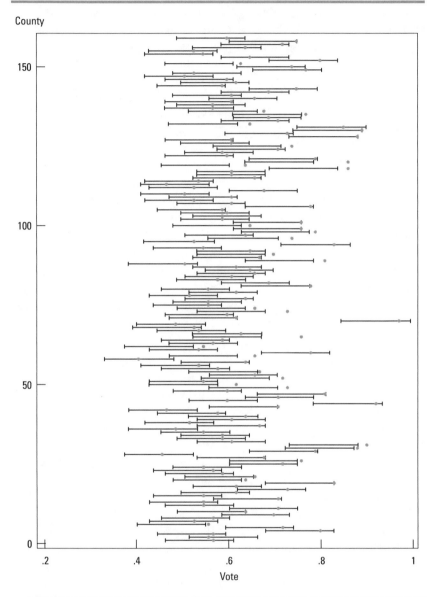

County

Vote

a. The dots represent the actual Democratic share of the vote in the election, and the bars are the 95 percent confidence intervals for the forecast model using presidential vote and percentage nonwhite in the county, fitted on the previous pair of elections.

statistically trained research faculty in local colleges or universities to undertake the type of analysis we used in this chapter.

However, there is one important prerequisite for this type of analysis: access to electoral data from many elections. Unfortunately, the quality of data reported today by many election officials is not sufficient for even the type of county-by-county study we do in this chapter.[23] At a minimum, counties and other election jurisdictions should report, for each election, basic statistical information regarding the administration of that election, including registration, turnout, and valid votes cast for each candidate or measure on the ballot. Even better for outlier detection analysis would be precinct-by-precinct data and data by voting system in each precinct. Finally, these data should be made available in readily usable formats (Excel spreadsheets, comma-delimited ASCII files, or other common database formats) that researchers can download.

Finally, the research community should continue to investigate the use of statistical techniques to study election anomalies, especially where there are allegations of fraud. Our analysis here uses powerful but common statistical tools; future work should explore other statistical approaches for studying election anomalies and outliers, for example, using random-effects and semiparametric models.

Notes

1. Andrew Gelman and Gary King, "Why Are American Presidential Election Campaign Polls So Variable When Votes Are So Predictable?" *British Journal of Political Science* 23 (2003): 409–51; James E. Campbell and James C. Garand, *Before the Vote: Forecasting American National Elections* (Thousand Oaks, Calif.: Sage, 2000).

2. Tadayoshi Kohno, Adam Stubblefield, Aviel D. Rubin, and Dan S. Wallach, "Analysis of an Electronic Voting System," *Security and Privacy, 2004, Proceedings*, IEEE Symposium on Security and Privacy, May 9–12, 2004 (http://ieeexplore.ieee.org/iel5/9120/28916/01301313.pdf?isnumber=28916∏=STD&arnumber=1301313&arnumber=1301313&arSt=+27&ared=+40&arAuthor=Kohno%2C+T.%3B+Stubblefield%2C+A.%3B+Rubin%2C+A.D.%3B+Wallach%2C+D.S. ([January 2008]).

3. John Schwartz, "Executive Calls Vote-Machine Letter an Error," *New York Times*, May 12, 2004.

4. See, for example, P. H. Argersinger, "New Perspectives on Election Fraud in the Gilded Age," *Political Science Quarterly* 100 (1985): 669–87.

5. Loomis Mayfield, "Voting Fraud in Early Twentieth-Century Pittsburgh," *Journal of Interdisciplinary History* 24, no. 1 (1993): 59–84.

6. Gary W. Cox and J. Morgan Kousser, "Turnout and Rural Corruption: New York as a Test Case," *American Journal of Political Science* 25 (1981): 646–63.

7. D. Baum, "Pinpointing Apparent Fraud in the 1861 Texas Secession Referendum," *Journal of Interdisciplinary History* 22 (1991): 201–21.

8. R. F. King, "Counting the Votes: South Carolina's Stolen Election of 1876," *Journal of Interdisciplinary History* 32 (2001): 169–91.

9. L. N. Powell, "Correcting for Fraud: A Quantitative Reassessment of the Mississippi Ratification Election of 1868," *Journal of Southern History* 5 (1989): 633–58.

10. George E. Miller, *Absentee Voters and Suffrage Laws* (Washington: Daylion, 1948); on allegations of voter registration fraud, see Joseph P. Harris, *Election Administration in the United States* (Brookings, 1934); and Alexander Keyssar, *The Right to Vote* (New York: Basic Books, 2000).

11. Larry J. Sabato and Glenn R. Simpson, *Dirty Little Secrets: The Persistence of Corruption in American Politics* (New York: Times Books, 1996).

12. Fabrice Lehoucq, "Election Fraud: Causes, Types and Consequences," *Annual Review of Political Science* 6 (2003): 233–56.

13. F. Lehoucq and I. Molina, *Stuffing the Ballot Box: Fraud, Election Reform and Democratization in Costa Rica* (Cambridge University Press, 2002); M. L. Anderson, *Practicing Democracy: Elections and Political Culture in Imperial Germany* (Princeton University Press, 2000); Hilda Sábato, *The Many and the Few: Political Participation in Republican Buenos Aires* (Stanford University Press, 2001); R. Graham, *Politics and Patronage in Nineteenth-Century Brazil* (Stanford University Press, 1990); Lehoucq, in "Election Fraud," provides a more extensive literature review, covering sources in French and Spanish, in addition to English.

14. See Walter R. Mebane Jr. and Jasjeet S. Sekhon, "Robust Estimation and Outlier Detection for Overdispersed Multinomial Models of Count Data," *American Journal of Political Science* 48 (April 2004): 391–410; Jonathan Wand and others, "The Butterfly Did It: The Aberrant Vote for Buchanan in Palm Beach County, Florida," *American Political Science Review* 95 (2001): 793–810. While this new interest is developing among methodologically sophisticated social scientists, the basic idea of using outlier detection to identify potential electoral fraud has appeared earlier in some historical studies of fraud, including Baum, "Pinpointing Apparent Fraud"; R. C. Oberst and A. Weilage, "Quantitative Tests of Electoral Fraud: The 1982 Sri Lankan Referendum," *Corruption and Reform* 5 (1990): 49–62; and Powell, "Correcting for Fraud."

15. Sometimes it is possible to examine actual ballots, as was the case in 2000 in Palm Beach, Florida. Other jurisdictions (such as Los Angeles County) have in the past made available "ballot-image" data, which could be used for forensic analyses.

16. This type of analysis has been used repeatedly in the relatively small literature on election anomaly detection. For a recent example see Charles Stewart III, "Declaration of Charles Stewart III on Excess Undervotes Cast in Sarasota County, Florida,

for the 13th Congressional District Race," November 20, 2006 (http://electionupdates. caltech.edu/SH81421120.pdf [January 2008]). For another perspective on this approach, see Mebane and Sekhon, "Robust Estimation and Outlier Detection."

17. Walter R. Mebane Jr., "Detecting Attempted Election Theft: Vote Counts, Voting Machines and Benford's Law," paper presented at the 2006 Midwest Political Science Association Annual Convention, Chicago.

18. See, for example, Kim Zetter, "Did E-Vote Firm Patch Election?" Wired News, October 13, 2003 (http://www.wired.com/news/politics/0,1283,60563,00.html [January 2008]).

19. Andrew Gelman and Gary King, "A Unified Method of Evaluating Electoral Systems and Redistricting Plans," *American Political Science Review* 38 (1994): 514–54.

20. Angus Campbell, "Surge and Decline: A Study of Electoral Change," *Public Opinion Quarterly* 25 (1960): 397–418.

21. For an overview of approaches to election forecasting in the context of the 2004 presidential election, see the special issue of *PS: Political Science & Politics* (October 2004): 733–67.

22. David Marks, writing on the message tactics involved in the 2002 Senate and governor's races in Georgia, concluded that Chambliss's message strategy played some role in his ability to defeat Cleland, but that "political events outside the Senate race helped: In the Georgia governor's race that year, the Democratic incumbent Roy Barnes had made changes to the state flag, which minimized its Confederate emblem, an issue that would depress turnout for the governor and by extension the remainder of the Democratic ticket. In the same vein, Cleland's loss was tied, in part, to the sorry fortunes of Georgia Democrats on Election Day 2002, which included the surprise defeat of Barnes, the loss of two new congressional seats expected to go Democratic, and the felling of several prominent state legislators." David Marks, *Going Dirty: The Art of Negative Campaigning* (New York: Rowman and Littlefield, 2006), p. 138.

23. R. Michael Alvarez, Stephen Ansolabehere, and Charles Stewart III, "Studying Elections: Data Quality and Pitfalls in Measuring the Effects of Voting Technologies," *Policy Studies Journal* 33, no. 1 (2005): 15–24.

ten

Election Forensics:
The Second-Digit Benford's Law Test and Recent American Presidential Elections

Walter R. Mebane Jr.

Arguably we are not much closer than we were one hundred years ago to understanding how to administer elections that not only are secure and fair but are widely believed to be secure and fair. As long as there have been elections there have been election scandals, and certainly throughout the history of the United States.[1] Notoriously, serious defects in election administration produced the wrong outcome in the 2000 American election for president.[2] These events sparked a rush to replace older mechanical voting technologies with machines based on electronic computers. Some states made such changes on their own, notably Florida.[3] Others were prompted to change by provisions of the Help America Vote Act of 2002 that made using punch-card ballots and lever machines illegal and provided funds to help pay for their replacement.

Equally important, the 2000 election controversy has prompted the development of new methods for detecting election irregularities. These methods (which I call *election forensics*) are based on statistical tools and are intended to examine elections after the fact. Election forensics focuses on the recorded votes, asking whether there are significant anomalies. Do the votes relate to covariates in ways we should expect, or are some votes outliers?[4] Are there other regularities the votes should exhibit? An earlier study of the conse-

An earlier version of this paper was presented at the Election Fraud Conference, Salt Lake City, Utah, September 29–30, 2006. I thank Herbie Ziskend, Charlie Gibbons, and Gideon Weissman for assistance.

quences of the butterfly ballot in the 2000 presidential election features both of these kinds of analysis.[5] That study finds that the vote for Pat Buchanan in Palm Beach County was a significant outlier, that the vote for Buchanan on election day ballots in Palm Beach County did not relate to the vote on absentee ballots in the same way that it did in other Florida counties, and that the vote for Buchanan did not track the vote for other Reform Party candidates running in Palm Beach County.

Of course the most challenging ambition for election forensics is to detect election fraud. An examination merely of recorded votes and their correlates can never by itself prove that regularities or irregularities the recorded votes may exhibit are the result of fraudulent intentions. But allegations of fraud may identify specific methods purportedly used to perpetrate the fraud, and the forensic analysis may be able to check for traces of those methods. Such an analysis may help reduce suspicions that election results are fraudulent. A study of votes cast in Ohio in the presidential election of 2004 commissioned by the Democratic National Committee documents many problems with the way the election was administered, but it does not find evidence to support charges that George W. Bush won only because tens of thousands of votes that were cast in favor of John Kerry were instead counted as votes for Bush.[6]

The ideal method for conducting election forensics would be one that depends neither on special assumptions about the particular political configurations contesting the election nor on any particular theory about how the election was conducted. Ruled out, for instance, would be ideas about the coalitions supporting a particular party or candidate. In general we should expect a method that is based on particular theories to be more powerful than a method that eschews such foundations, at least if the theories are correct. But any particular theory is likely also to be controversial. A diagnosis of election fraud—or of its absence—that depends on such theorizing may be only as convincing as the theory it depends on.

An ideal method for conducting election forensics would also be one that could be applied routinely, perhaps even automatically, without requiring special expertise or sophisticated technical judgment. Such a method might be the foundation for routine election audits. For instance, election officials might apply a simple test to publicly available information and then perform some kind of intensive manual inspection of places or equipment that performed poorly on the test. All precincts would have a positive probability of undergoing an audit immediately after the election that includes verification of ballot and machine chains of custody and a full manual recount, with the selection probabilities being substantially higher where the routine test had a significant result.

Although such an ideal method may well not exist, in this chapter I want to illustrate the use of one possible candidate. A method that may come close to satisfying our ideal set of requirements is based on an offshoot of Benford's Law. Benford's Law states that in a list of statistical data, such as vote tallies from different precincts, the digits of the numbers that make up those data points follow a specific distribution. In each significant digit position, smaller numerals appear more often than larger numerals. In a set of data that follow Benford's Law, the first significant digit is the number 1 roughly 30 percent of the time.[7] There is what I call a second-digit Benford's Law (2BL) distribution when the first digits have no particular pattern but the second digits of the data points do follow the pattern given by Benford's Law. In this case the second significant digit is 0 (zero) about 12 percent of the time.

Elsewhere I study this second-digit Benford's Law test for vote counts.[8] I identify a pair of flexible mechanisms that may generally characterize vote counts and that satisfy the 2BL distribution in a wide range of circumstances. I show that the 2BL test is sensitive to many patterns of vote count manipulation, including patterns that would occur in some kinds of election fraud. I argue that while the 2BL test may be generally suitable for precinct-level data, it is not useful for vote counts at the level of individual voting machines.

The 2BL test is not precisely theory free, and its suitability for a wide variety of electoral contexts has yet to be demonstrated. But it does fulfill the goal to free tests for election fraud from being bound to a particular idea about the substance of the campaigns or about the grounds for voters' decisions. The 2BL test uses only the vote counts themselves. No covariates are involved, and no statistical models need to be estimated. Given precinct-level vote count data, the test is very quick to compute (the hard part is obtaining the precinct data). But the test results are not sharply diagnostic: using simulations, I show the test can be triggered when votes are not being manipulated at all, and even if manipulation is occurring the test cannot indicate whether the manipulation is due to fraudulent actions.[9]

The relationship between the 2BL test and manual recounts is unclear. While the 2BL test is far from perfect, there are also limits on the kinds of fraud a manual recount may detect. Joseph Harris discusses many kinds of fraud, but there is a basic distinction between two broad classes. One class of fraud involves miscounting the ballots. For example, Harris writes, "The old form of voting fraud—that of repeating—has largely disappeared. It is safer and cheaper to have the election officers steal the election. This may be done by turning in an election return which is not based upon an actual count of the ballots, and does not at all correspond to the votes cast."[10] The other class of fraud involves falsifying ballots: "Another method of stealing an election is to stuff the ballot box with marked ballots, writing in the poll books the names of voters who failed to vote or who have died or moved away."[11] A routine recount may uncover a fraud of the first kind, but it would do nothing to reveal a fraud of the second kind. But the 2BL test may be sensitive to either kind of fraud. A statistical test, such as the 2BL test, and a program of manual recounts may reinforce one another but they are not redundant.

This potential capacity for the 2BL test to signal frauds that a recount cannot catch is of course one of the strongest arguments in its favor during a time, such as now, when many jurisdictions are using electronic voting machines that do not produce a reliable audit trail and so do not allow useful recounts. There is very little reason to think such systems are secure. If malicious software is installed on the machines, then all the vote counts and every available electronic record may be falsified.[12] Such falsification may be done in ways that would escape detection by the 2BL test. Neither the 2BL test nor any other statistical test is a panacea.

I illustrate use of the 2BL test by applying it to some of the precinct-level votes reported in recent American presidential elections. Because the controversies attending some of these election outcomes have been examined using other tools, this kind of survey will, one hopes, help build intuition about what the 2BL test can and cannot do. After briefly describing how to perform the 2BL test and considering some motivation for it, I return to the 2000 election in Florida to see whether the test flags any of the problems that are well documented to have happened there. Notwithstanding Florida's comprehensive reform of election administration after 2000, problems occurred in some places—for example, in Miami-Dade and Broward Counties during the 2002 gubernatorial election[13]—and allegations arose regarding suspected manipulation of the presidential votes in 2004. So I look at data from the 2004 election in Florida. Next I consider whether 2BL test results support the conclusions reached by Mebane and Herron about the 2004 election in Ohio.[14] After that I take a look at 2BL test results for presidential votes from across the United States in 2000 and 2004.

The Second-Digit Benford's Law Test for Vote Counts

The 2BL test for vote counts uses the distribution of second digits shown in table 10-1. The intuition behind the 2BL test is that if the actual distribution of second digits in a set of vote counts differs significantly from the expected distribution, some manipulation may have taken place.[15] Why should Benford's Law

Table 10-1. Frequency of Second Digits according to Benford's Law

Digit	0	1	2	3	4	5	6	7	8	9
Frequency	.120	.114	.109	.104	.100	.097	.093	.090	.088	.085

apply to the second digits of vote counts? This is a challenging question that I address more fully elsewhere.[16] Vote counts are complicated, being produced by several intersecting processes. Individuals decide whether to vote at all and, if so, they decide which candidates or ballot initiatives to choose. Laws and administrative decisions present a menu of alternative methods each person may use to vote: election day voting in person, early voting, provisional ballots or mail-in ballots; on paper, with machine assistance, or some combination of this list. Various rules and practices constrain which methods each person may choose and how the votes recorded in each category are aggregated. Conditions vary across polling places: relatively poor administration in some locations may cause errors to occur more frequently in those places. To motivate the 2BL test we need an argument that shows that such a complex of processes in general implies that the resulting vote counts have digits that follow the 2BL distribution.

Elsewhere I suggest that one way to construct such an argument is to focus on the moment just before each vote gets recorded.[17] When all is said and done, most voters will look at each option on the ballot and have a firm intention either to select an option or not to select an option. Then for whatever reason—momentary confusion, bad eyesight, defective voting technology—a small proportion of those intended votes will not be cast or recorded correctly. A small proportion will be "mistakes." Differences in partisanship, economic class, mobilization campaigns, administrative rules, and other details cause the proportion of voters who intend to choose each candidate or ballot question to vary across precincts. If such variations are combined with small and also varying probabilities of "mistakes" in making or recording each choice, then the resulting precinct vote counts will often follow the 2BL distribution. Simulations illustrate that such a mixture of processes—where the support for each alternative on the ballot varies over precincts and there are varying "mistakes"—can produce 2BL distributions of vote count digits even when the number of voters is constant across precincts. A related mixture process produces 2BL-distributed vote counts when both the support for each alternative and the number of voters varies extensively across precincts.[18] Presumably a wide variety of combinations of these kinds of mechanisms produces 2BL-distributed vote counts. Such a variety presents a rich family of processes that may correspond to what happens in real elections.

In what sense can the 2BL test detect election fraud? Elsewhere I show that if we start with vote counts that follow the 2BL distribution, then add or subtract votes from those counts in various ways, the test statistic used to measure the significance of deviations from the 2BL distribution (the Pearson chi-squared statistic, or $X^2_{B_2}$) will be large.[19] In particular, I present simulations to show that if votes are systematically added or subtracted in precincts where a candidate is already receiving more than the number of votes expected according to the vote-generating process, then the test statistic will tend to be large. In a scenario where the baseline, uncorrupted election process is expected to produce a tied outcome, increasing the vote counts in the manipulated districts by as little as 2 or 3 percent can trigger a significant test result. The test can also be triggered when votes are added or subtracted in precincts where, before the manipulation, the candidate received less than the number of votes expected according to the vote-generating process.

If the amount of manipulation is sufficiently small, the 2BL test will not signal that manipulation has occurred. The 2BL test is not sensitive to manipulations that involve adding or subtracting votes from a moderate number of precincts selected entirely at random. But the test would be triggered if somehow all the votes were replaced with counts generated using some simple random process (for example, Poisson, binomial, or negative binomial counts).

In general we will not be examining only one set of precincts or one set of vote counts. We may be interested in the sets of precincts in different counties or different electoral districts. We may want to look at the votes cast for different candidates, for different offices, or for different ballot items. To get a simple omnibus test result, one could pool all the different vote counts together. But especially in the case where the test rejects the hypothesis that the second digits of all the vote counts follow the 2BL distribution, it will be more perspicuous to test each natural subset of precincts separately. Doing so may allow one to identify for which set of precincts the test is signaling a problem. So the votes recorded for a presidential candidate in all the precincts in a county may be considered a set and tested together, but each county is treated separately.

When computing the 2BL test for multiple sets of precincts, we need to adjust any assessment of statistical significance for the fact that we are looking at multiple tests. The method I use to do this is to adjust the test level applied to hypothesis tests to control the false discovery rate (FDR).[20] Let $t = 1, \ldots, T$ index the T independent sets of precincts being tested. For instance, if we were testing the precincts in a state separately for each county, T might denote the number of counties in the state. Let the significance probability of the test statistic for each set be denoted S_t. In our case this probability is the

upper tail probability of the chi-squared distribution with 9 degrees of freedom (χ_9^2). Sort the values S_t from all T sets from smallest to largest. Let $S_{(t)}$
denote these ordered values, with $S_{(1)}$ being the smallest. For a chosen test
level α (e.g., $\alpha = .05$), let d be the smallest value such that $S_{(d+1)} > (d + 1)\alpha/T$.
This number d is the number of tests rejected by the FDR criterion. If the sec-
ond digits of the vote counts in all of the sets do follow the 2BL distribution,
then we should observe $d = 0$.

Florida 2000 and 2004

For the votes recorded for president in 2000, I have data for precincts in all of
Florida's sixty-seven counties.[21] These data exclude absentee ballots. Five
counties have too few precincts to support a useful analysis (for example,
Baker County has eight precincts). I use the sixty-two counties that have at
least ten precincts.

I computed the 2BL test for the votes recorded for George W. Bush and for
Al Gore. I treated each county's precincts as a separate set, and I also treated
separately the Bush and Gore vote totals. For sixty-two counties and two candidates we have $T = 124$ separate test statistics. Controlling the FDR gives
30.2 as the critical value the largest 2BL statistic must exceed to signal a significant departure from the 2BL distribution.

None of the 2BL test statistics comes close to exceeding that FDR-controlled
critical value. The largest statistic is $X_{B_2}^2 = 28.7$ for the vote for Gore in Charlotte
County. Nine other statistics are larger than the single-test critical value of 16.9:
four statistics are for votes recorded for Bush and five are for votes recorded for
Gore. None of those counties (Calhoun, Charlotte, Dixie, Hendry, Hillsborough, Levy, Manatee, Orange, and St. Johns) is among those associated with the
biggest controversies in 2000. Notably, Duval County has small statistical values
($X_{B_2}^2 < 8$), and the statistics for Palm Beach County are not large. For Palm
Beach, $X_{B_2}^2$ is 11.3 for Gore and 16.8 for Bush. In both counties high proportions
of ballots were spoiled by overvotes.[22]

For the major-party presidential votes recorded in Florida in 2000, then,
the 2BL test does not signal any significant problems. Clearly the test is not
responding to some major distortions that happened in some of the counties.
Neither the overvotes nor the undervotes that plagued voters in the state
cause the test to trigger.

Let's fast forward, then, to 2004.

By 2004, all of Florida's counties used either precinct-tabulated optical scan
or electronic touch-screen voting machine technology. Although these and other

changes significantly improved election administration and reduced the frequency of errors,[23] allegations nonetheless arose that vote totals had been manipulated using both modalities. Allegedly the scanners that tabulated the paper ballots were hacked so that a suspiciously large number of registered Democrats were recorded as voting for Bush.[24] These allegations largely evaporated in light of the finding that registered Democrats had long been voting for the Republican presidential nominee in the referent parts of Florida.[25] Moreover, careful comparisons between parts of the state that used different kinds of voting technology but were otherwise similar failed to turn up significant differences in voting patterns.[26] Finally, a manual reinspection of the ballots in three of the supposedly affected counties found no signs of manipulation.[27] At the other end there were allegations that some counties that used electronic voting machines recorded a surprisingly large number of votes for Bush.[28] The statistical analysis supporting these allegations was widely discredited as unsound, but nonetheless the suspicions they abetted remained in the air.[29]

For computing the 2BL test in Florida in 2004, I have usable precinct data from fifty counties.[30] I compute the 2BL test for the votes recorded for Bush and for Kerry. I include the totals reported for absentee ballots and for early voting, treating these totals as if they are from separate precincts as given in the reported data. For fifty counties and two candidates we have $T = 100$ separate test statistics, which implies an FDR-controlled critical value for the largest 2BL statistic of 29.7.

Once again, none of the 2BL test statistics is larger than the FDR-controlled critical value. One value comes close. For the vote for Bush in Manatee County, $X_{B_2}^2 = 28.5$. The next largest value is $X_{B_2}^2 = 21.4$, for the vote for Bush in Collier County. In all there are eight statistics larger than the single-test critical value of 16.9—three statistics are for votes recorded for Bush and five are for votes recorded for Kerry. Because we are looking at so many different tests, however, these single-test results are not a compelling indication of departures from the 2BL distribution. For the major-party presidential votes recorded at the precinct level in Florida in 2004, the 2BL test does not signal any significant problems.

Ohio 2004

When measured in terms of controversies and challenges, clearly the most important state in the 2004 American presidential election was Ohio. The state's electoral votes were pivotal in determining the Electoral College winner, and indeed the votes from the state were challenged in Congress when the electoral votes were counted.[31] That challenge was prompted in part by a report that documented extensive and serious difficulties voters in the state experienced due to partisan and poor election administration.[32] The Democratic National Committee (DNC) sponsored a study to further document and diagnose what happened in Ohio.[33]

One of the principal findings of the DNC study is that an examination of precinct vote totals from across the state produces "strong evidence against the claim that widespread fraud systematically misallocated votes from Kerry to Bush."[34] This conclusion was based on a study that matched precincts and wards that did not change boundaries between 2002 and 2004 and then examined the relationship between the vote shares for Kerry in 2004 and the vote shares for the Democratic candidate for governor (Tim Hagan) in 2002.

Does the 2BL test support this analysis? To compute the 2BL test, I use the data collected as part of the DNC study for all Ohio precincts. To enhance comparability with the earlier study, I exclude separately reported absentee vote counts. I compute the 2BL test for the votes recorded for Bush and for Kerry. For eighty-eight Ohio counties and two candidates we have $T = 176$ separate test statistics, which implies an FDR-controlled critical value for the largest 2BL statistic of 31.1.

Now, at last, we find a 2BL test statistic that is larger than the FDR-controlled critical value. Of the 176 statistics, one is greater than 31.1. This is the statistic for the vote for Kerry in Summit County, which is $X^2_{B_2} = 42.7$. The next largest value is $X^2_{B_2} = 25.2$, for the vote for Kerry in Scioto County. In all there are twenty-one statistics larger than the single-test critical value of 16.9—nine statistics are for votes recorded for Bush and twelve are for votes recorded for Kerry. Three counties have statistics greater than 16.9 for both candidates' votes, namely, Cuyahoga, Paulding, and Summit Counties.

These results do not in a strict sense call into question the conclusions of the earlier study. Summit is not one of the counties that had constant precinct boundaries from 2002 to 2004, so precincts from Summit County were not included in that analysis. But the high proportion of the statistics that are greater than the critical value for a single test may indicate that there was vote manipulation that the earlier analysis failed to detect. Having set a single-test level of $\alpha = .05$, we might expect about 5 percent of the statistics to exceed the corresponding critical value. But about 12 percent ($21/176 = .119$) of the statistics exceed that value. Of the eighteen counties that have such a statistic, seven are not among the counties that had constant precinct boundaries. Nonetheless, finding that thirteen of the ninety-four statistics that do come from such counties are larger than the single-test critical value is not especially reassuring. Since none of these thirteen statistics is close to the FDR-controlled critical value—for ninety-four tests this would be 29.5—the situation with the constant-boundary counties is one where the test signal has not been turned on but it is not clear that it is firmly off.

Presidential Votes across the United States in 2000 and 2004

We have looked at 2BL test statistics from Florida in 2000 and 2004 and from Ohio in 2004, and we have found only one that is large once we take into account the fact that we are considering many such statistics. Are significant 2BL test results in general rare? If so, it might mean either that election fraud that involves manipulation of the votes is genuinely rare, or that the 2BL test is just not sufficiently sensitive. Or perhaps it is simply that, despite all the controversy attending the voting in Florida and Ohio in recent elections, those states are exceptional in having relatively little of the kinds of vote shifting that the 2BL test in principle is able to detect. Perhaps in other places—or in other notorious places—more large 2BL test statistics will appear.

To get some perspective on this, I analyze precinct data reporting votes for president across the United States in 2000 and 2004. Again I compute the 2BL test for the votes recorded for Bush and for Kerry. Precinct data are not readily available from every state, or necessarily from every county in states for which some data are obtainable. I use data obtained from Dave Leip—for thirty-five states in 2000 and for forty-two states in 2004—supplemented with other information.[35] I compute the 2BL test separately for the precincts in every county that has at least ten precincts. If at least ten precincts remain in the rest of a state, I also compute the test for those precincts together in one set. Except for the data from Ohio in 2004, I include any totals that are reported for absentee ballots as separate precincts. Counting the residual precincts from the small counties in each state as one county, the analysis uses data from 1,726 counties and 130,827 precincts in 2000 and from 1,743 counties and 143,889 precincts in 2004.[36] Controlling the FDR for counties over the whole country in each year—that is, $T = 3,452$ and $T = 3,486$—gives FDR-controlled critical values of about 38.4.

From the box plot display of the distribution of the 2BL test statistics shown in figure 10-1, one can see that there are not many statistics as large as that global FDR-controlled critical value. Indeed, in all there are six counties that have 2BL statistics larger than 38.4: Los Angeles, Calif., and Cook, Ill., in both 2000 and 2004; DuPage, Ill., and Hamilton, Ohio, in 2000; and Summit, Ohio, and Davis, Utah, in 2004. The largest statistics in both years occur for

Figure 10-1. Precinct-Level U.S. 2000 and 2004 Presidential Vote 2BL Test Statistics, by County[a]

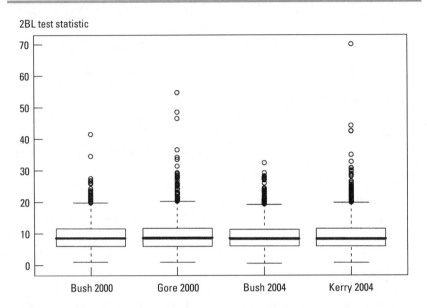

2BL test statistic

a. Each box plot shows the distribution of the 2BL statistics for a candidate's precinct-level vote counts over the 1,726 counties in 2000 and 1,743 counties in 2004.

Los Angeles: the statistic for the votes for Gore is $X^2_{B_2} = 54.8$, and for the votes for Kerry it is $X^2_{B_2} = 70.2$. Four other counties have statistics smaller than 38.4 but large enough to be rejected by the FDR criterion ($d > 1$). These are Latah, Idaho; Lake, Ill.; Hancock, Ohio (the votes for Gore); and Philadelphia (the vote for Bush) in 2000, and DuPage, Ill., (the vote for Kerry) in 2004.

The omnibus FDR-controlled critical value is lofty indeed. More pragmatically—but less skeptically—we might consider each county together with only the other counties in the same state. Such a perspective would be relevant, for instance, if each state's election officials were to use the 2BL test to screen the election results from their state. In this case it is reasonable to determine the FDR-controlled critical values for each state by taking into account only the number of test statistics that may be computed for that state. That is, *T* equals the number of counties in the state for which there are usable data, multiplied by the number of candidates for whose vote totals we are computing the test. Table 10-2 shows the results of applying state-specific FDR control. The list includes a mix of urban and rural places.

Table 10-2. Counties with Significant 2BL Tests Using State-Specific FDR Control

County	J	2000 Gore votes d_2	$X^2_{B_2}$	Bush votes d_2	$X^2_{B_2}$
Los Angeles, Calif.	5,045	5,011	54.8	4,930	20.3
San Bernardino, Calif.	910	854	28.0	865	6.9
Kent, Del.	61	61	9.0	61	22.2
Latah, Idaho	34	31	36.7	34	3.8
Cook, Ill.	5,179	5,097	46.7	4,145	24.4
Dupage, Ill.	714	714	28.0	714	41.6
Lake, Ill.	403	403	33.7	402	16.1
Passaic, N.J.	295	295	27.7	294	5.6
Hamilton, Ohio	1,025	1,020	48.7	988	8.9
Hancock, Ohio	67	67	34.3	67	9.9
Summit, Ohio	624	624	31.6	612	11.6
Summit, Ohio	624	624	31.6	612	11.6
Lancaster, Pa.	225	225	29.1	225	8.3
Philadelphia, Pa.	1,681	1,680	29.5	1,249	34.7
King, Wash.	2,683	2,665	27.0	2,641	8.9

County	J	2004 Kerry votes d_2	$X^2_{B_2}$	Bush votes d_2	$X^2_{B_2}$
Alameda, Calif.	997	890	26.7	862	9.7
Glenn, Calif.	23	23	2.8	23	27.9
Los Angeles, Calif.	4,984	4,951	70.2	4,929	12.4
Nevada, Calif.	134	123	13.5	121	24.0
Orange, Calif.	1,985	1,887	26.2	1,904	32.6
San Francisco, Calif.	577	577	28.7	568	16.9
Jefferson, Colo.	324	323	30.0	323	10.4
Kootenai, Idaho	75	75	30.9	75	12.1
Cook, Ill.	4,562	4,561	44.5	4,026	27.8
DuPage, Ill.	732	732	35.2	732	9.1
Rock Island, Ill.	121	121	24.2	121	8.4
Clay, Mo.	76	76	28.4	76	4.0
Summit, Ohio	475	475	42.7	474	21.0
Davis, Utah	213	212	42.6	213	6.0
Utah, Utah	247	241	9.2	246	27.6
Benton, Wash.	177	168	29.2	173	14.8

In 1934, Harris presented case studies detailing election frauds in four cities: Philadelphia, Chicago, Pittsburgh, and Cleveland. He wrote, "Recent investigations have brought to light election scandals in the particular cities covered, but it would be a mistake to assume that other cities are free of election frauds."[37] Nearly seventy years later, the 2BL test marks three of these cities as worrisome. Of course the county containing Chicago (Cook) and its adjacent neighbors (DuPage and Lake) has already been flagged as having significant 2BL test statistics even when the omnibus FDR control is imposed, as has Philadelphia in 2000. Summit, Ohio, is adjacent to Cleveland. Cook, DuPage, and Summit appear in table 10-3 in both 2000 and 2004. In 2004 the statistics for Philadelphia exceed the single-test critical value but are not larger than the FDR-controlled critical values. Philadelphia has $X_{B_2}^2 = 21.8$ and $X_{B_2}^2 = 23.4$ respectively for Kerry's and Bush's vote totals. Pittsburgh escapes inclusion.[38]

The 2004 result for Davis, Utah, highlights the importance of knowing how reported vote totals are being produced. The precise set of choices presented to each voter can strongly affect the 2BL test. Utah allows voters to cast a "straight party" vote. A voter who does this automatically casts a vote for every candidate who is affiliated with the indicated party. For Davis County the number of straight party votes is available for each precinct.[39] For both the Republican Party ($X_{B_2}^2 = 6.6$) and the Democratic Party ($X_{B_2}^2 = 8.1$), the 2BL test statistics for the straight party vote counts are not large. The statistic is also not large for the candidate-specific votes cast for Bush ($X_{B_2}^2 = 13.2$). The 2BL statistic for the candidate-specific votes cast for Kerry just exceeds the critical value for a single test ($X_{B_2}^2 = 17.0$). It is intriguing that the 2BL test statistic for the precinct sums of the straight party Democratic votes and the candidate-specific votes for Kerry ($X_{B_2}^2 = 42.6$) is so much larger than the statistics for the separate components. Because the straight party and candidate-specific options reflect distinct choices each voter can make, my more general analysis of the 2BL test motivates applying the test separately to each kind of vote total.[40] In that analysis I identify mechanisms that generate 2BL-distributed vote counts for a wide range of parameters that represent the votes' behavioral context, but that analysis does not imply that sums of such counts will be 2BL-distributed when the counts come from heterogeneous contexts. Indeed, too much heterogeneity will conflict with the formal requirement that the counts are mixtures of a small number of random distributions.[41] A choice to vote the party line is on its face very different from a choice not to vote the party line but instead to vote separately for the party's presidential candidate. Presumably this point applies to vote counts for partisan offices from any jurisdiction that allows a straight party option, which would include the vote data from all of Utah. But the point does not apply in an entirely straightforward way. For Salt Lake County the 2BL test statistics are not large if applied to the total of all votes counted for Bush ($X_{B_2}^2 = 15.3$) or for Kerry ($X_{B_2}^2 = 8.9$), but the statistic for the counts of the Kerry-specific votes is large ($X_{B_2}^2 = 37.2$).

The large 2BL statistics for Los Angeles County certainly catch one's attention. Subdividing the data from the county mitigates the significant results to

Table 10-3. Selected 2BL Tests for Parts of Los Angeles County, California

| | | 2000 | | | |
| | | Gore votes | | Bush votes | |
Part of county	J	d_2	$X^2_{B_2}$	d_2	$X^2_{B_2}$
Absentee group	82	48	8.4	40	9.1
Not absentee	4,963	4,963	55.6	4,890	21.4
Los Angeles City	1,757	1,757	27.0	1,719	19.0
Not Los Angeles City	3,206	3,206	38.6	3,171	18.4
		2004			
		Kerry votes		Bush votes	
Part of county	J	d_2	$X^2_{B_2}$	d_2	$X^2_{B_2}$
Absentee group	382	349	11.2	328	11.3
Not absentee	4,602	4,602	68.4	4,601	12.1
Los Angeles City	1,658	1,658	19.4	1,657	6.1
Not Los Angeles City	2,944	2,944	55.0	2,944	11.2

some extent. Table 10-3 shows, first, that significant 2BL statistics do not occur for the absentee groups in the data, but very large statistics occur for the collection of all the remaining precincts in each year. Treating the nonabsentee precincts from the city of Los Angeles separately, we find significant statistics both for the Los Angeles city precincts and for the remainder of the precincts. If we go further and treat each city in the county separately, then the number of cities that have at least ten precincts is eighty-eight in 2000 and eighty-three in 2004. For this analysis I group the smaller cities together and treat them as a set (encompassing 293 precincts in 2000 and 308 precincts in 2004). No city has a value of $X^2_{B_2}$ larger than the FDR-controlled critical values for each respective year. In 2000, nine 2BL statistics are greater than the single-test critical value; in 2004, twenty statistics are greater. This gives proportions of nominally large values of respectively $9/178 = .05$ and $20/168 = .12$. Perhaps the proportion of .05 is reassuring for the 2000 data, but the proportion of .12 echoes the naggingly worrying proportion observed for the 2004 data from Ohio.

For counties over the whole country, the frequency of large 2BL test statistics does not greatly exceed the nominally expected values. There are 234 2BL test statistics greater than the single-test critical value in 2000, and there are 226 test statistics in 2004 that are that large. These counts imply proportions of large statistics not much greater than the single-test level of $\alpha = .05$ would suggest. We have $234/3,422 = .068$ in 2000 and $226/3,448 = .066$ in 2004. Even more then, perhaps, does the much higher proportion of nominally large 2BL statistics found for Ohio 2004 stand out.

Conclusion

The good news is that, as measured by the 2BL test, signs of election fraud in recent American presidential votes seem to be rare. Several of the places that turn up with significantly large 2BL test statistics have been notorious for a century or more. That the 2BL test finds these places suggests it may be on to something. It is beyond the scope of this simple test to tell whether that something is a set of serious problems or a set of innocuous anomalies. If one wishes to lean on some of the places' notoriety, then these results using data from actual American elections may tend to reinforce the simulation results that show the 2BL test can spot many patterns of manipulation in vote counts.[42]

A significant 2BL test result is not in itself proof of fraud. For the vote counts from Davis, Utah, the test picked up the fact that two different kinds of votes were being added together in each precinct—the vote counts were sums of straight party votes and candidate-specific votes; but once the component votes were separated, indications that the votes were manipulated mostly dissipated. The marginally significant 2BL statistic found for the candidate-specific votes for Kerry might justify additional checks to verify the vote counts' accuracy, but in light of the large number of test statistics being examined from different places, the value of $X^2_{B_2} = 17.0$ is not significant if the FDR is controlled. Indeed, taking into account only the test statistics for the straight-party Democratic votes and the votes for Kerry in Davis County, so that $T = 2$, the FDR-controlled critical value corresponding to a single-test level of $\alpha = .05$ is 19.0.

The 2BL test is strikingly insensitive to some kinds of distortions that we know affected many votes. The most interesting case here is Florida in 2000. Notwithstanding the well-established fact that tens of thousands of votes were lost to undervotes and overvotes throughout the state, the 2BL test does not signal any significant problems with the precinct vote totals. The 2BL test gives a mixed message about Ohio in 2004. We can clearly reject the hypothesis that precinct vote counts throughout the state follow the 2BL distribution. The 2BL test statistic for Summit County is significantly large even when we take the FDR fully into account. Also, suspiciously many counties have 2BL test statistics that exceed the critical value we would use if we were looking at only one test. The 2BL test results do not overturn previous judgments that manipulation of reported vote totals did not determine the election outcome in Ohio, but neither do they completely dissipate the odor of suspicion that continues to hang over the state's results.

On the whole, this look at recent presidential election results through the lens of the 2BL test enhances the case that the test is worth taking seriously as a statistical test for election fraud. The 2BL test cannot detect all kinds of fraud, and significant 2BL test results may occur even when vote counts are in no way fraudulent. But, considering the results from Florida in 2000, the test seems not to be confused by some kinds of distortions in elections that do not involve manipulating the vote totals. Further investigations of the test's performance are clearly warranted.

In any case, the 2BL test on its own should not be considered proof either that election fraud has occurred or that an election was clean. A significant 2BL test result can be caused by complications other than fraud. Some kinds of fraud the 2BL test cannot detect. Indeed, in the worst imaginable case, where someone is able to fake an entire set of precinct vote counts, it would not be difficult to use fraudulent counts with second digits that follow the 2BL distribution. If simulation mechanisms similar to those I have discussed in previous work were used,[43] it would not be difficult to produce completely faked vote counts that also satisfy additional constraints such as having the artificial vote totals match the number of voters who actually turned out to vote on election day. But the larger the number of independent constraints the counts must satisfy, the more difficult it may be to produce faked counts that can escape detection. This is where statistical testing for fraud, with analysis using covariates and beliefs about relationships the vote counts should satisfy, may be helpful. When suitable data are available, additional analysis using covariates, robust estimation, and outlier detection should be conducted.[44] Such analysis may help to diagnose the origins and perhaps put bounds on the scope of any anomalies in the vote counts.

Ultimately, however, statistical analysis after the fact can accomplish only so much. To permit statistical testing to occur in a way that can make a difference, it is crucial that the highly disaggregated data needed to support analysis be made available in as timely a manner as possible. This includes not only the precinct level vote totals needed for the 2BL test, but also information about voting machines, poll workers, voter registration, the number of ballots cast, ballot formats, and other data that other analytical methods can use. Candidates, parties, political activists, citizens, and other observers may need to take steps well in advance of the election to make sure local election administrators will be able to supply the necessary data in time to inform any election contests that may occur. But to prevent election fraud, appropriate practices need to be used while the election is being conducted. Insecure or opaque voting technology or election administration procedures should not be used. The election environment should not foment chaos and confusion. Not only should elections be secure and fair, but everyone should know they are secure and fair.

Notes

1. Andrew Gumbel, *Steal This Vote* (New York: Nation Books, 2005).

2. Jonathan Wand, Kenneth Shotts, Jasjeet S. Sekhon, Walter R. Mebane Jr., Michael Herron, and Henry E. Brady, "The Butterfly Did It: The Aberrant Vote for Buchanan in Palm Beach County, Florida," *American Political Science Review* 95 (December 2001): 793–810; Walter R. Mebane Jr., "The Wrong Man Is President! Overvotes in the 2000 Presidential Election in Florida," *Perspectives on Politics* 2 (September 2004): 525–35.

3. Susan A. MacManus, "Goodbye Chads, Butterfly Ballots, Overvotes and Recount Ruckuses! Election Reform in Florida: 2000–2003," in *Election Reform: Politics and Policy*, edited by Daniel J Palazzolo and James W. Ceaser (Lanham, Md.: Lexington Books, 2004), pp. 377–58.

4. Walter R. Mebane Jr. and Jasjeet S. Sekhon, "Robust Estimation and Outlier Detection for Overdispersed Multinomial Models of Count Data," *American Journal of Political Science* 48 (April 2004): 392–411.

5. Wand and others, "The Butterfly Did It."

6. Walter R. Mebane Jr. and Michael C. Herron, "Ohio 2004 Election: Turnout, Residual Votes and Votes in Precincts and Wards," in *Democracy at Risk: The 2004 Election in Ohio*, edited by Democratic National Committee Voting Rights Institute (Washington: Democratic National Committee, June 2005).

7. Ralph A. Raimi, "The First Digit Problem," *American Mathematical Monthly* 83, no. 7 (1976): 521–38; Theodore P. Hill, "A Statistical Derivation of the Significant-Digit Law," *Statistical Science* 10 (1995): 354–63.

8. Walter R. Mebane Jr., "Election Forensics: Vote Counts and Benford's Law," paper presented at the 2006 Summer Meeting of the Political Methodology Society, University of California, Davis, July 20–22, 2006.

9. Ibid.

10. Harris, *Election Administration*, p. 262.

11. Ibid.

12. Ariel J. Feldman, J. Alex Halderman, and Edward W. Felten, "Security Analysis of the Diebold AccuVote-TS Voting Machine" (http://itpolicy.princeton.edu/voting [September 13, 2006]).

13. Dana Canedy, "Again, Sunshine State Is in Dark a Day after the Vote," *New York Times*, September 12, 2002, online edition; Dana Canedy, "Order Soundly Defeats Chaos as Florida County Goes to Polls," *New York Times*, March 12, 2003, online edition.

14. Mebane and Herron, "Ohio 2004 Election."

15. Let $q_{B_2 i}$ denote the expected relative frequency with which the second digit is i. These $q_{B_2 i}$ values are the values shown for each digit in table 10-1. Let d_{2i} be the number of times the second digit is i among the J precincts being considered, and let $d_2 = \sum_{i=0}^{9} d_{2i}$ denote the total number of second digits. If some precincts have vote counts of less than 10, then those small counts lack a second digit and $d_2 < J$. The statistic I use for a 2BL test is the Pearson chi-squared statistic:

$$X_{B_2}^2 = \sum_{i=0}^{9} \frac{(d_{2i} - d_2 q_{B_2 i})^2}{d_2 q_{B_2 i}}.$$

These statistics may be compared to the chi-squared distribution with 9 degrees of freedom (χ_9^2), which has a critical value of 16.9 for a .05-level test.

16. Mebane, "Election Forensics."

17. Ibid.

18. Ibid.

19. Ibid.

20. Yoav Benjamini and Yosef Hochberg, "Controlling the False Discovery Rate: A Practical and Powerful Approach to Multiple Testing," *Journal of the Royal Statistical Society* Series B, 57, no. 1 (1995): 289–300.

21. Data come from Florida Legislative Staff, "FREDS 2000 data set, PlanStatistics T00.zip," 2001 (http://www.flsenate.gov/senateredistricting/freds_data.cfm,file precinct00_pl.zip. [November 16, 2001]).

22. Effects of the butterfly ballot on the vote recorded for Buchanan in Palm Beach are apparent: $X_{B_2}^2 = 19.4$. Because Buchanan received so few votes, this result is a bit suspect. The votes for Buchanan exceed 10, so the vote count has a second digit in only 113 of the 534 Palm Beach County election day precincts for which the FREDS 2000 data set (Florida Legislative Staff) includes data.

23. MacManus, "Goodbye Chads."

24. Manuel Roig-Franzia and Dan Keating, "Latest Conspiracy Theory—Kerry Won—Hits the Ether," *Washington Post*, November 10, 2004, p. A2.

25. Walter R. Mebane Jr., ``Communications Regarding Optical Voting Machines in Florida, 2004" (http://macht.arts.cornell.edu/wrm1/commondreams/common dreams.html [November 8, 2004]) and (http://macht.arts.cornell.edu/wrm1/us together/ustogether.html [November 12, 2004]).

26. Jasjeet S. Sekhon, "The 2004 Florida Optical Voting Machine Controversy: A Causal Analysis Using Matching" (http://sekhon.berkeley.edu/papers/SekhonOptical Match.pdf [November 14, 2004]); Jonathan N. Wand, "Evaluating the Impact of Voting Technology on the Tabulation of Voter Preferences: The 2004 Presidential Election in Florida" (http://wand.stanford.edu/elections/us/FL2004/WandFlorida2004.pdf [November 15, 2004]).

27. Meg Laughlin and David Kidwell, "No Flaw Is Found in Bush's State Win," *Miami Herald*, November 28, 2004, online edition.

28. Kim Zetter, "Researchers: Florida Vote Fishy," *Wired* (http://www.wired.com/news/evote/0,2645,65757,00.html [November 18, 2004]).

29. Mark Crispin Miller, *Fooled Again* (New York: Basic Books, 2005).

30. The counties are Alachua, Bay, Bradford, Brevard, Broward, Calhoun, Charlotte, Citrus, Clay, Collier, Columbia, Dixie, Duval, Escambia, Flagler, Gadsden, Gilchrist, Gulf, Hamilton, Hardee, Hendry, Highlands, Hillsborough, Holmes, Indian River, Jackson, Lake, Lee, Leon, Levy, Manatee, Marion, Martin, Miami-Dade, Nassau, Okaloosa, Okeechobee, Orange, Palm Beach, Pasco, Pinellas, Putnam, Sarasota, Seminole, St. Johns, Sumter, Suwannee, Taylor, Wakulla and Walton counties. Data are from Dave Leip (http://www.uselectionatlas.org).

31. Sheryl Gay Stolberg and James Dao, "Congress Ratifies Bush Victory after a Rare Challenge," *New York Times*, January 7, 2005, online edition.

32. House Judiciary Committee Democratic Staff, "Preserving Democracy: What Went Wrong in Ohio" (http://www.house.gov/judiciary_democrats/ohiostatusrept 1505.pdf [2005]).

33. Voting Rights Institute, Democratic National Committee, *Democracy at Risk: The 2004 Election in Ohio* (Washington: Democratic National Committee, June 2005).

34. Mebane and Herron, "Ohio 2004 Election," p. 2.

35. Data for Florida in 2000 and Ohio in 2004 are as described above. For Pennsylvania in 2004 I use data obtained from the Pennsylvania State Election Commission (in a file named PA-2004G-Presidential.xls). For Nebraska in 2004 I use data from the secretary of state. I downloaded data for Cook County, Ill., in 2004 from the Cook County and Chicago election board websites.

36. The states with at least one county in the analysis in 2000 are Alaska, Alabama, Arkansas, Arizona, California, the District of Columbia, Delaware, Florida, Hawaii, Iowa, Idaho, Illinois, Indiana, Kansas, Louisiana, Maine, Michigan, Minnesota, Montana, North Carolina, North Dakota, New Hampshire, New Jersey, New York, Ohio, Pennsylvania, Rhode Island, South Carolina, South Dakota, Tennessee, Virginia, Vermont, Washington, Wisconsin, and Wyoming. For 2004 the states with at least one county in the analysis are Alaska, Alabama, Arkansas, Arizona, California, Colorado, the District of Columbia, Delaware, Florida, Georgia, Hawaii, Iowa, Idaho, Illinois, Indiana, Kansas, Louisiana, Maryland, Maine, Michigan, Minnesota, Missouri, Montana, North Carolina, North Dakota, Nebraska, New Hampshire, New Jersey, New Mexico, Nevada, New York, Ohio, Oregon, Pennsylvania, Rhode Island, South Carolina, South Dakota, Tennessee, Texas, Utah, Virginia, Vermont, Washington, Wisconsin, and Wyoming.

37. Harris, *Election Administration*, p. 320.

38. Allegheny County has $X^2_{B_2} = 21.2$ for the votes for Gore but 2BL statistics less than 16.9 for Bush in 2000 and for both Bush and Kerry in 2004.

39. I downloaded the data from the website of the Davis County Clerk.

40. Mebane, "Election Forensics."

41. If too many heterogeneous counts are summed, then the law of large numbers will mean the sum has approximately a normal distribution. A normal variate does not have 2BL-distributed digits.

42. Mebane, "Election Forensics."

43. Ibid.

44. Mebane and Sekhon, "Robust Estimation and Outlier Detection."

eleven

On the Trail of Fraud: Estimating the Flow of Votes between Russia's Elections

Mikhail Myagkov, Peter C. Ordeshook, and Dimitry Shaikin

Although the outcome of Russia's 2004 presidential election was never in doubt, the balloting nonetheless yielded surprises. For example, in Ingushetia and Kabardino-Balkaria, ostensibly 98 percent of the eligible electorate voted, with 96 percent supporting the winner and incumbent Vladimir Putin. Even higher numbers were officially registered in various parts of Tatarstan, Dage-stan, Mordovia, Adigeya, Chechnya, Bashkiria, Karachaevo-Cherkessya, and North Ossetia. Of course, no one questions that Putin's 71 percent share of the vote was a decisive reflection of his popularity. Yet we should ask whether such numbers are consistent with previous voting patterns. And if they are not, do such inconsistencies constitute evidence of the strategic maneuvering of political elites and of substantial fraud?

In this chapter, we argue that these questions can be addressed in part by estimating the flow of votes across elections, based on official election returns. In other words, we estimate whom the voters for one party in a given election turned to in the next (and how many voters simply stayed home). Such an analysis can highlight anomalies, suggesting, for example, that in some regions Putin's vote count may have been boosted by loyal local elites. More encouragingly, it can also reveal the stable components of an electorate—voters who

This research was supported by a grant to the California Institute of Technology by the National Council for Eurasian and East European Research.

vote consistently for parties and candidates of the same ideological ilk and who might then be the basis for a coherent party system.

Russia's Recent Elections

In the years since Russia's 2004 electoral cycle, questions have persisted as to the fairness of voting there and the extent to which manipulations facilitated Putin's landslide reelection. Surely in a state where the challengers to the Kremlin's authority were more likely to win a prison term than public office, allegations of fraud are credible. Such charges were made in the 2003 Duma contest wherein the Kremlin wrested away full control of that parliament. But the opposition's demand for a recount and reexamination of vote tallies went nowhere. In contrast, Putin's overwhelming victory in 2004 made protest of the outcome seem silly and any recount irrelevant.

Nevertheless, understanding what happened in those elections is impor-tant if only because we need to know whether Russia can still be a democracy or whether elections there have evolved into a Soviet-like sham, manipulated by Kremlin insiders or other elites as part of a reemergence of authoritarian rule. For example, how did Edinstvo in 1999, formed only months before the election, secure a plurality over the more established Otechestvo with its ostensible roots in the older Kremlin-sanctioned party in 1995? Why was the "party of power," United Russia, so much more successful in 2003 than its Kremlin-sanctioned predecessors? Did the drastic decline in support for the Communist Party and various liberal reformist blocs signal a wholesale aban-donment of the left and right for Putin's presumed middle-of-the road posi-tion, or did their supporters simply stay home, alienated from what had become the mainstream of Russia's electoral politics? Did United Russia suc-ceed in uniting the 1999 electoral bases of two earlier parties—Edinstvo ("Unity") and Otechestvo ("Fatherland")—or did it benefit from other, more sinister sources of votes? And to what extent did fraud, orchestrated by the Kremlin or engineered by regional elites courting favor with Putin, taint his victory in 2004?

We examine these questions by developing and applying an econometric method to official data to trace the electoral preferences of Russian voters from 1995 through 2004. Our data set consists of approximately 2,600 ob-servations—official returns for all *rayons* (read "counties") whose geo-graphic definitions remain essentially constant over the period considered. In the next section we briefly summarize some results reported elsewhere,

where the primary conclusion is that electoral preferences in Russia appear to have remained largely stable from 1995 to 2000, with vote flows between candidates and parties consistent with what we know about the ideological orientations of the electorate and elites.[1] That research, however, relied on a Goodman regression despite the use of rayon-level aggregated data. Therefore, we next offer a generalization of the Chambers-Steel methodology for treating such data.[2] We also reconsider the results of previous analyses and extend those results to 2003 and 2004. Briefly, the findings of earlier analyses remain largely unchanged, but we do find reasons for suspecting that Putin's 2004 vote was artificially augmented to avoid any need for a runoff. Our core conclusions, then, are that the Russian electorate has changed less significantly than the Kremlin's control of Russia's electoral processes, and that econometric techniques applied to official election returns can be used to reveal suspicious patterns in the data. We emphasize that our analysis is in no way intended as an alternative to conclusions derived from public opinion polls or expert observations of the internal machinations of Russia's politics. At the same time, though, we hope here to provide a methodology that can be used to support or question hypotheses established by other means, or to formulate hypotheses that require investigation using other methodologies, including hypotheses about the likelihood of falsified election returns.

Stability of the Russian Electorate, 1995–2000

Allegations of election fraud and dubious campaign tactics first appeared in the December 1993 Duma election and the referendum on Russia's new Constitution.[3] Nevertheless, voting patterns in each of Russia's parliamentary and presidential elections between 1995 and 2000 seem to reflect the electorate's well-studied preferences.[4] In addition, the estimated flow of votes from one candidate (or party) to another across elections matched what we know about Russian politics and electoral preferences based on both academic and anecdotal evidence.[5] Put simply, ideology correlated consistently and predictably with electoral choice, as have various socioeconomic variables such as age, income, level of urbanization, and so on. The primary difference between Russian and Western voters was the apparent tolerance of Russians for economic hardship. Rather than focus on the economic performance of incumbent governments, Russians appeared to pay more attention to the ideological stances of parties or candidates.[6] Even the unexpected success of the ultranationalist Vladimir Zhirinovskii and his Liberal Democratic Party of

Russia (LDPR) in 1993 was, arguably, the consequence of voter ideology and not some specific cost-benefit analysis about which party or candidate was most likely to benefit the voter economically.

Looking first, then, at Russia's parliamentary contests between 1995 and 1999, and avoiding expanding the scope of this essay to include any discussion of issues and personalities, I find several things worth noting about these Duma contests. First, electoral preferences and voting patterns appear to have remained remarkably stable and consistent throughout the period, as revealed by a crude breakdown of the support for various parties of the left, right, and nationalists. Briefly, the two major communist parties (Gennady Zyuganov's Communist Party of the Russian Federation [CPRF] and Viktor Ampilov's Communist Party of the Soviet Union [CPSU]) received 26.5 percent in 1999 and 26.8 percent in 1995. Liberal reformers (Grigorii Yavlinskii's Yabloko and the Union of Right Forces [SPS]) scored 14.5 percent in 1999 and thereby maintained almost the same level of support that reformers won four years earlier: 13.5 percent (Yabloko, Russia's Choice (RC), Boris Fedorov's Ahead Russia (AR), and Irina Khakamada's Common Cause (CC)). Only the nationalist Vladimir Zhirinovskii's LDPR saw its support decline from 11 percent to 6 percent, which still kept him (and his faction) represented in the Duma.

In interpreting these results keep in mind that because parties largely lacked any institutional substructure (except perhaps the CPRF), they consequently failed to utilize any electoral mandate to expand their electoral base. The electoral support of both the right and left electoral blocs, then, can be explained in 1999 by the same basic independent variables (rural/urban, age, education, residence in particular regions) as before, with the old cleavage between pro- and antireform movements remaining in force. Thus, if one neglects for a moment the appearance of Edinstvo and Otechestvo in 1999, a significant share of voters give the appearance of being frozen. An analysis of vote flows using a Goodman regression tells a similar story. In previous work we reported these estimated flows between 1995 and 1999 and estimated that virtually all of Yabloko's 1999 vote came from two sources, its own earlier vote (47 percent) and 10 percent of those who had voted for SPS, that the CPRF's vote came essentially from its own earlier supporters (64 percent) and from those who had voted for the LDPR in 1995 (29 percent), and that the LDPR's diminished vote came almost exclusively from its own original base (25 percent) plus a share of those voting for "other parties" (7 percent).[7] In contrast, the two competing "parties of power" appear to have garnered their support from a broader spectrum of voters. There are, however, two seemingly suspicious estimates—that Otechestvo won 116 percent of the vote from NDR ("Our Home Is Russia," the previous so-called party of power) and that Edinstvo secured a 34 percent share of "other parties."

Of course, one must treat these findings as merely suggestive, given their reliance on a method of estimation—a standard Goodman regression—that is susceptible to aggregation error (the over- or underestimation of coefficients) when the data are not homogeneous. Simply put, a homogeneous flow of votes means that transition coefficients (percentages of the vote that went from one party to another between elections) are normally distributed around the same mean across all observations. An aggregation error (related to the methodology presented here) occurs when the means-of-transition coefficients vary from observation to observation. Normally an aggregation error would present a serious problem when observations have different underlying factors or a different nature. For example, if one puts together observations from a wealthy suburb in the United States with data drawn from an inner city, serious aggregation errors are likely. In the Russian elections, aggregation bias is less of a problem because the distribution of voters is more or less homogeneous across electoral districts. In Russia one is likely to find voters of different occupations, wealth, and education in virtually all districts. There is no racial divide in the Russian electorate either. Of course, any serious aggregation error undermines any inferences we might make about either the presence or absence of fraud. Our methodology simply is not applicable to this particular task.

Given the statistical consistency of our methodology, we can draw inferences about election fraud using the following assumption. In a normal electorate, of course, no party or candidate can receive more than 100 percent of some other party or candidate's support, and unless a new party is explicitly formed as a coalition of preexisting ones, no party is likely to emerge in the short span of a single election to secure a significant share of small personality-based parties as Edinstvo did. Our point here, however, is that the (nearly) 40 percent of the vote secured by Edinstvo and Otechestvo in 1999 cannot be explained by any of the standard references to basic social cleavages. Instead, we can usually attribute such a large share of the vote to support from some local or regional elite.[8] With the 1999 contest seen largely as a prepresidential election contest between the Kremlin (Edinstvo) and supporters of a Luzhkov-Primakov alliance (Otechestvo), these parties are best viewed as coalitions of elites (governors, oligarchs, and others) who sought to back Yeltsin's likely successor and, by means fair and foul, sought to throw their resources behind the party most likely to yield the next president of Russia.

A preliminary estimate of the flow of votes from 1999 to the presidential contest of 2000, again using a standard Goodman regression, supports this view.[9] As most observers of Russian politics agree, Otechestvo's "defeat" in 1999 did not cause its elite base to scatter to various ideologically adjacent candidates; Otechestvo and its leadership had no ideology aside from wanting to back the winner. Hence its elite base and electoral support were delivered to the Kremlin's candidate, Putin. This is precisely what our earlier vote flow analysis reveals: Putin garners nearly all the support of both Edinstvo (108 percent) and Otechestvo (94 percent), whereas Zyuganov's support comes solely from the CPRF (92 percent), Yavlinskii's only significant support is from SPS (36 percent), Zhirinovskii gains nothing from other parties, and nonvoters come from other nonvoters or those who supported other parties in 1999 (55 percent).

The emergence of new and powerful players in 1999–2000 and Putin's landslide victory in 2004 raise the question of whether we are observing a fundamental shift in the character of the Russian electorate away from the left and right (or pro- and antireform) categories that characterized elections during the Yeltsin era, or the emergence of an electoral system whose processes, and indeed outcomes, are dictated by the Kremlin and its allies in regional politics. And although we are able use what we know about Russian politics to interpret the estimated vote flows derived from a standard Goodman regression, the emergence of suspicious coefficients (for example, estimated coefficients that award a party more than 100 percent of a predecessor's support) leads us to ask whether the explanation lies in the application of a flawed methodology or whether such estimates signal the existence of fraud. This is the issue we address next by extending our data to include the 2004 presidential contest and by applying a methodology more appropriate for the analysis of aggregate data than a standard Goodman regression.

Estimating the Flow of Votes

At this point our methodology requires a comment that will assist in explaining how it can be used to help detect fraud or at least electoral anomalies. As previously noted, the share of votes a candidate receives from some source (candidate or party) in an earlier election cannot exceed 100 percent or be less than 0 percent. Coefficients that lie outside this interval are commonly interpreted as evidence of aggregation error, in which case methods are devised that "force" coefficients to fall in the interval $[0, 1]$. Thus, since it is generally true that a standard Goodman regression yields coefficients between 0 and 1.0 only if the assumption of homogeneity is satisfied—only if the true coefficient corresponding to a candidate's share of some previous competitor's vote is the same in all rayons—a coefficient of 1.16 in our estimate of the vote flow from NDR to Otechestvo and of 1.08 in our estimate of the vote flow from Edinstvo to Putin might be taken to mean that our analysis is biased by aggregation error. This inference, however, while possibly true, is necessarily so only if there is no election fraud. Imagine a simple "regular" case in which all coefficients are constant across the observations (say, precincts) and where there are only two candidates plus nonvoters. In this instance a Goodman regression will reveal the "true" coefficients. Now suppose that the observed dependent variable (for example, Putin) is tainted by fraud and that the amount of fraud in each precinct is proportional to the vote Putin won in the previous elections (that is, fraud $= kX_i$). In the Russian case this would correspond to the reasonable scenario in which there is proportionately greater fraud in the republics than in, say, Samara. Finally, suppose that absent any fraud Putin would have secured 100 percent of the votes he won in the previous election (that is, the estimated coefficient at X_i would have been one). Under these conditions, a flow-of-votes analysis would, in effect, add fraud (kX_i) to both sides of the "true" equation so as to yield the observed dependent variable on the left and a coefficient at X_i that exceeds 1 (1 plus the constant) on the right. The intuition is simple: if fraud is proportional to X_i, it will all go into the coefficient at X_i, in which case if the "normal" coefficient at X_i is already high, our vote flow estimate will exceed 1.0. For example, suppose we take X_i for each observation and multiply it by, say, 1.2 to get Y_i. An OLS regression will yield 1.2 at X_i (note that if fraud is uncorrelated with any of the variables, its impact will be spread across all independent variables, but can still drive a coefficient above 1, although in this case R^2 will be lower than if fraud had not occurred).

The method we summarize here and apply to a reanalysis of our original data and data from the 2004 Russian presidential contest is a generalization of the Chambers-Steel method for ecological regression. That extension seeks, in effect, to render the data homogeneous in a statistically justifiable way so that we have greater confidence in supposing that "unusual" coefficients are not the consequence of aggregation error but, instead, indicate the likelihood of fraud. To begin, then, let X_i denote candidate or party i's share of the vote in any election, including n parties or candidates (with $i = 0$ denoting nonvoters) and let Y_j denote candidate or party j's share of the vote in some earlier election. Then

$$X_i = b_o Y_o + b_1 Y_1 + \dots + b_n Y_n,$$

where $Y_0 + Y_1 + \dots + Y_n = 100$. The difficulty with estimating this model, of course, is that the validity of any set of estimates of the b_j's depends on the assumption of homogeneous data—the assumption that the same coefficients apply to all observations. However, this assumption is violated if, for instance, the true coefficients depend on the extent of fraud in a region, as when fraud favoring a candidate is more prevalent in those regions where the candidate already has strong support.

The Chambers-Steel approach as applied here is, in effect, to form clusters of "similar" rayons according to such criteria as "percent urban" and the classification of regions as republics (those federal entities officially identified as "ethnic," commonly Islamic) or oblasts (those classified as "Russian"), to estimate coefficients within each cluster, and in effect to average those estimates.[10] Various goodness-of-fit measures are then applied to choose "the most appropriate clusters." To formalize this idea with a model we can statistically estimate, assume that n parties or candidates participated in election number one and that m parties or candidates participated in some subsequent election, number two. Assume the balloting results are available from R rayons and satisfy the following: X_{ri} with $1 < i < n$ denotes i's share of the vote in rayon r in election number one; $X_{r0} = 1 - \sum_{i=1}^{n} X_{ri}$ denotes the share of eligible voters who did not vote in election number one; Y_{ri}, $1 < i < m$ denotes the share of eligible voters who supported i in election number two; $Y_{r0} = 1 - \sum_{i=1}^{m} Y_{ri}$ denotes the share of eligible voters who did not vote in election number two; p_r equals the total number of eligible voters in rayon r; and z_r corresponds to a vector of variables (proxies) that provide information about the demographic character of r. Thus, for each rayon r and for each candidate i, the following equation must be satisfied:

$$Y_{ri} = \sum_{k=0}^{n} \alpha_{rik} X_{rk}. \tag{1}$$

In this equation, we arrive at α_{rik} by taking the voters in rayon r who voted for candidate k in election number one and then calculating the percentage of that subset who subsequently voted for candidate i in election number two.

What we require now is a specification of the total share of the votes that went from candidate k (in election number one) to candidate i (in election number two). That share is given by

$$\delta_{ik} = \frac{\sum_{r=1}^{R} \alpha_{rik} p_r X_{rk}}{\sum_{r=1}^{R} p_r X_{rk}}. \tag{2}$$

The first assumption we might make in estimating δ_{ik} is that of homogeneity across observations; specifically,

$$\alpha_{rik} = \alpha_{ik} + \epsilon_{rik}, \; E[\epsilon_{rik} \, / \, X_{r0}, \dots, X_{rn}] = 0. \tag{3}$$

In this case expression (1) can be rewritten as

$$Y_{ri} = \sum_{k=0}^{n} \alpha_{ik} X_{rk} + \epsilon_{ri}, \tag{4}$$

where

$$\epsilon_{ri} = \sum_{k=0}^{n} \epsilon_{rik} X_{rk}, \tag{5}$$

so it follows that

$$E[\epsilon_{rik} \, / \, X_{r1}, \dots, X_{rn+1}] = 0.$$

Thus, OLS can be used to estimate α_{ik} for $0 < k < n$, which yields consistent estimates of δ_{ik} since

$$\delta_{ik} = \frac{\sum\limits_{r=1}^{R} \alpha_{rik} p_r X_{rk}}{\sum\limits_{r=1}^{R} p_r X_{rk}} = \alpha_{rik} + \frac{\sum\limits_{r=1}^{R} \epsilon_{rik} p_r X_{rk}}{\sum\limits_{r=1}^{R} p_r X_{rk}}. \tag{6}$$

Other variants of OLS can be applied to this model, such as weighted least squares, but as is generally the case, the assumption of homogeneity across observations (rayons) is untenable. So assume instead that

$$\alpha_{ik} = f_{ik}(z_r) + \epsilon_{rik}, \tag{7}$$

where the f_{ik}'s are some (unknown) functions. These functions, though, can be estimated as follows:

$$\bar{f}_i(z) = \left\{ \sum_{r=1}^{R} k(H^{-1}[z_r - z]) X_r X_r' \right\}^{-1} \left\{ \sum_{r=1}^{R} k(H^{-1}[z_r - z]) X_r X_{ri} \right\}, \tag{8}$$

where

$$X_r = (X_{r0}, X_{r1}, \dots, X_{rn}),$$
$$\bar{f}_i = (\bar{f}_{r0}, \bar{f}_{r1}, \dots, \bar{f}_{rn}).$$

K is a "weight function" and H is a "window size" matrix. Briefly, for H we can choose

$$h3^{-1/2},$$

where 3 is a matrix of z_r covariates, and h is an exogenously chosen constant (selected here to set the "window size" equal to 200). For K we use the uniform density around z that contains exactly H neighboring data points in our sample. It is easy to see now that under some elementary assumptions, such as the smoothness of f_i, the estimates $f_i(z)$ are consistent and asymptotically normal as r 6 4 and h 6 0. Specifically,

$$\bar{\delta}_{ik} = \frac{\sum\limits_{r=1}^{R} \bar{f}_{ik}(z_r) p_r X_{rk}}{\sum\limits_{r=1}^{R} p_r X_{rk}} \xrightarrow{p} \delta_{ik}. \qquad (9)$$

The 2003 Duma Contest

To see now with this methodology whether the Russian electorate seemed any more or less stable than the picture painted by earlier research, we should specify first the proxy variables employed in our analysis. Briefly, those variables are as follows: for estimating the flow of votes between 1995 and 1999, the CPRF share in 1995, Zyuganov's share in 1996 (2nd round), Yeltsin's share in 1996 (2nd round), percent urban, and a dummy for republics; for votes between 1999 and 2003, Unity's share in 1999, Otechestvo's share in 1999, percent urban, and a dummy for republics; for estimating the flow of votes between 1999 and 2000, Yeltsin's share in 1996 (1st round), percent urban, and a dummy for republics; and for estimating the vote flow between 2003 and 2004, the proxy variables employed are Zyuganov's share in 1999, Putin's share in 2000, percent urban, and a dummy for republics.[11] Naturally, we should test for the sensitivity of our results to alternative proxies, but what we can say here is that although coefficients do vary somewhat when alternatives are considered, qualitative results and substantive conclusions remain largely unaffected.

We turn now to a brief reconsideration of voting patterns between the 1995 and 1999 elections and between 1999 and 2000. Table 11-1 gives the results of our reanalysis for 1995 to 1999 as well as the estimated flow of votes between 1999 and 2000. These estimates paint much the same picture as those in tables 11-2 and 11-3 using a simple Goodman regression. Indeed, there is even a bit more coherence to them now. For example, the coefficient of 1.16 as the estimated share of NDR's 1995 vote that Otechestvo captured in 1999 is now a more reasonable 0.63; Otechestvo is no longer credited with an otherwise inexplicable 32 percent of Yabloko's 1995 vote but rather with effectively 0 (−0.03); Yabloko and SPS continue to trade votes among themselves in these years; and Edinstvo's support is now spread more evenly across

Table 11-1. Reestimated Flow of Votes from 1995 to 1999 and 1999 to 2000

1995–1999 To/From	NDR	Yabloko	SPS	CPRF	LDPR	Nonvoters	Others
Edinstvo	0.13	−0.06	−0.01	0.05	0.46	−0.04	0.45
Otechestvo	0.63	−0.03	0.27	0.14	−0.22	0.09	−0.03
Yabloko	0.01	0.42	0.21	−0.01	0.01	0.03	−0.01
CPRF	0.00	0.06	−0.04	0.65	0.16	0.09	0.03
SPS	0.06	0.27	0.54	−0.03	−0.01	0.05	−0.01
LDPR	−0.01	−0.04	−0.02	−0.03	0.24	0.00	0.11
Nonvoters	0.02	0.32	0.04	0.21	0.23	0.73	0.22

1999–2000 To/From	Edinstvo	Otechestvo	SPS + Yabloko	CPRF	LDPR	Nonvoters	Others
Putin	1.09	0.95	0.07	−0.01	0.02	0.10	0.80
Zuganov	−0.22	0.02	−0.10	0.98	0.59	0.10	0.31
Yavlinskii	−0.01	0.13	0.38	−0.04	−0.05	0.01	−0.03
Zhirinovskii	0.00	−0.03	0.01	0.00	0.42	0.01	0.01
Nonvoters	0.01	0.03	0.15	0.02	0.16	0.74	−0.02
Others	0.12	−0.11	0.49	0.05	−0.10	0.03	−0.06

the old party of power, NDR (13 percent versus 5 percent), the LDPR's voter base, and "others." In the estimates reported in table 11-1, moreover, we add the estimate for the flow of votes to "nonvoters" and here we see what appears to be a wholly reasonable pattern. First, nonvoters tend to remain so: 73 percent of nonvoters in 1999 are estimated to have come from the ranks of nonvoters in 1995. But in addition, we begin to see the "melting away" of support for parties of the left and right. Specifically, 32 percent of Yabloko's 1995 support is estimated to have melted into the pool of abstainers, while 21 percent and 23 percent of those who voted for the CPRF and LDPR, respectively, in 1995 did the same.

If we turn to the vote flow between 1999 and the 2000 presidential contest (see the second part of table 11-1), we again see results that mimic what we found earlier using a standard Goodman regression: Putin, unsurprisingly, captured essentially all of Edinstvo and Otechestvo's vote. Indeed, once again we see a vote flow estimate that suspiciously exceeds 1.0. Hence, the only substantive difference is our revised estimate that Putin won none of the Communist vote but a majority of those who voted for minor parties in 1999. As before, Zyuganov's primary support comes from his party, the CPRF, and a majority share of the shriveling LDPR, while nonvoters in 2000 once again come predominantly from the ranks of nonvoters in 1999 plus a share of the LDPR, SPS, and Yabloko. Finally, the share of SPS's vote that went to Otechestvo in 1999 appears to have returned to Yavlinskii in 2000.

Table 11-2. Flow of Votes from 1999 to 2003

To/From	Edinstvo	Otechestvo	CPRF	Yabloko	SPS	LDPR	Nonvoters	Others
United Russia	0.65	0.63	0.19	0.18	−0.05	0.26	0.02	0.16
CPRF	0.00	−0.04	0.37	−0.01	0.09	−0.06	0.00	0.13
LDPR	0.09	−0.03	0.05	0.15	0.03	0.70	0.02	0.04
Rodina	0.07	0.14	0.08	0.15	0.14	−0.17	0.03	−0.02
Yabloko	0.01	0.06	−0.01	0.27	0.15	0.00	0.01	−0.02
SPS	0.00	0.04	−0.02	−0.01	0.37	−0.13	0.00	0.06
Nonvoters	0.08	0.03	0.23	0.37	0.07	0.29	0.93	−0.02
Others	0.10	0.17	0.11	−0.08	0.20	0.10	−0.01	0.66

The 10 percent of nonvoters that Putin and Zyuganov won should not be considered unusual since turnout is, as elsewhere, greater in presidential than in parliamentary contests. Thus, if there is a coefficient here that seems unusual, it is Putin's 109 percent share of Edinstvo's vote. Nevertheless, setting aside the potential significance of this estimate for the moment, let us turn to the 2003 parliamentary contest and table 11-2, which suggests that the stability of the electorate that characterized earlier elections appears to have disappeared. Of all the 2003 parties, United Russia enjoyed the most favorable environment and was viewed by many as Putin's party. Yet despite its privileged position, it received less than two-thirds of those who voted for either Edinstvo or Otechestvo in 1999. Even considering the overall relative success of United Russia in 2003, this "loss" amounts to approximately 8 million votes. These lost votes were almost equally split among LDPR, Rodina ("Motherland"), and voters who stayed home. However, United Russia's vote was augmented by nearly 20 percent of the 1999 Communist vote, a quarter of the LDPR's support base, and a good share of Yabloko's electorate. In fact, United Russia became the biggest beneficiary of the Communist Party's collapse. Overall, the CPRF lost about 60 percent of its electoral base between 1999 and 2003. In addition to United Russia voters, the CPRF's former voters could be found in 2003 among Rodina's electorate, among minor ("other") parties; CPRF's biggest loss of votes was a result of voters' staying home. Like the CPRF, the two proreform liberal parties (SPS and Yabloko) managed to keep only about one-third of their 1999 supporters. Both parties lost about 15 percent of their old support to the newly created Rodina, while one third of Yabloko's supporters simply stayed home. Indeed, the ranks of nonvoters were swelled by precisely those parties of the left, right, and nationalist persuasions (LDPR) who previously had given the Russian electorate at least the appearance of stability.[12]

Table 11-3. Flow of Votes from 2000 to 2004

To/From	Putin	Zuganov	Zhirinovskii	Yavlinskii	Nonvoters + Others
Putin	0.86	0.60	0.22	0.36	0.02
Kharitonov	0.06	0.34	−0.04	−0.24	0.03
Glaziev	−0.02	0.04	0.22	0.21	0.04
Khakamada	0.01	−0.01	0.09	0.39	0.02
Nonvoters	0.08	−0.02	0.04	0.05	0.87
Others	0.02	0.05	0.56	0.23	0.02

With regard to the 2004 presidential contest, tables 11-3 and 11-4 report the estimated vote flow coefficients from 2000 to 2004 and 2003 to 2004, and here we see fully Putin's impact. Looking first at table 11-3, we see that Putin's support comes from across the board and speaks to his essential destruction of the Kremlin's opposition from the 1990s: 60 percent of Zyuganov's vote, 22 percent of Zhirinovskii's, and 36 percent of Yavlinskii's base. Thus, although what little opposition exists to Putin derives its support from the obvious sources, we see here the further melting away, or at least scattering, of both the Communist and Yavlinskii's bases of support.

Turning to table 11-4 and the flow of votes between 2003 and 2004, keep in mind that when a party system is weak, with a strong presidency, parliamentary elections often serve merely as primaries for presidential elections. This is especially true in Russia, where parliamentary elections are conducted mere months before the presidential contest.[13] Hence, in 2000, the distribution of electoral support for presidential candidates more or less reflected political preferences as they were expressed in the 1999 elections to the State Duma (see table 11-1). Putin captured all of Edinstvo's vote and much of the vote of the party that was formed to further the national aspirations of two Moscow-based elites, Luzhkov and Primakov; Zyuganov captured essentially all of the vote of the CPRF; Yavlinskii's support came from his own party, SPS, and those who had voted for Otechestvo but who apparently were not yet enamored of the relatively unknown Putin; and Zhirinovskii's support came exclusively from the ranks of his LDPR. In contrast, the 2004 election was held under a different set of political circumstances. The Russian federal state had by then consolidated its position with regional elites, while Putin gained near total control over parliament by merging the two progovernment factions Edinstvo and Otechestvo into one large United Russia. The economic situation in the country was also dramatically differ-

Table 11-4. Flow of Votes from 2003 to 2004

To/From	United Russia	CPRF	LDPR	Rodina	Nonvoters	Others
Putin	1.14	0.08	0.02	−0.06	0.24	0.63
Kharitonov	0.02	0.98	0.10	−0.08	0.02	0.02
Glaziev	−0.02	−0.01	0.07	0.36	0.03	−0.02
Khakamada	−0.01	−0.01	−0.03	0.07	0.01	0.13
Nonvoters	−0.15	−0.04	0.60	0.69	0.67	0.16
Others	0.02	0.00	0.25	0.02	0.02	0.08

ent from post-crisis 1999, when economic hardship played a significant role in the political orientation of the population. By 2004, with Russia now becoming a profitable "gas station" for the West, the Kremlin had considerably greater monetary flexibility. Under these conditions, all major potential opponents of the incumbent Putin, who was certain to win regardless of who ran against him, chose not to participate in the presidential race. Nevertheless, the distribution of voters' preferences in the 2004 presidential election was very much different from patterns observed during the previous parliamentary elections.

Table 11-4 reveals both regular and some suspiciously irregular patterns. As expected, all of Putin's opponents kept the support of the parties they represented. The CPRF candidate, Nikolai Kharitonov, won 98 percent of votes cast for the CPRF three months earlier; Sergei Glaziev brought home 36 percent of Rodina's electorate; Irina Khakamada secured 37 and 43 percent of what was left of Yabloko's and SPS's supporters in 2003. However, the distribution of votes cast in support of Putin deviates from this pattern and patterns observed earlier. Owing no doubt to the absence of meaningful electoral competition, Putin attracted not only 114 percent (!) of United Russia's vote, but 24 percent of those who failed to vote and 63 percent of those who voted for minor parties in 2003.

These estimates are all the more unusual when one considers that the Communist Party is, at the grass-roots level, far better *officially* organized to mobilize its base of support than any other political entity in Russia. Yet the estimated vote flow from a Duma election to its presidential candidate never exceeds 98 percent. Equally interesting is the support ostensibly given to Putin by those who stayed home for the 2003 parliamentary elections. The largest share of nonvoters who previously had supported a presidential candidate was Putin and Zyuganov's 10 percent share in 2000. In 2004, in contrast, Putin succeeded in winning an unprecedented 24 percent. Thus, for an election that was a foregone conclusion even before the campaign officially commenced, our analysis shows that virtually *all* additional votes recorded in March 2004 were for Putin and virtually none for his opponents. That is, almost all members of the electorate who failed to vote in 2003 but who voted in 2004 cast their ballots as one for the incumbent. While in theory this is possible, the feasibility of such a monolithic preference is at best suspicious.

Republics versus Oblasts

With these suspicions in mind, it is important to understand that the coefficients reported thus far are averages calculated in accordance with expression (9) and, therefore, can disguise differences among types of rayons. And here we want to explore one categorization that has historically been of profound significance in Russian politics—the distinction between republics (and autonomous regions) on the one hand and oblasts (and *krais*) on the other. Elsewhere we note the differences between republics and oblasts: in particular, republics are characterized by more corruption and "boss rule."[14] Consider, then, table 11-5, which examines the flow of votes between the 1999 and 2003 parliamentary elections, with republics and oblasts analyzed separately.

The first comment we ought to add about these estimates is that those for Yabloko and SPS in the republics ought to be ignored. The support these parties received there (usually less than 1 percent) makes any estimate of vote flows for them wholly unstable and statistically meaningless. If we look, then, at the remaining estimates we see patterns within oblasts that mimic those in the republics and that mimic what we find when we combine all regions into a single sample: United Russia secures a majority of the vote of both Edinstvo and Otechestvo and a not-insignificant share of the CPRF, LDPR, and Yabloko vote. As before, nonvoters largely remain nonvoters, and both the CPRF and LDPR gain their support from their own past supporters. If there are differences revealed here, they are as follows: (1) United Russia wins a larger share of Otechestvo's vote within republics than among oblasts, which is unsurprising since a majority of the regional political bosses who initially supported Otechestvo were from the republics; (2) although United Russia is more successful in the republics at securing the votes of those who had previously supported the CPRF, a greater share of the CPRF's vote defects to the category of nonvoter in the oblasts; and (3) United Russia is far more successful in the republics at attracting the vote of those who previously had voted for minor parties (others).

Table 11-5. Flow of Votes from 1999 to 2003, Republics and Oblasts

To/From	Edinstvo	Otechestvo	CPRF	Yabloko	SPS	LDPR	Nonvoters	Others
			Republics and autonomous regions					
United								
Russia	0.77	0.94	0.54	0.99	−1.34	0.71	−0.10	0.24
CPRF	0.05	0.05	0.30	−0.47	0.46	−0.16	0.05	−0.07
LDPR	0.01	0.02	0.02	0.31	0.37	0.93	0.01	−0.11
Rodina	0.01	0.00	0.03	−0.09	0.41	−0.29	0.01	0.22
Yabloko	0.02	0.01	−0.01	0.31	0.19	−0.05	0.01	−0.04
SPS	0.04	−0.01	0.01	−0.51	0.59	−0.63	0.00	0.30
Nonvoters	0.03	−0.17	0.04	1.15	−0.50	0.51	0.93	0.08
Others	0.07	0.15	0.08	−0.69	0.82	−0.01	0.08	0.39
			Oblasts and krais					
United								
Russia	0.64	0.53	0.16	0.20	0.19	0.03	0.02	0.11
CPRF	0.00	−0.08	0.38	−0.06	0.03	0.06	0.00	0.16
LDPR	0.10	−0.08	0.06	0.65	0.11	0.00	0.03	0.07
Rodina	0.09	0.19	0.08	−0.14	0.15	0.15	0.03	−0.04
Yabloko	0.01	0.08	−0.01	0.00	0.24	0.17	0.01	−0.02
SPS	0.00	0.06	−0.03	−0.05	0.01	0.35	0.00	0.02
Nonvoters	0.06	0.09	0.23	0.30	0.27	0.15	0.94	−0.01
Others	0.10	0.21	0.12	0.11	−0.01	0.09	−0.03	0.70

The differences between republics and oblasts do not detract from the conclusion reached when we analyze all rayons as a whole; namely, that United Russia succeeded in upsetting the alignment of parties and voters that had characterized Russia in the 1990s. However, it is in the flow of votes between 2003 and 2004 that we see more substantial and suspicious differences between republics and oblasts. As shown in table 11-6, a few things here remain the same as when we combine oblasts and republics (see again table 11-4). Absent a candidate, the LDPR's support flows primarily to minor candidates or stays home. Also, Glaziev's vote comes primarily from Rodina and Kharitonov's from the CPRF. However, the division of rayons into two subsamples reveals some interesting differences and some suspicious patterns. First, Putin wins more than 100 percent of United Russia's vote in both subsamples, as well as a remarkable share of those who either failed to vote in 2003 or who voted for minor parties. Second, Putin's "demolition" of the CPRF occurs primarily in the republics and autonomous regions. Although Kharitonov wins all of the CPRF's vote in the oblasts, Putin actually out-polls him among those voters in the republics.

Table 11-6. Flow of Votes from 2003 to 2004, Republics and Oblasts

To/From	United Russia	CPRF	LDPR	Rodina	Nonvoters	Others
	Republics and autonomous regions					
Putin	1.07	0.80	−0.16	0.30	0.22	0.87
Kharitonov	−0.01	0.44	0.01	0.08	0.09	0.02
Glaziev	0.00	−0.01	0.06	0.26	0.02	−0.01
Khakamada	0.00	−0.10	−0.09	0.32	0.02	0.08
Nonvoters	−0.07	−0.12	0.89	0.00	0.62	0.01
Others	0.01	−0.02	0.29	0.04	0.03	0.03
	Oblasts and krais					
Putin	1.16	−0.07	0.05	−0.13	0.25	0.60
Kharitonov	0.03	1.09	0.12	−0.09	0.01	0.02
Glaziev	−0.03	−0.01	0.07	0.38	0.03	−0.02
Khakamada	−0.02	0.00	−0.03	0.03	0.01	0.14
Nonvoters	−0.17	−0.02	0.55	0.80	0.68	0.17
Others	0.03	0.00	0.24	0.01	0.02	0.09

Conclusions

In fact, a somewhat remarkable feature of the 2004 election is that Putin performs substantially better among earlier supporters of the CPRF, Rodina, and "others" in the republics than he does in Russia's oblasts. There is, however, a sinister interpretation of this fact. Regional political boss control is doubtlessly greater in the republics—especially in places such as Tatarstan, Dagestan, Bashkortostan, Chuvash, and Mordovia—than elsewhere. And with Putin the certain winner, it would be naive to suppose that these bosses did not exert extra effort to secure votes for Putin in order to curry favor with the Kremlin.[15] Of course, the estimated vote flows detailed in table 11-6 do not confirm that this extra effort constituted fraud. The methodology described and implemented here can only raise suspicions. But given what we already know about Russia and its electoral politics, including the special character of politics in its autonomous republics, it would also be naive to think that substantial fraud did not occur in various parts of Russia through the devices of stuffed ballot boxes and election protocols filled out without regard to actual ballots cast. Because the estimates reported in table 11-6 are consistent with such suppositions, the suggestion here is that our methodology can be applied both to the understanding of electoral behavior and political party development (our original intent when analyzing elections between 1995 and 1999) and as a tool for pointing us toward further explorations of the sources and extent of fraud in elections. Other follow-up or confirmatory methods are available and consist, for example, of looking at distributions of turnout, which we would expect to be normally distributed in a normal election, or at the relationship between turnout and a candidate's absolute share of the eligible electorate, which we would expect to be positive, and across homogeneous districts, represented by a simple regression equation where the coefficient between turnout and share equals the average proportion of vote the candidate actually won.[16] In other words, there are other tests one can apply to aggregate data. Our confidence in the inference that an election was marred by fraud would thereby increase to the extent that each of these tests revealed an anomaly (such as a bimodal distribution of turnout, which would suggest that a subset of the data has had its turnout artificially increased; or a negative relationship between turnout and a candidate's share of the eligible electorate, which would suggest that votes have been artificially subtracted from his or her total in a subset of the data).

Notes

1. See M. Myagkov, P. C. Ordeshook, and A. Sobyanin, "The Russian Electorate 1991–1996," *Post Soviet Affairs* 13, no. 2 (April–June 1997): 134–66; M. Myagkov and P. C. Ordeshook, "The Trail of Votes in Russia's 1999 Duma and 2000 Presidential Elections," *Communist and Post-Communist Studies* 34, no. 3 (September 2001): 353–70. For a parallel analysis of Ukraine, see M. Myagkov and P. C. Ordeshook, "The Trail of Votes in Ukraine's 1998, 1999 and 2002 Elections," *Post-Soviet Affairs* 21, no. 1 (January 2005): 56–71.

2. R. L. Chambers and D. G. Steel, "Simple Methods for Ecological Inference in 2x2 Tables," *Journal of the Royal Statistical Society*, Series A, 164, no. 1 (2001): 175–92.

3. A. Sobyanin, E. Gel'man, and O. Kaiunov, "The Political Climate of Russia's Regions: Voters and Deputies, 1991–93," *Soviet and Post-Soviet Review* 21, no. 1 (1994): 63–84; and A. Sobyanin and V. Suchovolskiy, "Elections and the Referendum December 12," in Russian, unpublished report to the Administration of the President of the Russian Federation, Moscow 1993.

4. See, for example, M. McFaul, *Russia's Unfinished Revolution: Political Change from Gorbachev to Putin* (Cornell University Press, 2001); and R. G. Moser, *Unexpected Outcomes: Electoral Systems, Political Parties and Representation in Russia* (University of Pittsburgh Press, 2001).

5. M. Myagkov, "The Duma Elections: A Step toward Democracy or the Elites' Game?" in *The 1999–2000 Elections in Russia: Their Impact and Legacy*, edited by V. L. Hesli and W. M. Reisinger (Cambridge University Press, 2003).

6. However, see A. Konitzer, *Voting for Russia's Governors* (Johns Hopkins University Press, 2006), for a dissenting argument with respect to regional and local elections.

7. Myagkov and Ordeshook, "The Trail of Votes in Russia's 1999 Duma," p. 362.

8. See A. Berezkin, M. Myagkov, and P.C. Ordeshook, "The Urban-Rural Divide in the Russian Electorate and the Effect of Distance from the Urban Centers," *Post-Soviet Geography and Economics* 40, no. 6 (September 1999): 395–406; and Berezkin and others, "Location and Political Influence: A Further Elaboration of Their Effects on Voting in Recent Russian Elections," *Eurasian Geography and Economics* 44, no. 3 (April–May 2003): 169–83.

9. See Myagkov and Ordeshook, "The Trail of Votes in Russia's 1999 Duma," table 4, p. 365.

10. *Oblast* is the Russian equivalent of a state in the United States. *Krai* has the same meaning as *oblast*. A republic is similar to an oblast in size and population but has more autonomy from the federal center and usually has an ethnic majority population (like Tatars in Tatarstan, for example).

11. Our proxy variables, which should correspond to those variables that characterize district (rayon) heterogeneity, are chosen so that, as much as we can ensure from our understanding of Russian politics, all of the variance in estimated transition coefficients that might be explained by a candidate's or a party's votes in the first election can also be explained by the proxy variables.

12. One substantively interesting question about the 2003 election is the source of support for Rodina. Created by Kremlin political consultants, this party was designed initially to cut into the CPRF's base and thus reduce its opposition to that of nuisance. Consequently, Rodina's preelection platform was built on a combination of socially oriented and nationalistic policy appeals. However, our analysis shows that its support came from places other than CPRF and LDPR. It won 7 percent of Edinstvo's vote, 14 percent of Otechestvo's, approximately 15 percent of Yabloko and SPS's vote, and only 8 percent of the CPRF's 1999 supporters.

13. See P. C. Ordeshook, "Reexaminimg Russia: Institutions and Incentives," *Journal of Democracy* 6, no. 2 (April 1995): 46–60.

14. M. Myagkov, P. C. Ordeshook, and D. Shaikin, "Fraud or Fairytales: Russia and Ukraine's Electoral Experience," *Post-Soviet Affairs* 21, no. 2 (June 2005): 91–131.

15. M. Myagkov, "The Duma Elections."

16. See, for example, Myagkov, Ordeshook, and Shaikin, "Fraud or Fairytales."

twelve

How International Election Observers Detect and Deter Fraud

Susan D. Hyde

International monitoring of elections is intended to promote democracy by providing an independent evaluation of whether a given election was democratic, detecting fraud when it exists, deterring fraud, and increasing voter confidence in the electoral process.[1] How do international observers accurately detect election fraud, particularly when election manipulators have the incentive to conceal their activities from observers? Do international observers have the ability to reduce election fraud? The goal of this chapter is to shed light on these questions. I first review the challenges international observers face in judging the quality of elections and then outline current best practices for fraud detection, including advances in observer methodology such as the parallel vote tabulation, the voter registration audit, media monitoring, and coordination with domestic election observers. I then turn to the potential for fraud reduction or deterrence and present the randomization of international observers as a methodological innovation that will aid in the detection and measurement of fraud and other irregularities.

The author is grateful to Eric Bjornlund, David Carroll, David Pottie, and Charles Stewart for comments on an earlier draft of this chapter, and to Avery Davis-Roberts, Clark Gibson, and Vladimir Pran for (informally) answering numerous questions about election monitoring. Any errors and omissions are my own.

The Challenges of Comparative Evaluation of Election Quality

Studies of individual behavior suggest that observers may deter fraud. Individuals behave differently when they know they are being watched, particularly when their intended behavior is illegal or otherwise socially objectionable. A recent study of U.S. voter behavior demonstrates that individuals are more likely to vote when their own voter turnout record is mailed to their neighbors.[2] Similarly, research has shown that sending more police officers to high-crime areas, called hot-spot policing, can have a significant deterrent effect on illegal behavior.[3] Proponents of election observation suggest that similar techniques can be used to promote election quality. In the presence of international observers, they argue, individuals are less likely to attempt to manipulate elections.

International election observers report on many aspects of an electoral process, sometimes providing technical assistance to domestic observer groups or aiding civic education programs. But they are best known for their postelection judgments. Immediately following an election, international observers issue a preliminary statement reflecting their judgment about whether the election was "clean," "genuine," "free and fair," "democratic," or "compliant with international standards." Since most elections are imperfect, deciding when an electoral process warrants a negative evaluation is a difficult task. Separate competent groups sometimes reach conflicting conclusions about the same election.

A central challenge facing election observers is determining the types and quantities of irregularities that collectively render an election fraudulent. Not all election irregularities are equally harmful to an electoral process. Moreover, it is often difficult for international observers to distinguish between unintentional administrative mistakes and blatant attempts to manipulate the outcome of an election. Most observer organizations would agree that it is not useful to call an entire process into question because of a few isolated incidents. Similarly, they do not believe that administrative incompetence by election officials is as malignant as intentional manipulation.

Observers have dealt with the challenges of aggregation in a variety of ways. One method is to use diplomatic terms such as "irregularities," rather than such loaded terms as "fraud" and "manipulation," unless observers are absolutely certain they have witnessed a stolen election. A second strategy has been to hold elections to different standards, depending on the margin of victory. Generally speaking, international observers are less severe in their criticism when it does not appear that observed irregularities would have influenced the election outcome, even in cases in which irregularities are widespread.[4]

However, before they can make such judgments, observers must first accomplish a basic task: they must be able to detect election fraud.

International Observers and Fraud Detection

Detecting election fraud is a difficult business. Political actors who manipulate elections have strong incentives to hide their activity from international observers. Other political actors may be motivated to falsely accuse their opponents of cheating. Methods of electoral manipulation vary widely between and within countries, and as international observers improve their methods of detecting fraud, cheating parties and candidates are likely to adopt methods that international observers are less likely to detect. Because each observer organization employs its own methodology, any general statement about how international observers detect fraud will only be partially accurate. Even within the same organization, practices are adapted for different countries in order to meet unique logistical and technical challenges. With these caveats, this section outlines best practice for fraud detection by international election observers.

Because election manipulation can take place at any point before, during, or after an election, most organizations now seek to observe the entire electoral process, including the registration of voters, the campaign period, election day, and the postelection announcement of results and resolution of disputes. Table 12-1 lists the many forms of election manipulation observers look for; these irregularities are often discussed in postelection reports as evidence of election fraud. Table 12-2 lists irregularities where the intention to manipulate the election is less clear. These ambiguous irregularities may be intentional attempts to bias the election toward a particular outcome but could also be the result of lack of experience with voting, administrative incompetence, or other randomly occurring mistakes that arise occasionally even in countries with well-respected and legitimate election processes.

Detecting Preelection Fraud

Signs of election manipulation in the pre-campaign period include failures in voter registration, particularly when problems disproportionately affect politically identifiable groups; banning of candidates or parties; an inadequate legal structure for handling election-related disputes; problems with the filing or appeals process; failure to prosecute previous violations of election law; and a politically biased election commission.

Table 12-1. Examples of Unambiguous Signs of Election Manipulation

Preelection period
—No registered opposition candidates
—Bans on candidates or political parties
—Refusal to update inaccurate and biased voter registration lists
—Gross misuse of state resources to support incumbent
—Restrictions on universal adult suffrage for politically targeted populations
—Campaign-related violence and intimidation
—Obviously biased campaign finance
—State-controlled media
—Intimidation or harassment of media
—Other unreasonable barriers to candidates wishing to communicate with voters
—Blatantly partisan election commission
—Selective use of legal sanctions against likely candidates
—Jailing of candidates or political party officials

Election day
—Insecure ballots
—Broken seals on ballot boxes
—Multiple individuals inside voting booths
—When ballot boxes are transparent: multiple ballots folded together, premarked ballots not in ballot box, too many ballots relative to number of voters checked on registration list, too few ballots relative to number of voters on list
—During count: lack of transparency to international observers
—Ballot boxes present outside of polling stations
—Large collections of voter identification, either on election day or before election day
—Carousel voting (also called the Tasmanian Dodge)
—Exchange of money or goods following voting
—Buses of voters from neighboring areas (multiple voting)
—Multiple ballots given to one individual
—Voters with proper identification turned away
—Voters with proper identification listed as deceased
—Deceased voters listed as having voted (usually reported through relatives and documented)
—Systematically late or missing materials in opposition strongholds
—Violence or intimidation against voters
—Intimidating crowds in or outside the polling station, particularly when their presence violates the election law
—Attempts to influence voter choice inside the polling station
—Interference by the military, police, or other unauthorized individuals
—During the count: falsifying results
—Arbitrary or inconsistent invalidation of votes cast
—Stolen ballot boxes
—Extra ballot boxes
—Destruction of ballots

Announcement of results
—Parallel vote tabulation that differs significantly from official results (determines winner within margin of error)
—Changes in official results between those recorded by observers on election day and those published
—Suppression of official results
—Refusal by losing candidate to accept the results
—Large discrepancies between number of ballots distributed and official tallies of votes cast
—Government violence against protesters or bans on protest

Table 12-2. Examples of Election Irregularities When Intention to Manipulate Is Unclear

Preelection period
—After international observers are invited, attempt to place restrictions on them
—Barriers in the accreditation process to domestic election observers
—Unbalanced media time for candidates
—Election laws that favor one candidate or party
—Controversial interpretation of election laws
—Lack of an independent judiciary
—Lack of transparency in election planning process
—Lack of a procedure for filing election-related complaints
—Lack of funding for elections
—Lack of training for polling station officials
—Excessive requirements for candidate registration
—Selective implementation of the law for particular candidates or parties
—Lack of transparency of voter registration list
—Voting practices or ballot design that present a barrier to voting for certain groups (for example, those who are illiterate, linguistic minorities)
—Campaign materials near the polling station
—Poorly designed voting booths that fail to ensure secrecy of the ballot
—Election commission with unbalanced partisan representation

Election day
—Underage voting
—Problems in identification verification
—Problems with indelible ink
—Family voting
—Partisan polling station officials
—Imbalance in political party witnesses or lack of political party witnesses
—Handing out of ballots to individuals who are not checked off the voter list or otherwise recorded
—Missing election materials
—Disorganized polling stations
—During the count, lack of political party observers or domestic observers, or both
—During the count, filling out official tallies in pencil
—At any period, unsecured ballot boxes
—Inconsistencies in interpretation of proper election day procedures

Postelection period
—Slow legal system to deal with postelection disputes
—Postelection protest

How do observers detect manipulation before the campaign period? Today, standard practice for organizations such as the European Union, the Organization of American States (OAS), the National Democratic Institute, the Organization for Security and Cooperation in Europe's Office for Democratic Institutions and Human Rights, and the Carter Center is to deploy an election assessment mission well in advance of the election. Although these missions vary widely in scope and timing, the most common purpose is to assess the possibilities for deploying a full-scale mission, determine the major issues surrounding the election and the broader political context, and negotiate with the host country on logistical issues such as access to polling stations and the provision of visas for international observers. Without officially granted access to polling stations and other areas deemed relevant by election monitors, observers cannot successfully observe an election. A government that prohibits access by international observers to polling stations and vote tabulation centers is often viewed as having something to hide and, generally speaking, such action is viewed as a violation of international norms.

Most reputable election observation missions include long-term observers (LTOs), whose job is to observe the entire electoral process. They are deployed throughout the country, often focusing on regions in which problems are anticipated. For some missions, components of the preelection period are also observed by larger delegations of short-term observers, such as the joint OAS/Carter Center mission to observe the signature verification process during the 2004 referendum to recall the Venezuelan president. LTOs watch voter and candidate registration, evaluate the legal framework for the election, monitor the actions of the election administration body, evaluate any perceived or actual bias of election administrators, and assess the preparations for the election throughout the country.[5] These qualitative judgments provide important context when observers evaluate the electoral process as a whole. When significant problems are noted in the preelection period, observers issue statements suggesting that the problems be addressed. Often simply calling attention to problems brings about a resolution. For example, controversy over the inadequacy of preelection preparations can result in the postponement of elections until the problems are remedied; this occurred in Guyana in 1992, Liberia in 1997, and Venezuela in 2000.

One widespread problem in the preelection period involves the registration of voters. Sometimes inaccuracies are the unintentional result of the difficulty of keeping records up to date. But they can also reflect attempts to alter the political balance. Voter registration fraud can be used by the government to boost its own vote share through the use of "ghost voters" or to decrease its opponents' abilities to register their own voters.[6]

Measuring the accuracy of a voter registration list is difficult, particularly when registration is voluntary. International and domestic nonpartisan election observers have used voter registration audits for this purpose. The most comprehensive method is a "two-way" audit, which is conducted by comparing the accuracy of information in two different random samples of the voting population.[7] This process is intended to catch registered ghost voters, to identify problems experienced by eligible voters who had difficulty register-ing, and to identify individuals who are registered but are not aware that they are registered.

In order to determine how many voters are included in the voter list but are no longer eligible to vote, a statistical sample of names and addresses is taken from the voter register and is then checked for accuracy in face-to-face inter-views (also called a "list-to-voters" comparison). In order to determine the rate of registered voters relative to the population of eligible voters and to determine whether voters who believed they were registered are actually registered (and vice versa), a statistical sample is also taken of all eligible voters. This "voter-to-list" comparison interviews eligible voters to determine whether they believe they are registered and compares this information with the actual voter regis-ter. This procedure is expensive and time-consuming but provides an impor-tant check on the accuracy of a voter register.[8]

Detecting Fraud during the Campaign Period

The campaign period can reveal other blatant attempts at manipulation, including vote buying, distribution of patronage, jailing of political candidates and activists, intimidation at political rallies, politically targeted violence or threats of violence, attempts by employers to require employees to vote for their favored candidate, and the use of state resources to campaign for the incumbent candidate or party. Open competition can also be limited by a cen-sored press (either officially censored or self-censoring). Depending on voter interest, normal channels of political communication, and the political culture of the country, these issues vary in the degree to which they limit open politi-cal competition. However, because they can have a substantial effect on elec-tions, the campaign period is closely watched by international observers.

Some observer organizations monitor the media or coordinate with a domestic nonpartisan organization engaged in media monitoring.[9] Methods of media monitoring vary but can include keeping precise records of airtime or print space given to each candidate, observing the relationship between state-controlled and private media, and tracking the accuracy of paid adver-tising and political reporting. Very basic media monitoring consists of re-cording general impressions of coverage and fairness. In countries that lack free and independent media, media monitoring can reveal the extent to which the communication of information to voters has been compromised. In extreme cases, opposition parties are all but prohibited from access to the news media and face significant hurdles in communicating with voters. Doc-umenting media access and radio or television time can sometimes reveal significant barriers to democratic elections, although precise international standards for media fairness are not yet developed.

Detecting Fraud on Election Day

On election day, short-term observers collect qualitative and sometimes quantitative information on practices inside and around voting stations. They are prohibited from interfering in the voting process in any way, even to correct ongoing problems. Short-term observers record their observations on standardized forms, which are compiled by the observation mission's central office. Each observer usually visits multiple polling stations. Many of their observations are impressionistic and difficult to aggregate. Direct observations of vote buying or voter intimidation do not always form part of a larger pattern.

Short-term observers typically collect information on the environment inside the voting station, including the availability of materials and whether the physical arrangement of the polling station protects the secrecy of the ballot; the provision of materials and the security of unmarked ballots and ballot boxes; the presence of individuals inside polling stations (and whether they are authorized to be there); the conduct of election officials; the flow of voters (and the rejection of eligible voters); the conduct of the voters and their compliance with electoral regulations; and the environment surrounding polling stations, including potentially intimidating individuals or interactions between voters and vote buyers.[10]

International observers also gain valuable information about election day by coordinating with domestic observers. Domestic election observers are considered by many practitioners to be better able to evaluate elections because they are familiar with local practices and culture and are usually able to deploy significantly more observers on election day.[11] However, they are not always able to generate the same international media coverage of their evaluation of the election, and are sometimes perceived as biased.

Neutral, nonpartisan domestic election monitors commonly deploy stationary election observers who remain in the same polling station for the entire election day. Although domestic election observers vary in their efficacy and commitment to nonpartisan election monitoring, well-respected domestic observers are an important check on election fraud and can be a source of information about the quality of the electoral process. When visiting a polling station, international observers note the presence of domestic observers and may record domestic monitors' observations of the process before the arrival of the international observers. Within problematic polling stations, they can help international observers document the extent of problems that occurred throughout election day.

Although observers often catch many forms of election day irregularities, there is still room for international observers to improve election day observation. Observers may be able to detect election day manipulation even when they are unable to observe it directly. In the final section of this chapter I detail a proposed methodological improvement to election day observation. But first the next section discusses the tabulation of election results, one of the components of the electoral process in which international and domestic observers have been most successful in catching election fraud.

Tabulation of Results

Short-term observers are typically deployed at the conclusion of election day to observe the first stage(s) of the vote tabulation process. To the extent possible, observers report on the transparency of the ballot counting process, the presence of political party agents, the impartiality of the election officials, the ability of voters to access the results, the secrecy of the vote, the adherence to voting regulations, and the general atmosphere. Observers have witnessed signs of fraud such as prebundled and uniformly marked ballots' being removed from ballot boxes and counted. They have also found evidence of ballot box tampering, such as broken seals, and have uncovered "missing" ballot boxes. In several cases they have witnessed the theft of ballot boxes, as well as the intentional destruction or disposal of valid ballots.

The parallel vote tabulation (PVT) has become one of the central means by which international and domestic observers detect fraud during the counting process.[12] In a PVT (also called a "quick count") the counting of votes from a random sample of individual polling stations or vote counting centers is observed directly, and the results are immediately communicated to a central location. Because the sample is random, a PVT provides an independent estimate of the outcome of the election. A PVT differs from an exit poll because it relies on direct observation of the vote count rather than on interviews with voters as they exit polling stations.

Parallel vote tabulations and exit polls often yield similar results. A notable exception involved the 2004 recall referendum in Venezuela, when huge differences between the PVT and exit poll results created widespread controversy following that election. Nonetheless, PVTs are generally more difficult to manipulate than exit polls. They are also preferable to exit polling in countries where voters have an incentive to misrepresent their vote to pollsters or are unwilling to answer questions outside polling stations (especially if the individuals who refuse to answer are disproportionately from one demographic or political group).[13]

In most cases, parallel vote tabulations match the official results and further legitimate the electoral process. However, in several notable cases, PVTs have exposed election fraud or are believed to have eliminated the possibility that the losing incumbent could engineer a last-minute theft of the election. In elections in the Philippines in 1986, Chile in 1988, Panama in 1989, Nicaragua in 1990, Zambia in 1991, and Georgia in 2003, PVTs are thought to have played a large role in creating the conditions for the transfer of power to the rightfully elected party.[14]

A PVT cannot be conducted effectively without observer access to the vote counting process, in particular the announcement of results by polling stations. Ideally, observers have access to a complete list of polling stations. If observers do not have access to a list of polling stations, a PVT may be conducted by sampling across other units such as neighborhoods, as in the 2004 presidential elections in Indonesia. Another challenge for PVTs is the move toward electronic voting, particularly those forms of electronic voting that do not provide a paper trail. If a paper trail is available, parallel vote tabulation should still be possible.

In addition to the PVT, some international observer missions have employed statisticians to monitor vote returns and turnout for suspicious patterns. Turnout that exceeds 100 percent of eligible voters in polling stations, impossibly large jumps in turnout over the course of an election day, or politically competitive areas in which one candidate receives close to 100 percent of the vote draw attention. This form of fraud detection during the vote tabulation process remains less systematic, but is likely to become a more sophisticated and more common part of election observation missions in the future.

Acceptance of Results and Postelection Dispute Resolution

An election observation mission ends with the widespread acceptance of the results. Whereas in the very early period of election observation, some missions left the country soon after election day, current best practice is for the mission to remain in the country until the official results are announced and certified. Some missions have deployed long-term observers to closely monitor the dispute resolution process, as took place in Ethiopia in 2005. The mechanics of the result certification process vary widely, but most missions focus on the acceptance of results by all parties, the use of official channels for dispute resolution, and the impartiality of the dispute resolution process.

International Observers and Fraud Deterrence

International observers clearly have numerous techniques for detecting election fraud. But do they also deter it? It is difficult to answer this question by observing elections in the aggregate. The knowledge that international observers will be present at an election may prevent political parties and candidates from attempting fraud, but in hindsight, it is extremely difficult to distinguish between an election that was clean because international observers were invited and an election that would have been clean regardless of their presence. A solution to this problem lies in randomizing the assignment of observers to polling stations on election day. Randomization makes it possible to measure whether (and when) observers deter election day fraud. It can also result in improved detection of fraud and thereby potentially contribute to more generalized deterrence.

Because individuals committing fraud, intimidation, or other electoral improprieties may not wish to carry out their intended actions in the physical presence of observers, the presence of observers in some polling stations on election day may reduce the level of vote manipulation in those polling stations. If observers visit a randomly selected sample of polling stations during the course of election day, election outcomes at the monitored and unmonitored polling stations can then be compared. If the presence of observers reduces election day fraud, there should be a statistically significant difference in the incidence of irregularities or in outcomes between observed and unobserved polling stations. If a difference is detected, it would be further evidence that manipulation is occurring, even if the total amount of fraud influenced by observers is quite small. On the other hand, if there is no observable difference in vote share, turnout, or other key variables between observed polling stations and unobserved polling stations, observers can be more confident in generalizing their observations to the entire electoral process.

The potential utility of this process is suggested by the outcome of the first round of the 2003 presidential elections in Armenia, in which observers were assigned in a near random manner. The incumbent presidential candidate earned an average of 54.2 percent of the vote in unobserved polling stations, but earned only 48.3 percent of the vote in polling stations that were visited by international observers.[15] There were widely documented instances by international observers of violations by the incumbent candidate and his supporters, including ballot box stuffing, intimidation, and vote buying. However, the evidence suggests that the presence of observers reduced the amount of election fraud that occurred on election day.

Despite its advantages, randomization of observers has only been attempted with these objectives in a handful of cases, including the 2004 Indonesian presidential elections and the 2006 Nicaraguan general elections.[16] In many cases, logistical factors may mean that a more sophisticated randomized deployment plan is appropriate. Depending on the nature of the logistical challenges, stratified, multistage, or clustered sampling may create a more realistic or more efficient design. For example, in many countries there are likely to be a number of polling stations or geographic areas that are unreachable on election day because travel is too difficult or because the delegation of observers is not large enough to cover the entire country. As a result, randomization across the entire country may be unachievable, but randomization within a subset of polling stations is usually possible and carries the same advantages. Similarly, it is likely that not all polling stations would actually be visited by observers. Because the "failure to treat" is a common problem in experimental work, there exists a well-developed set of statistical tools for comparing groups of polling stations even if not all randomly selected polling stations are visited by international observers.

There are several arguments against the randomization of international observers. The most commonly cited argument is that international observers should go to the polling stations where they expect to find problems. By targeting problematic polling stations, observers can focus their impact where it is needed most and get a better sense of the difficulties experienced in the worst areas, but their observations would be biased toward a negative evaluation and judging the extent of the problems would be guesswork. A similar argument is made for having observers visit as many polling stations as possible in order to maximize their visibility and thus their impact on the quality of the election. Observers using this method are likely to visit many polling stations that are very similar to each other, and are unlikely to reach a random sample of polling stations, thus creating a situation in which the direction of the bias is unknown. More important, both arguments rely on the assumption that observers have a positive effect on election day behavior. In many cases, this may not be true, and only random assignment of observers allows for an empirical evaluation of this claim.

It is possible to combine the random assignment of observers to polling stations with a targeted focus on certain regions. Observers may be randomized within geographically defined regions that are expected to be problematic. The results generated could only be applied to specific regions, but the advantages of randomization would hold.

Conclusion

International election observers have dramatically improved their ability to judge the quality of elections, both in their methods to detect fraud and in their ability to aggregate the information they collect into an overall evaluation of elections in a wide variety of circumstances.

Extensive long-term qualitative monitoring of the election process, voter registration audits, media monitoring, the widespread presence of short-term observers on election day, the parallel vote tabulation, and the potential randomization of observers during the voting process on election day are all methods used by international observers to detect fraud and to increase their ability to make summary judgments of elections. Because those engaging in election fraud will always have the incentive to find methods of manipulating the election that are less likely to be discovered, observers will face continuing challenges to their mandate to evaluate election quality. One large challenge is detecting fraud that occurs before election day. Improvements in election day observation have given election manipulators the incentive to focus their efforts on the period leading up to election day and on the post-election period. The effect of preelectoral attempts to bias the electoral process toward one candidate or party is more difficult to evaluate than ballot box stuffing or intimidation of voters. In addition, some forms of "fixing" an election, such as gerrymandering and buying news coverage, have become part of the game in developed democracies and are not as widely agreed upon as violations of democratic norms. Considering the entire "menu of manipulation" will be crucial as international observers continue to evaluate elections in a variety of contexts.[17]

Another important question concerns the role that international election observers and the practices they have pioneered can play in developed countries, such as the United States. Outside the United States, even election officials and incumbent leaders who know that the electoral process has not been compromised have found value in allowing unbiased election observers. In addition, some methods, like the parallel vote tabulation and the voter registration audit, would be innovations in the U.S. context and could be used to identify existing problems, and if none exist, would serve to increase voter confidence in the electoral process.

Notes

1. Eric C. Bjornlund, *Beyond Free and Fair: Monitoring Elections and Building Democracy* (Washington: Woodrow Wilson Center Press, 2004), p. 12; Thomas Carothers, "The Observers Observed," *Journal of Democracy* 8 (1997): 18–19.

2. Alan S. Gerber, Donald P. Green, and Christopher W. Larimer, "Social Pressure and Voter Turnout: Evidence from a Large-Scale Field Experiment," *American Political Science Review* (February 2008).

3. David Weisburd and Anthony A. Braga, "Hot Spots Policing," in *Crime Prevention: New Approaches*, edited by Helmut Kury and Joachim Obergfell-Fuchs (Mainz, Germany: Weisner Ring, 2003).

4. Jon Abbink, "Introduction: Rethinking Democratization and Election Observation," in *Election Observation and Democratization in Africa,* edited by Jon Abbink and Gerti Hesseling (New York: St. Martin's Press, 2000), pp. 11–12. Not all organizations consistently employ this strategy because even in elections with a decisive margin of victory, election fraud can have other negative effects, including decreasing public trust in the electoral process.

5. See, for example, European Union, *Handbook for EU Election Observation Missions* (Stockholm: Swedish International Development Cooperation Agency, 2005), chap. 11.

6. The term "ghost voters" is most commonly used to refer to names on the voter register that do not correspond to living eligible voters. The most commonly used ghost voters are previously registered voters who are deceased.

7. National Democratic Institute for International Affairs, *Advancing the Democratic Tradition in Indonesia: The Second Democratic Legislative Elections since the Transition* (Washington: NDI, 2004).

8. NDI, *Advancing the Democratic Transition*, p. 6, n7.

9. Robert Norris and Patrick Merloe, *Media Monitoring to Promote Democratic Elections: An NDI Handbook for Citizen Organizations* (Washington: National Democratic Institute for International Affairs, 2002).

10. OSCE/ODIHR, *Election Observation Handbook* (Warsaw: Office for Democratic Institutions and Human Rights, 2005); European Union, *Handbook for EU Election Observation Missions*.

11. National Democratic Institute for International Affairs, *How Domestic Organizations Monitor Elections: An A to Z Guide* (Washington: NDI, 1995).

12. Melissa Estok, Neil Nevitte, and Glenn Cowan, *Quick Count and Election Observation: An NDI Handbook for Civic Organizations and Political Parties* (Washington: National Democratic Institute for International Affairs, 2002).

13. For further discussion of the differences between exit polls and PVTs, see Eric Bjornlund, "Improving Vote Count Verification in Transitional Elections," *Electoral Insight* (March 2006).

14. Larry Garber and Glenn Cowan, "The Virtues of Parallel Vote Tabulations," *Journal of Democracy* 4, no. 2 (1993): 95–107.

15. Susan D. Hyde, "The Observer Effect in International Politics: Evidence from a Natural Experiment," *World Politics* 60, no. 1 (2008): 37–63.

16. Observers have been randomly assigned for other purposes in several other instances, including the 2006 Palestinian elections.

17. The phrase is borrowed from Andreas Schedler, "The Menu of Manipulation," *Journal of Democracy* 13, no. 2 (2002): 36–50.

thirteen

Unintended Consequences of Election Monitoring

Alberto Simpser

$\mathbf{A}$s elections have spread to most of the world's countries, organized efforts by nongovernmental groups and international organizations to discourage cheating have become the norm.[1] The centerpiece of such efforts, election monitoring, seeks to change the behavior of would-be cheaters, specifically to prevent cheating by rendering it more risky and more costly, ideally, prohibitively so. When cheating can be verified, for instance, redress becomes more plausible, rendering cheating a riskier proposition. But monitoring does not always succeed at discouraging cheating: it can also induce the monitored party to resort to means of manipulating elections that are more difficult to scrutinize.[2] The consequences of such strategic adaptation for the overall political and economic health of the country being observed have not been fully explored.

I argue here that those forms of electoral manipulation that are less amenable to detection and redress through monitoring can also cause important damage to political, legal, and governmental institutions and to media independence. Hence, insofar as monitoring induces the adoption of such forms of electoral manipulation, it can have negative consequences—unintended, to be sure—for political and economic well-being.

I thank the participants at the University of Utah–Caltech/MIT Voting Technology Project Conference, September 2006, in particular Michael Alvarez, Thad Hall, Walter Mebane, and Susan Hyde, who provided very helpful comments on a previous draft. I also thank Marusia Musacchio for a helpful discussion. The usual caveat applies.

Whether this danger is important in any one case or set of circumstances is, of course, an empirical question. Election monitoring has likely contributed to the promotion of political freedom in numerous instances, and there is no intention here to detract from its merits. The goal of this essay is merely to raise the question of unintended consequences in the minds of practitioners and scholars.

The Argument

The idea that monitoring can induce the monitored party to strategically adapt its behavior has been explored in a wide range of situations. It has long been pointed out, for one thing, that regulation can give rise to "offsetting behavior" that reduces or even reverses the intended effect. Samuel Peltzman, for example, argued that increasing car safety standards might encourage more risky driving, and he showed that, while driver deaths per accident declined as a result of the 1966 National Traffic and Motor Vehicle Safety Act, the number of accidents increased, as did the number of deaths of pedestrians and cyclists.[3] Brian Jacob and Steven Levitt provide evidence that laws that sought to improve student attainment by punishing or rewarding schools on the basis of student test scores led to more cheating in low-achieving classrooms in Chicago public schools.[4] As these examples illustrate, unintended consequences can go beyond merely offsetting the intended result—they may lead to additional negative effects. Such dynamics are not exclusive to the realm of government regulation. In a 1975 article, "On the Folly of Rewarding A, while Hoping for B," Steven Kerr provides examples of instances in which some valuable behaviors are neglected because incentives are provided for different kinds of behavior. His examples come from areas as diverse as politics, medicine, war, and higher education. Similar arguments about offsetting behavior have been advanced in many other areas, including the war on drugs, border controls, and various realms of government regulation, including the Freedom of Information Act, the regulation of pharmaceuticals, and schooling laws.[5]

The idea can be well illustrated by borrowing a page from the theory of employee compensation. Suppose that an employer hires an employee to carry out two different activities. If one of the activities is easily measurable by the employer, but the other activity is not, then conditioning compensation on the observable activity will divert the employee's attention away from the activity that is difficult to observe. The reason is simple: the employee will focus on those activities that are rewarded. In such a situation, the employer may be better off not conditioning compensation on the observable activity (for example, he may be better off paying a fixed wage rather than a piece rate that is conditioned on the observable activity).[6]

Similarly, suppose that an incumbent seeking to increase his chances of victory in an upcoming election can resort to two kinds of fraudulent or illegitimate activities: one readily verifiable as illegitimate by election monitors, should monitors be present, and the other difficult to verify as such even if monitors are present. The monitoring will increase the returns to the incumbent associated with the unverifiable activity relative to the verifiable one. In this scenario, monitoring could lead an incumbent to favor the unverifiable form of cheating, even though he might have preferred the verifiable one in the absence of monitoring.

To make this more concrete, suppose, for example, that the two potential activities are stuffing ballot boxes and padding the electoral commission with partisan supporters of the incumbent. While the stuffing of ballot boxes, when detected by monitors, can unambiguously be labeled as illegitimate or fraudulent, appointments to the electoral commission can be justified on a variety of grounds and so are difficult for election monitors to label outright as illegitimate. Therefore the presence of election monitors, even as it deters ballot box stuffing, could increase an incumbent's incentive to meddle with appointments to the electoral commission. So, even if the incumbent preferred ballot box stuffing over meddling with appointments, effective election monitoring could induce him to focus on manipulating appointments.

In addition, if padding the electoral commission with incumbent supporters has negative consequences that go beyond the election at hand—such as requiring the incumbent to undermine legislative independence (for example, through bribes or intimidation) in order to secure the necessary appointments to the electoral commission—then society as a whole might be better off with the ballot stuffing scenario, and hence better off with a less effective form of election monitoring (or none at all).[7]

Often the tying of rewards and punishments to measurable behavior has an unimpeachable normative basis, such as improving student attainment, car safety, or the quality of elections. But as the above example suggests, sometimes plugging one hole can open a bigger one—the unintended effects might offset the intended ones and cause more harm than good.

Stripped of all specifics, the argument can be cast as follows. Unintended negative consequences can result from attempts to control third-party behavior when the following two conditions hold. First, there exist substitute behaviors that are more difficult to control (possibly because they cannot be readily verified). Second, the substitute behaviors have negative externalities. In the following sections, I explore some of the ways in which these two conditions may arise in the realm of election monitoring.

The relative importance of the intended positive effects and the unintended negative ones should be judged in light of the specific circumstances of the case under consideration.

Adaptation and the Limits to Election Monitoring

That election monitoring induces strategic adaptation in the behavior of the monitored parties has been amply noted. Thomas Carothers writes that "efforts by entrenched leaders to manipulate electoral processes to their advantage have become more subtle as such leaders have been socialized into the new world of global democracy and internationally observed elections. The distortions now usually occur during the run-up to the election rather than on voting day itself."[8] More recent work continues to make the same point. Bjornlund writes that "where effective monitoring is permitted, rulers willing to cheat have learned to focus on other parts of the process, particularly in the pre-election period, that can be more easily manipulated and for which domestic and international monitors have yet to develop effective deterrents."[9] Emily Beaulieu and Susan Hyde argue that incumbents have improved their skill at hiding election fraud over time as international election monitoring has become more pervasive. They use the term "prudent manipulation" to denote the idea that incumbents strategically choose forms of manipulation that are "less likely to provoke negative reports from international observers."[10]

This raises the question whether strategic adaptation of the means of manipulating elections is a problem that could be prevented with good-quality monitoring. This is important to know because the standards of observation appear to be improving over time.[11] In what follows I examine this question in some detail. On this point I find that, as Bjornlund suggested, even good-quality monitoring is limited in its reach. I return to the core of the argument—the issue of institutional damage—in the next section.

Verifiable vs. Nonverifiable Forms of Manipulation

In practice, different forms of manipulation vary in their propensity to be verifiably detected by election monitors. One source of variation, of course, is the quality and the scope of the monitoring mission. Good-quality monitoring is surely better able to detect cheating in elections than bad-quality monitoring. But even the best-quality monitoring effort may not be able to verifiably detect all forms of electoral manipulation with the same ease, and some forms of manipulation may be beyond the reach of monitoring altogether.

To illustrate this point, consider the contrast between the Kenyan elections of 1992 and 1997, which often come up in debates on the quality of election monitoring. Even though the 1992 elections were monitored by a collection of international teams and domestic observers, the monitoring effort on the whole was found wanting in many ways. Many believed that "major manipulation practices took place during the stages prior to the actual polling day."[12] This was attributed in part to the fact that international monitors arrived in Kenya only a few days before the election and hence were not able to directly observe any form of manipulation that might already have taken place. In addition, the monitoring effort was limited by a lack of capacity, in part because of imperfect coordination among the different monitoring missions, with the result that many allegations of rigging were not even investigated.[13] In this election, monitoring quality could be said to have been low and of limited reach.

The monitoring effort in the 1997 election, in contrast, was well organized, with a view to avoiding a repeat of the 1992 situation, and was much more successful, to the point that it was subsequently held up by some as a model for future election monitoring. Many of the countries that planned to send monitoring missions collectively established a secretariat, the Election Observation Center, to coordinate the different missions and perform some complementary monitoring functions. In contrast with 1992, monitors were present months in advance of the election, and many stages of the election were observed, including voter registration, party primaries, candidate nomination, and the campaign period, in addition, of course, to election day.[14] One practitioner involved in the 1997 monitoring mission called for this "new model" of monitoring to become "an essential element of the new code of conduct for election observation," believing that "under the old model chances of legitimizing fraudulent elections are higher" and that therefore the old model "should be abandoned altogether."[15]

Beyond the context of Kenya, others, too, have expressed considerable hope in the capacities of high-quality monitoring missions. Carothers, for instance, has written that "very well designed observation efforts mounted by experienced organizations (with extensive preelection coverage, close coordination with domestic monitors, and a parallel vote count) do have a chance of catching the subtler forms of wrongdoing, such as manipulation of voter-registration lists, strategic ballot-tampering, and small but significant distortions in vote tabulation."[16]

Does high-quality monitoring, then, have the capacity to verifiably detect all the potentially worrisome forms of manipulation? Unfortunately, the answer is likely no. Even as high-quality monitoring can verifiably detect many forms of manipulation, the monitored parties have often found means of manipulation that election monitors are hardly, if at all, able to verify as such.

In fact, even as the 1997 monitoring effort in Kenya was put up as a model for monitoring in general, it was acknowledged that severe problems of manipulation were nevertheless present. It was said that the election failed to meet "normal democratic standards," that "voter registration was incomplete, the media, the TV and the radio controlled by the State did not provide balanced coverage." [17] Dick Foeken and Ton Dietz concluded that "despite the monitoring activities, the election process was not entirely 'free and fair.'"[18] Whether this particular instance reflected a deficiency in the monitoring effort or the inherent limitations of monitoring itself is an open question, but if substantial forms of manipulation took place even in the presence of what many labeled a model monitoring effort, there may be limits to what even good monitoring can achieve.

More generally, recent work on election monitoring has noted that some forms of manipulation elude the sweep of monitors, not because of a lack of quality in the monitoring effort, but for reasons related to the means of manipulation themselves. Susan Hyde, for example, has pointed out that some kinds of activities that may affect elections in important ways, such as manipulation through administrative procedures, are difficult to label as instances of cheating since "it is more difficult to prove that they are intentional manipulation . . . than administrative incompetence."[19] Inefficiency in cleaning up voter registration lists could fall under this category. Furthermore, Hyde points out, extreme kinds of election tampering, such as the mysterious death of an opposition candidate, may lie beyond the purview of what international monitors consider their sphere of competence.

Jonathan Hartlyn and Jennifer McCoy have made a related observation as part of what they call the "paradox of comprehensiveness," by which they mean that, as the period and the scope of the actions of the monitored party that are observed increase, the certainty with which one can judge the electoral effects of what is observed decreases. For example, sometimes it is difficult to say whether problems within the opposition resulted from "manipulative, undemocratic changes in election rules and intimidation" or more from "decisions within the opposition movements themselves"; it is also hard to tell whether a formal mechanism (such as a law or administrative procedure) was established "primarily to ensure greater control and oversight or to implement targeted disenfranchisement."[20] Laws ostensibly designed to disqualify particular contenders can, for instance, be justified under the guise of some normative principle. Examples include the disqualification of opposition candidates in the 2000 Kyrgyz presidential election on the basis of an "onerous language test," and the disqualification of an important opposition party in the 1995 Armenian parliamentary election.[21]

It is useful to sharpen these ideas by drawing a distinction between those forms of electoral manipulation that are potentially verifiable and those that are not. In reality these may be ideal types at opposite ends of a continuum, but drawing the distinction sharply is analytically useful. The rigging of voter registration lists, destroying or fabricating votes, and intimidating voters are all potentially verifiable in the sense that, if they are adequately documented, they constitute strong evidence of electoral manipulation. In contrast, regulations that somehow weaken or altogether disqualify an opposition candidate may not be easily verified as a form of electoral manipulation or cheating—for instance, when the regulation can be defended on other grounds. Similarly, the appointment by an incumbent of partisan members to the electoral commission or to the legislature, the tightening of government controls over the media, and the selective application of the law against opposition supporters are all activities that, even if they are electorally motivated and constitute illegitimate use of power, may not always be easily labeled as cheating.

Note that this distinction does not concern the potential *observability* of the efforts at manipulation. Verifiable forms of electoral manipulation must, of course, be observable in principle. But nonverifiable forms may also be observable: Election monitors are often aware of an incumbent's actions that are both illegitimate in flavor and likely to be electorally motivated; nevertheless monitors may not be able, for reasons such as those suggested by Hyde and by Hartlyn and McCoy, to *verifiably document* that such actions constitute electoral cheating, and therefore it may be impossible to attach consequences to them (in contrast, consequences can often be attached to verifiable forms of cheating). The effectiveness of monitoring, needless to say, hinges on its ability to pin consequences—trade sanctions, legal prosecution, the annulment of an election—to actions of electoral manipulation; hence the importance of verifiability.

A useful analogy exists in the study of employment compensation. A key idea in some influential work in that field is that an employee's *total* contribution to a firm's value may be difficult to measure. Activities such as helping or mentoring fellow employees, boosting team morale, identifying opportunities for efficiency, or, on the negative side, sabotaging production, may have both short- and long-term consequences that are difficult to ascertain. For this reason, it may be impossible to base a compensation contract on an employee's total contribution to the firm: even though an employee's total contribution could conceivably be estimated by some of her peers and immediate superiors, such a contract would be impossible to enforce in a court of law. In other words, an employee's total contribution could be said to be *observable but not verifiable*. In contrast, an enforceable employment contract could be written on the basis of performance measures (such as the number of hours billed or units produced). But such measures capture only part of an employee's total contribution—that part which is verifiable.[22] Just as, under such a contract, an employee's compensation depends on her verifiable performance, but not on that which, though observable, may not be verifiable, the consequences or sanctions associated with cheating in elections can be attached to those forms of cheating that monitoring is able to verify, but not to those which, while evident to many, cannot reliably be labeled as cheating.[23]

Unintended Consequences of Election Monitoring

I now examine some of the means for electoral manipulation that incumbents can resort to when simpler forms of manipulation are foreclosed, as well as their effects on political and economic welfare. Of course, electoral manipulation, regardless of the means used to manipulate, is unfair and can have consequences for the performance of the government and hence for the general welfare. But the welfare consequences of different forms of manipulation can differ considerably. Some means of manipulating elections are more damaging to freedom and democracy, and more distortive of economic incentives, than others. The manipulation of legal, judicial, and electoral institutions, the arbitrary rewriting of the constitution for electoral purposes, and the consolidation of government control over the media for electoral advantage presumably have deeper consequences for political and economic life than the stuffing of ballot boxes on election day.

Consider the case of Peru under Fujimori as an illustration. Knowing that the presidential election in 2000 would take place under intense scrutiny, as Fujimori ostensibly did, by the argument I have presented one would expect Fujimori to have used nonverifiable forms of electoral manipulation in preparation for that election. In contrast, in a counterfactual scenario *without* the expectation that the 2000 election was to be scrutinized (or that it would be less closely scrutinized), Fujimori might have made comparatively less use of nonverifiable methods of manipulation and comparatively more use of verifiable ones such as stuffing ballot boxes.

From the beginning of his second term in office, which began in 1995, Fujimori manipulated the legislature and the judiciary in order to enable a legal decision that would allow him to run for a third term in 2000. His actions presumably alerted the international community and attracted the attention of foreign powers and monitoring organizations, increasing their interest in tracking the upcoming 2000 election. Having been allowed to run, in order to ensure that he would win, Fujimori manipulated the electoral authorities by appointing people loyal to him to positions of control.[24] He also invested considerable resources and effort in controlling the media. For instance, in 1997, Fujimori expropriated the television channel Frecuencia Latina/Canal 2 from one of its owners and stripped him of his Peruvian nationality after the channel aired a show criticizing the government. On the basis of secret videos (that subsequently became public) taken by Vladimiro Montesinos, a close aide of Fujimori's and the chief of Peru's national intelligence services, McMillan and Zoido-Lobaton estimate that Fujimori spent over US$3 million per month on bribes to television channels.[25] The picture that emerges from these videos is one in which Fujimori and his aides severely manipulated the main institutions of democracy for electoral purposes to the point that they drained them of their democratic functioning.[26] Many Supreme Court judges were bribed by Montesinos, as were many congressmen. Judges received an estimated US$5,000 to US$10,000 per month, a sum several times their official salary. Congressmen received between US$5,000 and US$20,000 per month.[27]

How might the expectation that the 2000 election was to be intensely scrutinized have influenced Fujimori's strategy in the period before that election? This counterfactual question, of course, is difficult to answer, but it is possible to speculate that the knowledge that the 2000 election would take place under the attentive eye of international and domestic monitors had an impact on Fujimori's strategic choices during his second term in office. Fujimori might have come to think, expecting domestic and international monitoring, that the most straightforward means of manipulating the election would be more difficult to use, or more risky, or limited in scope. He might therefore have felt more pressure, once the legal possibility of reelection had been secured, to find means other than election day fraud to ensure victory, such as establishing a high level of control over the media, over the electoral institutions, and over the legislature and the judiciary. In addition to their direct effects on the election, such levels of control over institutions and the media presumably allowed Fujimori to get away with some degree of verifiable cheating, by reducing the possibilities for punishment or redress.

Had Fujimori expected simpler means of rigging elections to be even more widely available to him in the 2000 election than they were, his efforts to undercut the institutions of government might have been milder, and the cost to the Peruvian public in terms of political and media freedom, economic distortions, and the channeling of government effort to unproductive activities such as securing money for bribes, might have been lower.[28]

The potential losses associated with manipulation of the kind that Fujimori and his aides pursued are of various sorts. In addition to the damage that Fujimori caused to government institutions and media freedom in the years preceding the 2000 election, the president and his aides likely devoted considerable time and effort to cheating, which could have been used instead to govern more effectively.[29] Another loss concerns the distortions in economic incentives that likely ensued from Fujimori's need to secure the funds to bribe the media and the legislators. Andrei Shleifer and Robert Vishny have argued that one of the reasons why corruption is much more distortive of the economy than taxation is that it provides incentives for the government to allocate resources to sectors where corruption is easier, not to those that maximize social welfare.[30] Finally, the manipulation of the media can have important distortive effects as well. Simeon Djankov and his colleagues, for example, using a large cross-national database of media ownership, found support for the idea that government ownership of the media undermines political and economic freedom.[31]

The techniques used by Fujimori are a subset of those available to incumbents seeking to manipulate elections. Andreas Schedler has provided a catalog of means of electoral manipulation.[32] Of these, the following might conceivably be deterred by a high-quality monitoring effort: informal disenfranchisement (for example, making it difficult for voters to reach polls in certain regions), voter intimidation, vote buying, and manipulation of the vote count.

Other items on the list, while possibly more complicated for incumbents to enact, might also be more difficult for monitors to deter and therefore could be pursued by incumbents under scrutiny: preventing opposition forces from participating in the election, working to fragment the opposition, restricting political and civil liberties, restricting opposition access to media and money, enacting laws to restrict who can vote, using political appointments to replace elected positions, murdering opposition candidates, and tolerating or encouraging bureaucratic inefficiency in updating voter rolls whenever this is advantageous to the incumbent. It is the latter forms of manipulation—those that are more difficult for monitors to verify—that can have large spillover effects outside the electoral realm, as well as in the medium and long term. In this sense, the pursuit of electoral victory through such means can be said to have substantial negative externalities. Of course, verifiable forms of electoral manipulation, such as election day fraud, may also require resources and attention on the part of the perpetrators and hence induce distortions of their own. But such distortions would seem to be appreciably smaller than the institutional erosion and allocative distortions entailed by nonverifiable forms of manipulation.

Discussion

Several aspects of these arguments merit further elaboration. First, when is the danger discussed here—that is, that monitoring could induce alternative means of manipulation with substantial negative externalities—likely to be present? In order for such a danger to be present, several conditions must obtain. First, desirable *substitutes* must be available: because monitoring renders some forms of manipulation more costly (understanding *cost* broadly to encompass difficulty of implementation, risk, and severity of the potential punishment), an incumbent who hopes to cheat must have other means of manipulation at his disposal. When he does not—that is, when alternative means of manipulation are not within the reach of the incumbent once those that monitors can potentially verify have been ruled out—then monitoring can be said to have been successful. Second, the substitutes must have negative *spillovers*: the alternative means of manipulation must yield undesirable externalities. When they do not, then monitoring, regardless of its success at reducing the level of manipulation, will not have had unintended negative consequences.

Paradoxically, one way in which monitoring is unlikely to lead to the negative external effects I have discussed is when monitoring is of low quality. When this is the case, monitoring is unlikely to induce substitution of the more damaging forms of manipulation even if they are available to the incumbent.

In other words, monitoring may succeed when it is strict enough to prevent cheating (when alternative means of manipulation are too costly to the incumbent), or, to a lesser extent, when it is lax enough that it fails to induce counterproductive effects such as damage to institutions and the media.

In practice, the most pernicious forms of electoral manipulation are not equally available in all political systems. In advanced, wealthy democracies, for example, dismantling institutions and curbing media freedoms in any significant way would probably be too costly for any incumbent government or politician. In some developing countries, however, such actions may fall well within the realm of the possible.[33]

These ideas have implications for democratic consolidation and failure. In some parts of the developing world, pressures to hold clean elections could in theory lead not only to the erosion of democratic institutions, as in Peru, but also, potentially, to the rolling back of democracy itself. Moreover, the expectation that high-quality monitoring would be implemented if an election were held, by reducing the chances that an autocrat could win an election should he choose to hold it, could make it less likely that an election would be held in the first place. Of course, one might question whether a rigged election is more desirable than autocracy, but even rigged elections seem to introduce an element of unpredictability, and so even a rigged election might be viewed as an opportunity for democratic progress.[34]

Another issue of interest concerns the ideal level of election monitoring. The argument I have presented suggests that, in some cases, monitoring might be *over*provided—specifically, when the potential for unintended negative consequences is substantial. This raises the question: what or who determines the provision of election monitoring and the quality of the monitoring effort? Although a variety of factors come into play, I wish to raise the possibility that those parties with decision power over the presence and quality of monitoring—often foreign countries and democracy-promotion organizations—may not face exactly the same incentives as the society where the elections are to take place. Their differing interests could lead to the overprovision, or to the underprovision, of monitoring. For example, if those who decide whether and how to monitor fail to consider the possibility of unintended negative effects, they may provide more or stricter monitoring, or both, than the optimum for the society holding the election. In contrast, in a situation where unintended consequences are unlikely and monitoring could be beneficial, monitoring may be underprovided if those who decide whether and how to monitor fail to internalize all of the potential benefits of monitoring. In light of this, it is interesting to note that domestic monitoring efforts are generally greater in scope than international missions.[35] One could speculate that this is true because domestic groups internalize a larger share of the potential benefits of better-quality elections than international observers do.[36] On a related point, it has been widely noted that some monitors have interests of their own, such as when the monitors want to ensure that they will be allowed to observe future elections in the country in question or when the monitors' home country has a particular political agenda to push.

Finally, it is interesting to consider what potential policy solutions might exist when monitoring presents the risk of serious unintended consequences. I wish to suggest several possibilities, more as food for thought than as fully formed prescriptions. First, unverifiable forms of manipulation, while they are hard to punish through formal mechanisms, may be amenable to punishments and rewards that do not require verifiability, but instead are based on observability—in other words, punishments and rewards based on reputation. While it may be difficult to verify that an incumbent's actions constitute manipulation, it may be possible to observe an overall disposition of the incumbent as progressive or antidemocratic. At the risk of seeming naive, one could venture that some incumbents are sensitive to their reputations—for instance, an incumbent's reputation could affect his future career prospects in international or multilateral organizations. In a sense, published rankings such as the Transparency International (TI) international corruption index capture aspects of a phenomenon—corruption, in the case of the TI index—that are "observable but not verifiable." A similar emphasis on the democratic reputation of leaders might help to reduce the returns to incumbents from pursuing forms of manipulation that are observable but not verifiable.

This idea also has an analogue in the theory of compensation. Implicit incentive pay, namely pay that is not based on an objective measure of performance (such as a subjectively determined bonus) can sometimes be used to motivate employees to attend to tasks that are important but cannot be verifiably measured.[37] Similarly, as long as an incumbent understands that the "fuzzy"—that is, observable but not verifiable—modalities of electoral manipulation matter for his reputation, and hence could have personal consequences for him down the line, he would have some motivation to refrain from such forms of manipulation.

Another potential direction for thought about policy implications concerns post-conflict amnesty. Much as the prospect of judgment and punishment could lead an autocrat to seek to hold on to power even when he would let go if his personal safety could be assured, the prospect of restrictions on the possibilities for an incumbent to manipulate elections, and hence to win them, could lead such an incumbent to resort to damaging forms of manipulation that he would not necessarily pursue in the absence of monitoring. This suggests that, in situations where the most damaging forms of manipulation are open to incumbents, the international community might consider providing a commitment to the incumbent that election monitoring will be limited, at least temporarily, in order to prevent worse consequences. Similarly, an autocrat deciding whether to hold elections in the first place might be more inclined to do so if he could be assured that he would not be subjected to intense scrutiny immediately following "democratization." This idea could be misguided, but it is not too different from the idea that shielding an incumbent with a criminal track record from prosecution might encourage him to step down or to preserve the peace. In practice, of course, whether such a course of action is warranted will depend on the merits of the case in question.[38]

While this chapter has thus far focused on election monitoring, the logic of the argument applies more broadly. In the area of elections, monitoring is not the only kind of constraint that would-be cheaters might face: an independent electoral commission, laws governing campaign finance and spending and other aspects of elections, or the presence of independent watchdog groups, to name a few examples, can also restrict the behavior of politicians and parties. Therefore, like international monitoring, such constraints could potentially (but, of course, not necessarily) induce substitution to more pernicious forms of political behavior.

More generally, the argument speaks to the growing body of work on institutions as the motor of socioeconomic development. Institutions, according to one of the most famous definitions, are "constraints that shape human interaction."[39] While the virtues of good institutions—for example, those that place constraints on the use and abuse of power—are frequently emphasized, the possibility of unintended negative consequences often remains unexamined.[40] The argument in this chapter calls attention to the possibility that even seemingly good institutions could unwittingly give rise to negative consequences. Ultimately, what institutions—understood as constraints—actually do is to alter the schedule of prices associated with different courses of action: an independent electoral commission, for example, can substantially increase the price to be paid for engaging in verifiable forms of electoral corruption. By so doing, the institution might change the relative desirability of available alternatives. Prescriptions for institution building and reform, therefore, ought to consider not only their direct effects on the behavior of interest, but also those on the full schedule of available substitutes.[41]

Conclusion

I have argued that election monitoring, by focusing on aspects of an incumbent's behavior that are verifiable, can sometimes motivate the incumbent under scrutiny to substitute other, less easily verifiable forms of electoral manipulation. Scholars and practitioners have recognized that political actors often react strategically to election monitoring. Hyde, for example, suggests that monitoring has increased the likelihood of opposition boycotts.[42] Here, I explored a different kind of strategic reaction, namely the substitution of means of cheating that, while harder to verify as such, can have potentially serious negative effects. Examples of such means of cheating include the subversion of institutions of government, the misallocation of resources, and the restriction of media freedom. I suggested that when monitoring provides incentives for incumbents to substitute such pernicious forms of manipulation, monitoring could be self-defeating. This danger is only present where these damaging forms of manipulation are not prohibitively costly to the incumbent, as may be the case in some settings in the developing world. Whether such a danger should be a first-order concern is a matter for the analyst and policymaker to determine on a case-by-case basis. By bringing attention to these issues, this analysis is a modest attempt to provide some food for thought.

Notes

1. I will use the terms "cheating" and "manipulation" indistinctly. See also note 38.

2. See, for example, Thomas Carothers, "The Observers Observed," *Journal of Democracy* 8, no. 3 (1997): 17–31; Dick Foeken and Ton Dietz, "Of Ethnicity, Manipulation and Observation: The 1992 and 1997 Elections in Kenya," in *Election Observation and Democratization in Africa,* edited by Jon Abbink and Gerti Hesseling (New York: St. Martin's Press, 2000); and Susan Hyde, "Observing Norms: Explaining the Causes and Consequences of Internationally Monitored Elections" (Ph.D. dissertation, University of California, San Diego, 2006).

3. Samuel Peltzman, "Regulation of Automobile Safety" (Washington: AEI Evaluative Studies, American Enterprise Institute, 1975).

4. Brian Jacob and Steven Levitt, "Rotten Apples: An Investigation of the Prevalence and Predictors of Teacher Cheating," *Quarterly Journal of Economics* 118, no. 3 (2003): 843–77.

5. Steven Kerr, "On the Folly of Rewarding A, while Hoping for B," *Academy of Management Journal* 18, no. 4 (1975): 769–83; Samuel Peltzman, "An Evaluation of Consumer Protection Legislation: The 1962 Drug Amendments," *Journal of Political Economy* 81, no. 5 (1973): 1049–91; Peltzman, "Regulation of Automobile Safety"; Samuel Peltzman, "Regulation and the Natural Progress of Opulence," AEI-Brookings Joint Center for Regulatory Studies, Distinguished Lecture 2004.

6. Bengt Holmstrom and Paul Milgrom, "Multitask Principal-Agent Analyses: Incentive Contracts, Asset Ownership, and Job Design," *Journal of Law, Economics and Organization* 7, Special Issue (1991): 24–52.

7. The best situation, of course, would be one without either ballot box stuffing or the padding of the electoral commission, but in this example monitoring is not able to ensure such an outcome.

8. Carothers, "The Observers Observed," p. 22.

9. Eric Bjornlund, *Beyond Free and Fair* (Washington and Baltimore: Woodrow Wilson Center Press and Johns Hopkins University Press, 2004), pp. 282–83.

10. See Emily Beaulieu and Susan Hyde, "Election Boycotts, Election Observers, and Competition: Do International Election Observers Give Parties an Incentive to Boycott Elections?" presented at the APSA Annual Meeting, 2004; Bjornlund, *Beyond Free and Fair*; Hyde, "Observing Norms"; Susan Hyde, "Can International Election Observers Deter Election Day Fraud? Evidence from a Natural Experiment," paper presented at the Annual Meeting of the International Studies Association, 2006.

11. Beaulieu and Hyde, "Election Boycotts."

12. Foeken and Dietz, "Of Ethnicity, Manipulation and Observation," p. 147.

13. Africa Confidential 1992 and 1993, quoted in Marcel Rutten, "The Kenyan General Elections of 1997: Implementing a New Model for International Election Observation in Africa," in *Election Observation and Democratization in Africa*, edited by Abbink and Hesseling.

14. The monitoring effort began even before the Election Observation Center started to operate. See Rutten, "The Kenyan General Elections," for a detailed timeline.

15. Ibid., pp. 316–17.

16. Carothers, "The Observers Observed," p. 19.

17. *Daily Nation*, January 8, 1998, cited in Foeken and Dietz, "Of Ethnicity, Manipulation and Observation," p. 146.

18. Foeken and Dietz, "Of Ethnicity, Manipulation and Observation," p. 147.

19. Hyde, "Observing Norms," chap. 8.

20. Jonathan Hartlyn and Jennifer McCoy, "Free Enough? Fair Enough? Assessing Electoral Manipulation in Democratizing Contexts," presented at the APSA Annual Meeting, 2004; Jonathan Hartlyn and Jennifer McCoy, "Observer Paradoxes: How to Assess Electoral Manipulation," in *Electoral Authoritarianism: The Dynamics of Unfree Competition*, edited by Andreas Schedler (Boulder, Colo.: Lynne Rienner, 2006).

21. Organization for Security and Co-operation in Europe/Office for Democratic Institutions and Human Rights, "Kyrgyz Republic Presidential Elections, 29 October 2000," pp. 5–6; and Commission on Security and Co-operation in Europe, "Armenia's Parliamentary Election and Constitutional Referendum, July 5 1995." The interpretation in the text, of course, is contested. For more details, see Simpser, "Making Votes Not Count: Strategic Incentives for Electoral Corruption" (Ph.D. dissertation, Stanford University, 2005), pp. 17–18.

22. See, for instance, Robert Gibbons, "Incentives in Organizations," *Journal of Economic Perspectives* 12, no. 4 (1998): 115–32; Holmstrom and Milgrom, "Multitask

Principal-Agent Analyses"; George Baker, Robert Gibbons, and Kevin Murphy, "Subjective Performance Measures in Optimal Incentive Contracts," *Quarterly Journal of Economics* 109, no. 4 (1994): 1125–56.

23. This is not to say that the unverifiable cannot constitute a basis for compensation; it can. In fact, it might be a good idea to base rewards and punishments on unverifiable aspects of an incumbent's performance. I elaborate this point later in this chapter.

24. Steven Levitsky, "Fujimori and Post-Party Politics in Peru," *Journal of Democracy* 10, no. 3 (1999): 78–92.

25. John McMillan and Pablo Zoido-Lobaton, "How to Subvert Democracy: Montesinos in Peru," *Journal of Economic Perspectives* 18, no.4 (2004): 82.

26. Ibid., p. 69.

27. Ibid., pp. 77–79.

28. After winning the election, Fujimori was brought down. The counterfactual comparison in the text is one between the actual events and a hypothetical scenario in which Fujimori would not have manipulated institutions to the same degree, would have won in 2000 using election day fraud, and would have been brought down after winning, as actually happened (of course, it could be argued that Fujimori's actual behavior contributed to his fall after the 2000 election, but it is not implausible to argue that his fall was overdetermined—that is, that there would still have been sufficient reasons for him to fall even if he had not engaged in institutional manipulation to the degree that he did). The fact that Fujimori did use election day fraud in addition to manipulating elections does not invalidate the implication of the counterfactual comparison: In the counterfactual scenario, Fujimori would also have used election day fraud, but the damage to institutions would have been smaller. Of course, this counterfactual scenario is one among many possible ones; regardless of its plausibility, it helps to illustrate the argument.

29. This observation presumes, of course, that more attention to governing would have led to better decisions. Of course, the same critique could apply to some extent to candidates who do not cheat, but spend time campaigning that could be used for governing.

30. See Andrei Shleifer and Robert Vishny, "Corruption," *Quarterly Journal of Economics* 58, no. 3 (August): 599–617. Moreover, if monitoring leads incumbents to choose different means of manipulation, by a revealed-preference argument such substitutes must on the whole be less desirable to the incumbent, possibly because implementing them requires more resources. If so, the additional costs of implementing the substitute methods could potentially be passed on, at least in part, to the public.

31. Simeon Djankov, Caralee McLiesh, Tatiana Nenova, and Andrei Shleifer, "Who Owns the Media?" Harvard University, 2001.

32. Andreas Schedler, "Elections without Democracy: The Menu of Manipulation," *Journal of Democracy* 13, no. 2 (2002): 39.

33. In such cases, of course, incumbents may have a relatively high degree of control over the institutions of government and possibly also over the media in the first

place, regardless of monitoring. Nevertheless, there is often scope for further consolidation of such control.

34. Thus far I have operated under the intuitive assumption that monitoring decreases (or has no effect on) the level of manipulation. But it is also possible that monitoring could increase incentives for electoral manipulation. This could happen, for example, if monitoring helped the incumbent to signal strength. For a fuller exposition of this argument see Simpser, "Making Votes Not Count"; and Alberto Simpser, "A Theory of Corrupt Elections," University of Chicago, 2006. This could help explain some of the otherwise puzzling cases in which incumbents invite monitors even though they plan to engage in fraud (an alternative reason is that failing to invite monitors has simply become too costly; see Hyde, "Observing Norms," for an elaboration of this argument).

35. Carothers, "The Observers Observed," p. 26.

36. Another reason might be that domestic observation efforts have positive externalities that international efforts do not have. Bjornlund, for instance, writes that "domestic election monitoring can energize citizen involvement, empower nongovernmental organizations, and transform public attitudes toward national politics. The local organizations and networks that are created to monitor elections often go on to promote democracy in other ways, by fighting corruption, monitoring government performance, or engaging in civic education" (Bjornlund, *Beyond Free and Fair*, p. 308). Also, domestic monitors, because they are more culturally attuned, can often see things that international ones cannot. Domestic monitoring can also have its downside: since large numbers of people are involved, the level of professionalism can suffer, and monitors can be easier to bribe (I thank Susan Hyde for this point).

37. Paul Milgrom and John Roberts, *Economics, Organization and Management* (New York: Prentice-Hall, 1992); Baker, Gibbons, and Murphy, "Subjective Performance Measures."

38. Throughout this chapter, I have referred to a wide variety of forms of manipulation or fraud under the rubric of "cheating" (or, indistinctly, "manipulation"). It could be argued that it is not appropriate to lump together in one same category actions as different as, for instance, stuffing ballot boxes and bribing a congressman. The reason for doing so is that, in the framework I have presented, those two actions, while very different, would represent different means to the same end—that is, they are to some extent substitutes. A second issue that is often raised in discussions about cheating in elections is that it is not always clear where the line should be drawn between legitimate ways to seek victory and cheating. The legitimacy of some forms of campaign finance, or of some redistricting practices, for example, is the subject of ongoing debate. At bottom, the issue is a definitional one. For two prominent attempts at specifying what constitutes cheating in elections, see Jorgen Elklit and Paale Svensson, "What Makes Elections Free and Fair?" *Journal of Democracy* 8, no. 3 (1997): 32–46; and Schedler, "Elections without Democracy." The issue, however, has not been satisfactorily resolved (see Simpser, "Making Votes Not Count," chap. 2, for further discussion). Nevertheless,

while some kinds of electoral behavior fall in the gray area between that which is legit-imate and that which constitutes cheating, a large proportion does not; most analysts would agree that rigging voter registration lists, intimidating candidates, and stuffing ballot boxes are instances of cheating.

39. Douglass North, *Institutions, Institutional Change and Economic Performance* (Cambridge University Press, 1990), p. 3.

40. For the view that institutions are fundamental to economic growth, see ibid.; Douglass North and Barry Weingast, "Constitutions and Commitment," *Journal of Economic History* 49, no. 4 (1989): 803–32; and Daron Acemoglu, Simon Johnson, and James Robinson, "Institutions as a Fundamental Cause of Long-Run Growth," chap. 6 in *Handbook of Economic Growth*, edited by Philippe Aghion and Steven N. Durlauf, vol. 1A (Amsterdam: Elsevier, 2005). For a dissenting view see Edward Glaeser, Rafael La Porta, Florencio Lopez-de-Silanes, and Andrei Shleifer, "Do Institutions Cause Growth?" Harvard University, June 2004.

41. In fact, for some analytical purposes an institution can be usefully defined as a schedule of prices attached to behaviors. Such a definition has the advantage that it automatically calls attention to the possibility of substitution.

42. The argument is that if opposition parties have information about an incum-bent's cheating that is not visible to outside monitors, a boycott can signal their pos-session of such information. Hyde, "Observing Norms," chap. 8.

Conclusion

R. Michael Alvarez, Thad E. Hall, and Susan D. Hyde

Our intention when we decided to hold a small conference on election fraud and then organize the contributions from that conference into this edited volume was to kindle scholarly research on a subject we think is academically and politically important. A common frustration for academics who have been involved in election reform activities in recent years is the lack of hard empirical data on election fraud. We have a difficult time answering even basic questions about election fraud: What types of election fraud exist? What factors explain the variation in election fraud across time and space? And perhaps most important, is election fraud pervasive enough to call election results into question (especially in recent elections)? In our opinion, few scholars have taken Fabrice Lehoucq's call for more research on election fraud to heart, even as recent events illustrate how claims of fraud continue to proliferate.[1]

The work represented in these pages is impressive, both in answering these basic questions and in raising new ones. The contributors encourage researchers to develop a broad scientific strategy for better understanding election fraud, in particular, ways to detect and deter it in future elections. It is critical that this research be presented with an eye toward its effective implementation. This volume has already provided the fuel for new collaborations and new conversations, and we are confident that the foundation provided here will serve as a springboard for additional scholarship on the important topic of election fraud.

However, despite the progress made here, we are left with a series of questions and topics for new research. In this conclusion, we focus on these questions with the hope of providing some structure for the next stages in research on the detection and deterrence of election fraud.

The first question raised in this book concerns how we define *election fraud*. On one hand, there is a simple, legalistic answer to this conceptual quandary: we can simply define *election fraud* as anything that runs counter to the explicit legal apparatus that exists in a particular time and place. Thus, for example, if a nation's election law carefully defines the requirements for exercise of the franchise and if individuals who are outside that definition attempt to cast ballots—for example, noncitizens, convicted felons, or other categories of individuals who are in some places denied the right to vote— that action would constitute election fraud.

But as several contributors point out, such a legalistic definition does not provide a complete understanding of election manipulation. On one hand, as Çavdar, Simpser, and Hyde note, in nations with new or evolving democratic institutions, incumbent governments may use extralegal tactics to make it difficult for political challengers to run full-fledged campaigns, and in some cases intentionally and artificially limit political competition. Or, as Alvarez and Hall imply in their chapter on perceptions of fraud, there may be campaign tactics or political maneuvers that are perfectly legal within the context of a jurisdiction's election code but that are perceived by citizens, voters, or political opponents as illegal, antidemocratic, and outside the boundaries of "fair" political competition. Finally, there are also activities that are legal, and perceived by stakeholders as legal, such as political protest, that as Kiewiet, Hall, Alvarez, and Katz note can be used to disrupt or block legitimate election administration operations. A narrow legal definition of election fraud would ignore such phenomena and could lead to incorrect policy prescriptions for preventing election fraud.

Thus, to focus the next stage of research on election fraud, we need conceptual and theoretical work that clarifies the subject across a variety of contexts, and that differentiates election fraud from legitimate campaign tactics. Some of our contributors argued that a narrow legalistic definition is a suitable starting point, but we chose to allow for a broader conceptual definition of what constitutes election fraud. Armed with a better conceptual definition of election fraud, scholars need to develop a stronger theoretical framework for studying fraud. Although we are agnostic as to whether stronger deductive theory should come from a rational choice perspective, from a philosophical perspective, or from a more empirically driven one, we do hope that scholars will begin to develop a priori theories of election fraud that can be applied to future empirical studies of fraud. Such theorizing might focus on basic questions such as the relationship between political competition and the incentives for committing fraud (is the relationship strictly linear, or is it curvilinear?); on whether there are different incentives for committing different types of election fraud in newly institutionalizing democracies and in established democracies; and on what impact different democratic rules and procedures might have on the incentives and abilities of political agents to commit various types of election fraud. We think that the rich political-economic literature on political corruption might serve as an excellent starting point for approaches to developing theoretical models of election fraud.[2]

A second question regards data and method: how can we work with election officials to improve the timeliness, quality, and quantity of data that they report? The research on election "forensics" and outlier analysis conducted in the contributions from Mebane, Myagkov, Ordeshook, and Shaikin, and by Alvarez and Katz is all predicated on the availability of specific types of data. County-level, precinct-level, and especially voting-machine data are needed, for both election outcomes and election administration, as well as information about other factors that can be used as explanatory variables in models for predicting election outcomes. Accurate and useful determinations of vote patterns that are truly anomalous require large quantities of high-quality data. In many cases necessary data are not reported at all, and some reported data are difficult to use or difficult to understand.[3] In order to detect and study election fraud, we need to be able to find election anomalies, and to separate the anomalies into oddities and cases of clear fraud or manipulation.

Along with improvements in data collection, the social science community should improve the methods for analyzing these data. The contributors to this book (and others who presented at our earlier conference) are pushing the methodological frontiers in their work, using complex nonlinear statistical models and novel tools of statistical inference (see, for example, Mebane's analysis here). Others are combining sophisticated graphical tools, statistical modeling, and social science theory to find outliers and thus to identify fraud (Myagkov and Ordeshook; Alvarez and Katz). The social science community needs to study all of the statistical tools that have been—and could be—used to detect anomalies and outliers, and to better understand the circumstances under which these tools work, when they do not work, and the situations in which some are superior to others.

Third, even if advances are made in methods and dissemination, there will still exist a disjunction between research and practice. Many of the tools that social scientists use to study election anomalies and detect outliers are quite sophisticated and complex; but election officials do not hold social science Ph.D.s, and not many are trained in statistics. Thus the social science community should work on ways to make these methods understandable and usable by election officials. One obvious way is for academics and election officials to collaborate: the academics can do the statistical work and disseminate it in a form that election officials can use. Another idea is for the two groups to communicate through conferences and workshops and in other venues—where the tools can be disseminated and discussed in an open and productive way.

A third idea is to invest resources in implementing simple software tools, say, on the Internet, or perhaps eventually as part of an election administration software "suite" for use by election officials. Such a "fraud detection" program would allow election officials to input specific election data into a program on the Internet that would conduct outlier detection or other forms of fraud detection analysis. The results of the analysis would allow election officials to know whether they should investigate specific aspects of the election more thoroughly. Such analyses might become a permanent part of the post-election auditing regimes that many states have adopted since the 2000 election. One caveat to this proposal is that it will likely need continuous updating. As Simpser suggests, detection of election fraud may create incentives for other forms of election manipulation.

There is also a need for the credibility of data and research to be established. Academic research achieves credibility through peer review, dissemination, and replication. Unfortunately, these processes are time-consuming; in the social sciences it can often take one or two years for original research to go through the peer-review process and reach publication. The replication of research questions as aspects of the political process change—such as changes in voting technology and election laws—and the examination of specific questions in subsequent research can take many more years.

Election officials need answers immediately after an election, especially when an election is under dispute, litigation is looming, and the media are camped outside their offices. Election officials cannot wait—nor can the media, candidates, and the public—for academics to ponder the issue, generate a study, write up their results, get the work peer-reviewed and published, and then have colleagues replicate the methods and analysis. Studies need to produce rapid analysis of data for outlier detection, but also need to ensure the credibility of the researchers and their work. Possible ways to do this include using technology for speedy review and publication, establishing postelection nonpartisan "SWAT teams" to study anomalies, and developing a certification program for researchers. The academic community needs to figure out how to publicize credible work, and to do so while the work is still relevant to the question at hand.

Finally, one of the most important lessons we learned from organizing the election fraud conference and from the chapters in this book is that we have much to learn from each other. Many of the academics, such as those who specialize in American politics, were interested in what those who study international politics could tell them about the detection of election fraud outside the United States. The election officials were often surprised by how much the academics had to offer; and of course the academics were often surprised by the insights of election officials (not to mention their offers of data sharing).

We as editors agree that the conversation between those who run and those who study elections must evolve. As many of the contributions to this volume show, the study of election fraud, and methods to detect it, are often better developed outside the United States. Mexico, for example, has a formal system of electoral courts; and most elections in other developed democracies are monitored by nonpartisan teams using special techniques.[4] In some U.S. states, election observation and monitoring is relatively easy (California, for example), but in others it is difficult or impossible. We think that the development of easier and routine independent monitoring of elections in the United States will increase public trust in U.S. electoral institutions. Another desirable goal is to implement some of the methodologies that have been utilized internationally, such as "quick counts" or parallel vote tabulation procedures. These methods gather election results from a sample of precincts before they are aggregated and independently produce an estimate, within a specified margin of error, of the election outcome. We are not aware that this method has been applied to elections in the United States, even though it is viewed by many international practitioners as superior to exit polling.[5] The application of the "quick count" methodology could help improve confidence in reported election outcomes, though it might require new procedures in many American jurisdictions.[6] Thus it is clear to us that researchers and election officials in the United States have much to learn from their colleagues in other nations, and can benefit from developing collaborations and studying overseas election procedures.

The internationalization of research on election fraud is also likely to become more important as many of the voting techniques common in the United States—such as no-excuse absentee voting and electronic vote tabulation—are adopted overseas and innovations such as Internet voting become more widespread. The issues and sensibilities that make these techniques and reforms work in one jurisdiction may not work as well in another, and election officials need to understand these issues before they implement reforms. For example, the British government implemented no-excuse absentee voting in 2005 after a series of pilot projects, only to discover that fraud complaints increased as a result. Had the British consulted U.S. practices more rigorously, they might have addressed some of the chain-of-custody and related issues that are associated with absentee voting. In short, internationalizing election research can help both the United States and other nations learn about the benefits and pitfalls of election reforms, and ultimately improve both public confidence in electoral processes and the overall quality of elections.

Notes

1. Fabrice Lehoucq, "Election Fraud: Causes, Types and Consequences," *Annual Review of Political Science* 6 (2003): 233–56.

2. See, for example, Susan Rose Ackerman and Jana Kunicova, "Electoral Rules and Constitutional Structure as Constraints on Corruption," *British Journal of Political Science* 34 (2005): 573–606; Torsten Persson, Guido Tabellini, and Francesco Trebbi, "Electoral Rules and Corruption," *Journal of the European Economic Association* 1 (2003): 958–89. Both of those articles also have excellent reviews of other theoretical and empirical research on political corruption.

3. In addition, see R. Michael Alvarez, Stephen Ansolabehere, and Charles Stewart III, "Studying Elections: Data Quality and Pitfalls in Measuring the Effects of Voting Technologies," *Policy Studies Journal* 33 (2005): 15–24. For discussion of how better data collection might be implemented, see R. Michael Alvarez and Thad E. Hall, "Improving the Election Day Survey," Caltech/MIT Voting Technology Project, March 31, 2006 (http://vote.caltech.edu/reports/EAC-eds.pdf [January 2008]).

4. For discussion of Mexico's electoral courts, see Todd A. Eisenstadt, *Courting Democracy in Mexico: Party Strategies and Electoral Institutions* (Cambridge University Press, 2004). International election monitoring, and how it can detect and mitigate fraud, has been discussed in Eric C. Bjornlund, *Beyond Free and Fair: Monitoring Elections and Building Democracy* (Johns Hopkins University Press, 2004).

5. A full exposition of the "quick count" methodology can be found in Melissa Estok, Neil Nevitte, and Glen Cowan, "The Quick Count and Election Observation,"

National Democratic Institute for International Affairs (www.accessdemocracy.org/library/1417_elect_quickcounthdbk_1-30.pdf [January 2008]).

6. For example, for a "quick count" to be conducted in a jurisdiction, the ballots cast in a precinct need to be tabulated locally before being transported to a collection station or the tabulation location; in many jurisdictions, ballot reconciliation does not include the actual tabulation of candidate races or ballot measure votes, but merely the number of ballots cast and spoiled.

Contributors

R. Michael Alvarez
California Institute of Technology

Delia Bailey
Washington University in St. Louis

Frederick J. Boehmke
University of Iowa

Gamze Çavdar
Colorado State University

Todd Donovan
Western Washington University

Craig C. Donsanto
U.S. Department of Justice

Thad E. Hall
University of Utah

Susan D. Hyde
Yale University

Jonathan N. Katz
California Institute of Technology

D. Roderick Kiewiet
California Institute of Technology

Walter R. Mebane Jr.
University of Michigan

Mikhail Myagkov
University of Oregon

Peter C. Ordeshook
California Institute of Technology

Dimitry Shaikin
Academy of National Economy (Moscow)

Alberto Simpser
University of Chicago

Daniel A. Smith
University of Florida

Tova Andrea Wang
The Century Foundation

Index